Game Development Tools

Game Development Tools

Marwan Y. Ansari, Editor

CRC Press
Taylor & Francis Group
Boca Raton London New York

CRC Press is an imprint of the
Taylor & Francis Group, an **informa** business

AN A K PETERS BOOK

Cover Image: "The Iron Worker and King Solomon," engraving by John Sartain after the painting by Christian Schussele, courtesy of the Scottish Rite Masonic Museum and Library.

The image depicts the story of an ancient tool maker. According to Jewish legend recorded with the painting:

When the temple of Jerusalem was completed King Solomon gave a feast to the artificers employed in its construction. On unveiling the throne it was found that a smith had usurped a seat of honor on the right of the king's place, not yet awarded, whereupon the people clamored and the guard rushed to cut him down.

"Hold! Let him speak," commanded Solomon.

"Thou hast, O King, invited all craftsmen but me, yet how could these builders raise the temple without the tools I have fashioned?"

"True," decreed Solomon, "The seat is his of right. All honor to the iron worker."

Like the vital but underappreciated iron worker whose tools made possible the building of the temple at Jerusalem, creators of game development tools may too often go unnoticed but their tools are the essential prerequisites to all that is possible in computer games.

CRC Press
Taylor & Francis Group
6000 Broken Sound Parkway NW, Suite 300
Boca Raton, FL 33487-2742

First issued in hardback 2018

© 2011 by Taylor and Francis Group, LLC
CRC Press is an imprint of Taylor & Francis Group, an Informa business

No claim to original U.S. Government works

ISBN 13: 978-1-138-42861-4 (hbk)
ISBN 13: 978-1-56881-432-2 (pbk)

Library of Congress Cataloging-in-Publication Data

Game development tools / Marwan Y. Ansari, editor. -- 1st ed.
    p. cm. -- (An AK Peter book.)
    Summary: "This book brings the insights of game professionals, DCC creators, hardware vendors, and current researchers together into a collection that focuses on the most underrepresented and critical part of game production: tools development. The first gems-type book dedicated to game tools, this volume focuses on practical, implementable tools for game development professionals. Topics range from asset tracking to improving remote version control performance to robust and efficient IO. Technical artists, as well as game play, audio, and graphics programmers will find new tools to improve work flow and help build games faster"-- Provided by publisher.
    Includes bibliographical references and index.
    ISBN 978-1-56881-432-2 (hardback)
    1. Computer games--Programming. I. Ansari, Marwan.

    QA76.76.C672G3587 2011
    794.8'1526--dc22
    2011009334

Visit the Taylor & Francis Web site at
http://www.taylorandfrancis.com

and the A K Peters Web site at
http://www.akpeters.com

For my sons,

Mason and M.J.

The difficult we do right away; the impossible takes a little longer

Contents

Preface

Many might expect the preface of this book to try to convince the prospective reader of the importance of tool creation and design in the hopes of making a sale. Although a sale would be nice, I think the fact that you are reading the preface in contemplation of a purchase (or even after the purchase) shows that you already know the value of tools in games and software development. So, rather than preaching the value of the topic, why don't I spend these few pages the way Jim Blinn suggested, writing a preface that serves as a link between the author's mind and the reader's wallet in an effort to convince the reader not of the premise of the book, but rather that it will be a valuable addition to their library.

Originally, I wanted each article to describe something that the reader would be able to build. Now, however, it's obvious that was flawed thinking. A number of contributors submitted proposals on third-party tools (such as Genetica, Mudd Box, and FBX) that were clearly valuable because they give the reader another insight into how these tools may be used in their development pipelines.

Not only are there articles on third-party tools, I also received many articles on philosophical topics such as managing complexity, planning game streaming, and continuous integration. Due to the quality of these proposals, it became clear that the book would become more than just a set of recipes for do-it-yourself tools.

Many articles have relevant and valuable insight to aid in decision making and planning your asset pipeline such as "Workflow Improvement via Automatic Asset Tracking" (Chapter 3) and "Real Time Tool Communication" (Chapter 6).

Just as important is the sampling of third-party tools where developers of Intel's Threading Building Blocks (TBB) library discuss "Optimizing a Task-Based Game Engine" (Chapter 17) and Autodesk provides an article on vector displacement maps and using FBX (Chapter 16).

In the area of do-it-yourself tools, we have an equally impressive lineup. The "Low Coupling Command System" (Chapter 13) is explained as well as a method for "Improving Remote Perforce Usage" (Chapter 15). Our authors also contributed in-depth articles on "Real-Time Constructive Solid Geometry" (Chapter 8) and "Shape-Preserving Terrain Decimation and Associated Tools" (Chapter 10). Virtually all games programmers have heard of or already use COLLADA. Even though the wide-range implementations can make it difficult to write robust code, "A COLLADA Toolbox" (Chapter 9) will help make your code more bulletproof.

You will find the book is divided into three parts. Out of the gate, we have philosophical articles in the first part, followed by the do-it-yourself tools in the second part, and finally, third-party tools in the last part. Ultimately, time will tell if this is as useful as I hope it will be.

My choice in the cover art was made for several reasons. Originally I was going to pick a screen shot from one of the tools covered in the book, but after some reflection, I remembered seeing a painting at a Masonic temple where my lodge used to meet in Riverside, Illinois. Right away, it struck me as the perfect cover art.

Essentially, the moral of the painting is about recognizing the labor of the tool maker. The story goes that at the completion of King Solomon's Temple, a great feast was held in honor of the craftsmen and artisans who accomplished the great undertaking. Having sat in the honored location at the right of King Solomon, the ironworker earned the ire of the craftsmen and artisans. After his breach of protocol was brought to the king's attention, the ironworker was asked to account for his taking the seat of honor before the king could invite someone to take it. Not discounting the work of the craftsmen and artisans, the ironworker explained that without his tools, they would not have been able to build such as magnificent structure. Acknowledging the ironworker's point, King Solomon let him stay in the seat of honor.

Now, I did not start my career in the hopes of being a tool maker. You might agree with me that very few of us in the field of video games do. Tools still need to be made though, and we can't all be engine programmers, shader writers, and artisans. Having been a driver developer, a demo developer, a shader writer, a physics programmer, a video game developer, and even a data base developer (long ago!), what I have noticed is that every company needs a tools developer. Invariably, though, the tools developers always feel (and actually are, IMHO) that they are undervalued.

Not many people can get excited about a new 3D Studio Max exporter or a nice library that handles exceptions well. Given the need for the role, and being undervalued, I thought the painting of "King Solomon and the Iron Worker" a perfect choice for this book.

Every large undertaking, such as this, is done with the help and support of many friends and family. Listing each person would, of course, be prohibitive and would probably take up half the book. Sadly, I'm sure that I'll leave someone out, and I hope they don't take it personally. Everybody forgets something, right?

First and foremost, I would like to thank my family for their support in this process. I am lucky to have been given the time to organize this work when I probably should have been doing things like cutting the grass or washing the dishes. Thank you Jackie, Mason, and M.J.

The staff at A K Peters was invaluable during this process. Going from contributor to editor is a bit daunting, and Alice Peters' and Sarah Cutler's faith and support was incredible. Selecting the articles was no small feat. Drew Card, Dave

Gosselin, and Jon Greenberg kept me from cutting some articles that turned out to be about a thousand times better than I would have foreseen on my own: thanks fellas. Of course, the authors of this book are not to be forgotten. Each of them gave up personal time as well as time with their friends and families to help. I must give a special thank you to Sebastien Noury, Jaewon Jung, and Amir Ebrahimi for helping me proofread some of the drafts. Also, thank you to Craig Barr and Mark Davies for spending the time talking out some fine points of their articles and working particularly diligently to ensure that their articles were as forthcoming as possible. A personal thank you to Victor Lerias and Mike Irby, colleagues of mine, whose levity during a work crunch (which interfered with this project) made everything a little less stressful. A thank you cannot be forgotten for the Scottish Rite Masonic Museum and Library and especially for Maureen Harper for helping us get the rights for the artwork on the front cover.

Also, I'd like to just list a few folks who have helped me in little or big ways over the years but I simply don't have enough space to include the reasons: R.W. Br. Raymond J. Babinski, R.W. Br. Vytoutas V. Paukstys, the members of Azure Lodge 1153, Western Springs, Illinois, A.F. and A.M., Eric Haines, Dr. Roselle Wolfe, Dr. Henry Harr, Mr. Dan Keibles, Mr. James Deacy, Narayan Nayer, Maher and Marty Ansari, and C. Scott Garay (last but never least).

Finally, a special thank you to Wolfgang Engel. Wolfgang first got me started publishing articles in *Shader X^2* and has kept in touch ever since. His high standard of excellence in the ShaderX and GPU Pro series is something that everyone has come to expect and something that all books of that nature now strive for. Thanks Wolfgang.

—Marwan Y. Ansari

Part I

Philosophy and Methodology

It's never easy trying to decide which path to take when starting a large project. Should you write your own exporter? Should you use something off the shelf? Each has its own set of advantages and drawbacks, but unless you have gone down that road before, it's often difficult to know what the cost of the pitfalls really are.

This part offers some guidance into how you might structure various parts of your next large project or how you might begin to approach refactoring some areas of your current code base.

To name just a few, we start with Chapter 1: "Taming the Beast: Managing Complexity in Game Build Pipelines" to discuss different approaches that will be useful in various aspects of your next or current game. Chapter 3 discusses "Workflow Improvement via Automatic Asset Tracking." However, general strategies can be applied to lower-level functionality as we see in Chapter 7: "Robust File I/O."

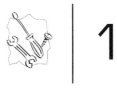

1

Taming the Beast: Managing Complexity in Game Build Pipelines

Fernando Navarro

1.1 Introduction

It is not a secret. Game companies face fierce competition to attract gamer's attention. Every holiday season, many products compete for the honor of being played. As a consequence, games need to be bigger, nicer, even funnier! Their plots need to be deeper and longer. Game scripts use many more levels, scenarios, and quests. Engines struggle to squeeze all the computing power to render highly detailed textures, models, and animations. Playing online and using downloaded content is also a must. In short, games have become awfully complex.

From a technical point of view, each title requires more assets and increasingly more complex relations among them. For artists to raise the quality level, they need to rely on tools that allow quick iteration. Releasing a multiplatform game is also the norm for many publishers.

Every aspect of the current generation of games proves more challenging for the production pipeline. Traditional designs are no longer capable of handling such pressure, and these not-so-old models do not scale well. New approaches are required.

The importance of new solutions is so obvious that terms such as *content management* or *asset pipeline* have become frequent guests in the agenda of many management meetings.

With this in mind, we are going to discuss different approaches that will be helpful during the design, implementation, and refactoring of content processing and asset build pipelines. Even if these notes do not represent a specific implementation, they describe generic methods that can be used to reduce downtime and improve efficiency. Many of them are orthogonal and can be implemented independently without requiring a full revamp of the system. These guidelines are a combination of common sense tips, answers to the evaluation of practical "what if...?" scenarios and information scattered across the Internet.

1.2 The Asset Build Pipeline

The term *asset build pipeline* can be found in many wordy flavors: content pipeline, asset build pipeline, build pipeline, pipeline or simply build. Under this concept, each company can fit a radically different implementation of a system whose main duty is transforming assets. In order to give a clear overview of what it represents, we will briefly describe its contents and its (sometimes) blurry limits.

1.2.1 What Is Included and What Is Not

As far as this chapter is concerned, we will consider the asset build pipeline as covering any processes designed to transform raw assets as produced by the *digital content creation tools* or DCCs (3D modeling or animation packages, image painting software, audio editing suites, in-house editors, ...) to the files that can be loaded by the *game* in a fully cooked or temporary form. In their simplest form, the associated processes are executed at each user's workstation and are the main method to push content from the DCC into the game. Figure 1.1 shows the location of the system as part of the global set of production tools and how the system connects to each one.

In general terms, the asset build is a framework that allows the execution of generic transformation tasks. Each square node in Figure 1.2 represents a single step that massages a set of inputs into one or many output files. This conversion is the result of executing a compiler, a script, or a tool that transforms data so it can

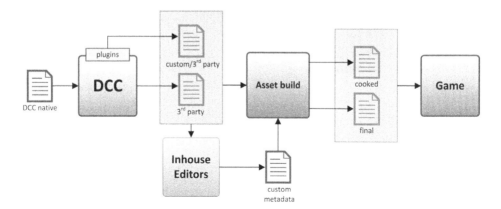

Figure 1.1. Block diagram of a content production pipeline, showing the tools and exchange formats involved in the production of game assets.

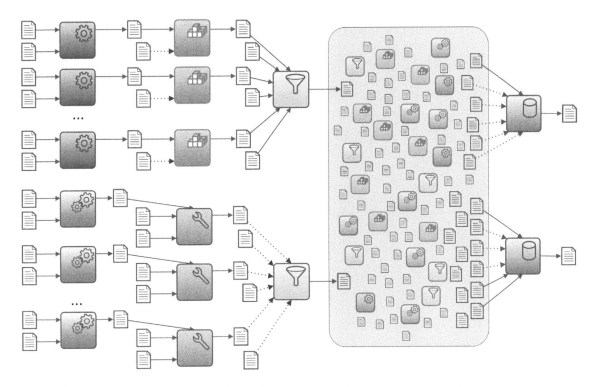

Figure 1.2. Diagram showing an imaginary dependency graph. Compilers are displayed as rounded boxes, with a different color representing alternative transformation steps. Dependencies connect compilers, input files, and output files. Explicit and implicit dependencies are drawn as solid and dotted lines respectively. (See Color Plate I.)

be consumed by the game. Each input is modeled as a *dependency* for the node, the node becomes a direct dependency for each of the outputs, and the outputs themselves are dependencies for later processing steps. In its minimal implementation, the system will be composed of a method to extract the dependencies, so a set of tasks can be *scheduled* and *executed*.

Our focus will be on the framework itself, not on the details of each individual compiler. Each compiler can integrate complex conversions involving geometry, image and sound processing, database accesses, etc. which can also probably be implemented using alternative methods. Together with custom editors and tools, they deserve an independent discussion and will not be covered in this chapter.

We have implicitly assumed that the target of a build is the production game assets. From a broader point of view, other professional environments use conceptually similar frameworks that are wired to compile source code, render and postprocess CG images, process natural language, crunch physics simulations, or untangle the mysteries of DNA sequences [Xoreax Advanced Grid Solutions 01, Sun Microsystems 11, Pande lab Stanford University 11]. These frameworks can also benefit from what is explained in the following sections.

1.2.2   Features and Design Decisions

In this section, we list the requirements for a hypothetically ideal system. We also group the requirements according to degrees of desirability. Most of them are purposely open and, in some cases, vague. You as a designer need to find what each of them means depending on your particular environment and the characteristics of your project.

As a common-sense rule, you should clearly determine the constraints, complexity, and targets of your system. A careful study will help in answering the single most important question you need to ask yourself: *Do I really need to implement my own solution, or can I use an off-the-shelf product like XNA Build, SCons, Makefiles, Jam, ...?* Even if the vast majority of projects require some sort of build pipeline, adapting an existing package can be a wise decision that may eventually save your company a significant amount of development and support time.

Your project will also impose alternative requirements and priorities. The following list tries to cover a wide set of situations. Even if some of them are just guidelines, they have to be seriously considered, as they are the source of project failures and frequent design pitfalls. As general as they are, use them as a starting point after which you will probably want to consider more specialized features that are not included here.

Required features of a build.

- Given a set of input and target files, the build must be able to automatically determine what files need to be processed and in which order.

- It must be able to handle the amount and complexity of transformations required to process each file.

- It must be able to detect processing errors and report them accordingly.

- It must be able to handle a variety of sources of data. A generic system needs to be agnostic of the contents of the processed files.

- It must be able to produce assets for a number of target platforms.

- It must finish within a reasonable time frame and always within the constraints defined by the project.

- Finally, a key factor for its success: It must provide a smooth user experience. Even if internally complex, an effort needs to be made to make it look simple, clear, fast, or at least to keep users informed.

Desirable features of a build.

- Provide granularity and allow executions on reduced sets of assets.

- Allow quick iteration for the most common asset types or at least provide alternative tools for them.

- Signal any issues as early as possible. Any user should be able to understand any errors, warnings, and important messages.

- Handle broken or missing data. On any issues, a partial build may be a valid result. A failed build should be the last option.

- Design it to be resilient to machine failure. Hundreds of users may be relying on the service, so on server failure, it must continue working even if it is in a degraded mode.

- Implement fine file control. Avoid *master files* that cannot be simultaneously edited or automatically merged. They will become a bottleneck.

- Design it to be extensible and scalable. Games are dynamic environments and evolve over time. Expect new requirements at the final stages of the project.

- Use conceptually simple models. It will allow more efficient execution, debuging, and maintenance. Remember that complexity has a direct impact on development costs. Downtime and support also determine the final budget of a project.

- Do not reinvent the wheel. Use existing libraries, reuse modules, apply design patterns and follow known good practices.

Optional features of a build.

- Support changes in the file formats of input and output files. Otherwise, full rebuilds may be required.

- Reduce the overhead of the system. Allow fast starts and retries. Null builds should be quick.

- Offload computation. Large sets of similar assets and complex or slow transformations can be processed by *number crunching machines* or *computing farms*.

- Focus on efficiency. Rely on advanced techniques such as caching, file reusing, and proxying.

- Provide methods to prevent pollution from broken or malfunctioning hosts and tools to clean and purge caches.

- Split the pipeline into several independent steps. Frequently, dependency
  extraction can start and end without executing any compilation steps. A task
  scheduler can be fed based on an execution plan built from the dependencies.
  Packaging of development versions, daily builds, and release candidates may
  be postprocesses.

1.3 Dependencies

Automatic asset building can be thought of as the execution of a series of steps
determined by a complex recipe. A given step can be safely executed only after all
its requirements, or dependencies, are satisfied. On the other hand, a node needs
to be reevaluated only when its direct dependencies or the dependencies of their
direct dependencies differ in a significant way. Knowing that, the order in which
the tasks are executed will be fully determined by the overall set of dependencies.

1.4 How to Determine Dependencies

Establishing the correct build dependencies is a conceptually simple process: it
requires the construction of a directed acyclic graph (DAG) resulting from the ag-
gregation of each node's dependencies. Frequently, these dependencies are modeled
at the file level, but finer grained approaches can also be used. In the later case,
dependencies are extracted from the files themselves.

We will assume each processing step is deterministic; that is, it always produces the same output for a given set of inputs. Even if this is not a requirement,
advanced techniques such as caching and proxing can be greatly simplified. Therefore, any processing that relies on random number generation, timestamps, IDs,
and references to other objects will need to be carefully designed.

There are two basic methods that can be used to determine the full set of
dependencies.

Hardcoded dependencies. This is the most primitive approach, as dependencies
and order of execution are hardcoded into the scripts. As such, each new entity
requires an update of the system. The asset build simply executes every known
step in the order determined by static dependency data. Because files are compiled
assuming every dependency is ready, this approach restricts flexibility. Missing
inputs due to user error may be difficult to avoid and debug. Smart scheduling
is also out of the capabilities of the framework. This method is the equivalent to
batch and shell scripts or really simple makefiles. It can only be used in simple
scenarios where dependencies are described at file level only.

Automatic extraction. Each compilation step is represented as a templated description of the inputs that are required, the outputs that are produced, and the
parameters used in the execution of the compiler. The full set of inputs and the

templates are used to generate a full graph of explicit dependencies. These dependencies are gathered without any knowledge of the contents of the source files by applying the recipe that matches a given set of input and output file types.

The build will rely on dynamic dependency extraction when the dependencies cannot be known in advance, they are stored inside a file, or this file is produced during the build process itself. In these cases, a scanner will read, parse and extract the relevant implicit dependencies to be added to the overall set. This means that areas of the DAG are not known until the build has started and the corresponding scanners are triggered. Implicit dependency scanning has been successfully used in systems such as SCons and Waf [Knight 11, Nagy 10].

In general, everything that can possibly modify the result of a compilation step needs to be tracked as a dependency. As such, it may be desirable to track the version, compiler command line, and execution environment.

1.5 How to Use Dependencies to Your Benefit

1.5.1 Determine Dependencies as Early as Possible

There are many advantages to establishing dependencies as early as possible in the pipeline. Knowing the dependencies even before the asset build is invoked can potentially reduce the complexity of the system and the size of any transient data. The cost of extracting asset dependencies in the DCC is small and will be amortized by the amount of times they are used. Scanner execution is minimized, and larger areas of the graph can be fully determined in advance. This makes the system more predictable, increases system stability, and reduces processing time. Both early data validation and smart scheduling become more feasible. This same data can be used by DCC plugins to track references and allow the production team to forsee the implications of changing a given asset.

As desirable as this is, early determination can only extract the dependencies from the assets that are directly processed inside the DCCs. Figure 1.2 represents the nodes without input dependencies on the left side of the graph. In most scenarios, static determination can define large areas of the DAG but needs to be complemented with alternative methods.

1.5.2 Dependency Granularity: Coarse or Fine Level

In many situations, a file can be considered an atomic entity that provides a high enough level of granularity. In some other cases, when, for example, hundreds of compiler instances share the same file as an input, finer dependencies can be an interesting option. By using file-specific scanners, the graph can be populated with detailed information. In case the original file is updated, only the tasks in the path whose refined dependencies have changed will need to be reevaluated. This may imply a reduction of orders of magnitude in the number of tasks compared to tasks using coarser dependencies, just by avoiding redundant compiler executions.

1.5.3   Out-of-Order Evaluation

The DAG contains patterns that provide interesting advantages. Certain asset types, mainly those located on the left of Figure 1.2, are usually numerous, independent of any other assets, and their compilation steps are similar. Textures, meshes, skeletons and skinning data, animations, prerendered videos, audio and speech files are examples of these assets.

By precompiling these files, complete areas of the graph can be evaluated offline, so the processed files are available even before an instance of the asset build is started. Since no interdependencies exists, these tasks can be easily distributed and calculated in parallel. For this to be effective, any output files need to be stored and reused using caching techniques (see Section 1.6.1). Existing packages can reduce the complexity of the implementation [Xoreax Advanced Grid Solutions 01, Electric Cloud, Inc. 11, Sun Microsystems 11].

Continuous integration techniques that have traditionally been employed with source code [Duvall et al. 07] can also be used with certain asset types. Changelists added to a versioning system can be monitored for assets that can potentially be built and cached. As with the original approach, a farm of servers may be responsible for the execution of the corresponding tasks.

The need for this approach and the associated complexity has to be considered in light of the characteristics of each particular scenario, but in general they can be easily implemented once a caching strategy is in place.

1.5.4   Limiting the Scope of the Build

In the same way that certain asset types can be precompiled, we can also reduce the extension of the dependency graph by ignoring specific asset types. Builds focused on providing quick iteration may not require the generation of a fresh copy of every single output file, even if their dependencies say otherwise. For example, audio files can be safely ignored when the intention is testing meshes and textures. In other cases, the build can be reduced following gameplay-related divisions: levels, quests, cutscenes, and global assets are frequently self-contained and independent.

For this to work, with the dependency graph already determined, every node that will produce a file that can be ignored is tagged as inactive. Any dependencies that lead to these nodes can be safely disabled, given that they are not required by any other active nodes. After the DAG has been processed, only nodes that are still active are scheduled for execution.

In some other situations, it is interesting to consider regions of the graph as a whole. Any dependencies entering the selected area can be considered inputs for an alternative node representing the region. The same occurs with outputs and the dependencies that originate inside and crossing this area's borders. If none of the inputs have changed, the area can be safely tagged as fully processed.

Knowing that the number of dependencies can be as large as several million, pruning areas can provide big savings both in the size of the data sets and the number of tasks that will ultimately be executed. The advantages will become evident after knowing the details of the proxying techniques of Section 1.6.3.

1.5.5   Dump the Dependency Graph

Once the dependency graph has been built, dump it to a file! Later builds can read it and use the contents as a starting point. An updated DAG can be built at a reduced cost, allowing faster start-up times. Moreover, many implicit dependencies will be ready, with a considerable reduction of the number of scanner executions. The chances of performing conceptually simple but technically difficult tasks, such as giving an estimate of a build time, are also improved. If none of the task templates have been modified, any subsequent builds will only need to regenerate the areas of the graph whose inputs have changed. "What has changed" can be redefined based on the expectations of the current build: a quick, incremental build focused on a single level, a full build, replacement of a few objects, etc.

Another important consequence is the fact that graph generation and task scheduling are now decoupled. This provides interesting opportunities: Tool updates become more localized, and the determination and evaluation of tasks become independent. It is even possible to use alternative schedulers optimized for quick turnaround, make use of heavy parallelism, or rely on the facilities of certain computing hosts, or use simple heuristics such as first-come, first-serve, etc.

Finally, the information contained in the dependency graph can be invaluable for finding and studying bottlenecks, locating areas for improvement, and fine-tuning the system. Understanding how such a complex system is performing may be a daunting task in the absence of execution data and clear logs. Simple formats such as plain text, xml, .doc, or GraphML and tools like Microsoft Excel and languages supporting xquery or even the command grep can be invaluable.

1.6   Advanced Techniques

1.6.1   Caching

This method focuses on file reuse and is heavily inspired by the equivalent systems for source-code compilation. A successful example is the CCache package [Tridgell 11].

With a caching scheme, the outputs of compilation steps are stored in a repository. During the evaluation of each node, the scheduler checks for the existence of a cached result that corresponds to the given set of input nodes. In the event of a cache hit, the result can be efficiently retrieved. Cache misses fall back to a standard compilation that includes uploading the results to the cache server. It is up to the designer to allow the method of populating the server from users' workstations and dedicated machines. In general, any result is acceptable, independent of its origin.

Establishing how the set of input dependencies are determined, stored, and queried is a fundamental decision. Simple methods such as filenames and timestamps may be inaccurate as they do not fully represent the contents of the files. Hashes, signatures, and file digests are popular alternatives. They can be calculated using different variations of the CRC, MD5, or SHA algorithms. In general, any method capable of converting a variable-length stream into a fixed-length key is valid. For our practical needs, the methods need to generate keys with low collision probability; that is, for two different files, the probability of generating the same key is really low.

Hashes can also be combined together, so several dependencies can be represented by a single key. For a combined hash, a successful search in the database will retrieve a file that has been compiled from all the inputs whose hashes were merged.

Cached results can be stored in many ways. Two of the most common methods are versioning systems and dedicated servers:

Versioning systems. Compiled results are stored in a versioning system (Perforce, Alienbrain, CVS, SVN, Git). Cache population and cache hits are, in fact, repository check-ins and retrievals.

This approach works well in those cases where each file is compiled with a single set of inputs and where the most recent version is generally usable by any build. Every source and its compiled results can be checked in at the same time. Syncing to the latest version of the repository will mostly retrieve files that do not need further recompilation. This approach is not so flexible when files are processed with variable compiler flags and dependencies. In these cases, the versioning system needs to be complemented with an external database capable of linking each hash with a given version.

Dedicated servers. The use of dedicated servers represents the most flexible approach. A cache server can integrate sophisticated algorithms, but in its most basic configuration it can be built from a database and a file server. In some circumstances the hash management system is accessed through an ad hoc interface that implements advanced querying features. They will be described in the following sections.

Not to be overlooked: These machines must be able to support high disk/network loads as well as to efficiently handle concurrent uploads and downloads. In general, file accesses will range from a few bytes to several gigabytes. However, the distribution is usually biased to files containing metadata and art assets due to these files being more numerous and having reduced variability in their input dependencies.

As pointed out before, with the server being a central resource, in the case of failure the build needs to rely on alternative servers or be able to work in a degraded mode.

1.6.2 Results That Are Close Enough

In some cases, it is desirable to use compiled files, cached or not, even if they have not been generated from exactly the same set of dependencies. For certain types of nodes, and assuming the game code supports it, a result that has been generated from the closest set of inputs may be used without significant differences in the game experience. This option is especially interesting with files that are generated after long compilation processes. Examples of this are precomputed lighting, baked ambient occlusion, collision meshes, and navigation data. The advantages are clear compared to the standard approach, where a change in a single mesh triggers a complete reevaluation.

Without loss of generality, file hashes can be calculated using smart methods that ignore the parts of the file that cannot modify the compiled result. Good candidates are comments, annotations, and object and material names that are not externally referenced.

1.6.3 Proxies

This second technique tries to avoid unnecessary work, namely, compilations and cache transfers, by performing lightweight evaluations of regions of the DAG. While similar in nature to the optimizations considered in Section 1.5, proxies are designed so the build can operate using file hashes instead of the original files.

The relationship between a file and its hash can be exploited in many different ways:

- During dependency generation and early scheduling, a file can be fully represented by its hash. The file needs to be transfered to the client's hard disk in just a few situations. For example, cache retrievals can be delayed until we have clearly determined that the file is going to be read by a compiler or a scanner.

- The hashes of the outputs of a compilation can be stored and retrieved from a cache server. This allows the dependency graph to be updated without requiring the execution of any compilers.

- Implicit dependencies can also be cached, so the evaluation of certain scanners may not be needed.

A build can avoid unnecessary compilations by simply determining the hashes of inputs and outputs and using them to update the dependency graph. Cascading this process can complete large regions of the DAG. In the best cases, a build may replace several compiler executions by repeated hash retrievals, completely bypassing any intermediate results that are needed to produce the final files.

1.7   Minimizing the Impact of Build Failures

In a production environment, it is as important to implement the right technology as it is to ensure a seamless operation of the system. Build systems are operated as part of organic environments where new content is delivered in increasingly tighter deadlines. The evolution of every project will impose a relaxation of the assumptions that were accepted during the initial design process. All of this pushes against the stability of the system and may imply frequent system updates.

As worrying as it looks, a progressive degradation of the system is to be expected. On the brighter side, there are simple approaches that can improve the chances of success. These methods, without tackling the source of the problems, will surely raise user satisfaction.

1.7.1   Exploit the Difference between an Error and a Warning

Most content creators are interested in propping and previewing their assets in game and are not so concerned about the latest version of *every* asset. With this in mind, the system's priority becomes completing partial builds that accurately represent views of a reduced set of assets. This is true even if, on the global picture, some other second priority areas may display artifacts.

Let's assume every system incidence is treated as an error and, as such, forces the build to stop. Applying simple statistics, if we consider that each asset is processed with a nonzero probability of failure, the chances of successfully completing a build are extremely low.

It becomes evident that a correct level of criticality needs to be assigned to each build message. For example, in the context of a geometry compiler, finding polygons with irregular shapes may be a reason to avoid generating the processed mesh. In the context of the whole build, this situation certainly has a less dramatic relevance.

Fatal errors should be the exception. In many cases, failed compilations can be logged as a warning, and their outputs replaced with placeholder assets. These fallback mechanisms do not fix the source of the problem, so additional maintenance will be added to the workloads of the support team. The issues may be solved via changes in the code and data, or, in some other cases, they will involve the artist updating the assets. Clearer messaging will increase the opportunities for the content creators to be able to identify and fix the problems by themselves.

In this context, multiple message categories need to be defined. Each information displayed will fall into one of them. A trivial approach that is commonly accepted classifies messages, in order of increasing importance, as *debug, verbose, information, warning, error*, and *fatal error*. Logs tagged using this simple method can also be easily filtered.

1.7.2 Early Data Validation and Reporting

Early validation can improve the user experience in many ways. First, it will quickly point out problems that otherwise would only be found after minutes or even hours of computation. It can also give a better idea of if the build will finish successfully or if fundamental pieces of data are missing or corrupted.

Efficient data validation may focus on metadata files: entity and hierarchical data, compilation and run-time information, and gameplay balancing among others. On the other hand, asset contents tend to be too specific for a generic system, and they represent big volumes of data, so it is not always suitable for early validation.

As such, metadata can be processed using simple tests aimed at finding duplicates and detecting missing references and assets, empty data records, inconsistent hierarchies, files with unexpected sizes, or malformed XML data.

Even if early validation is not a complete solution and does not cover all possible data paths, it can be complemented with asset data validation as part of the export process. The next section explains this approach.

1.7.3 Prevent Data Corruption

Data corruption is always a possibility in a environment where files are edited concurrently using tools that are under constant development. In the worst cases, corrupted data can produce a meltdown of the whole system and bring the team to a halt.

In order to limit the extent of the damage, local data validation must be performed before metadata and assets can be submitted to the versioning system. In some cases, the checks detailed in Section 1.7.2 will suffice. In other cases, a quick compilation at the time the asset is exported from the DCC will be beneficial. However, the ultimate proof of damage is a full build. For efficiency reasons, this approach is not always feasible. In all cases, every check-in must be properly labeled, and in the event of data corruption, user builds can be forced to use the latest data known to be safe.

Fixing corrupted data and eliminating build warnings are usually manual processes. They need to be performed by staff capable of checking the integrity of each file format and applying the corresponding updates. We encourage the use of human readable formats such as XML that allow simple editing, diffing, and merging operations.

It is also worth considering the fact that a defective tool may generate corrupted data that can pollute the caches. In these cases, any derived files need to be purged and replaced by recompiled assets. Cleaning operations are frequent, not only due to errors, but also as a maintenance operation. Removing the files compiled with a given version of a tool, uploaded from a certain client, or not referenced for a period of time are common duties in any system.

1.8 Conclusions

In this chapter, we have presented a series of approaches that can improve the chances of setting up an asset build pipeline that is both efficient and resilient to failure. These directions will prove useful for both new and existing frameworks.

As initially stated, these are a set of guidelines and checkpoints that can anticipate common pitfalls and design issues, the reader may be faced with when implementing a complex systems like this.

The never-ending search for the perfect AAA game will eventually challenge each of these ideas. However, we think this chapter offers some insight into different alternatives that build engineers can use to keep their systems up and running and enjoy a satisfied user base.

Bibliography

[Duvall et al. 07] Paul Duvall, Stephen M. Matyas, and Andrew Glover. *Continuous Integration: Improving Software Quality and Reducing Risk.* Addison-Wesley, 2007.

[Electric Cloud, Inc. 11] Electric Cloud, Inc. "Electric Cloud Home." Available at http://www.electric-cloud.com/, 2011.

[Knight 11] Steven Knight. "SCons: A Software Construction Tool." Available at http://www.scons.org/, 2011.

[Nagy 10] Thomas Nagy. "Waf: The Flexible Build System." Availabkle at http://code.google.com/p/waf/, 2010.

[Pande lab Stanford University 11] Pande lab Stanford University. "Folding@Home." Available at http://folding.stanford.edu/, 2011.

[Sun Microsystems 11] Sun Microsystems. "Grid Engine." Available at http://gridengine.sunsource.net/, 2011.

[Tridgell 11] Andrew Tridgell. "CCache: A Fast Compile Cache." Available at http://ccache.samba.org/, 2011.

[Xoreax Advanced Grid Solutions 01] Xoreax Advanced Grid Solutions. "Incredibuild." Available at http://www.xoreax.com/, 2001.

2

Game Streaming:
A Planned Approach

Jeffrey Aydelotte and Amir Ebrahimi

2.1 Introduction

The game industry has gradually been shifting away from traditional boxed titles and toward digital distribution. As of the writing of this chapter, Steam, a digital distribution service operated by Valve, currently has over 1,100 titles available through its service [Steam 10]. You might be hard pressed to find that many titles on the shelves at your local retail store. It's no surprise that this shift is occurring, as the numbers are there to back it up. In early 2010, Valve announced that it saw a 205% increase in Steam's unit sales year over year [O'Connor 10]. On September 20th of that very same year, NPD announced that PC digital game downloads surpassed retail unit sales by three million units [Riley 10]. Traditional game retailers finally took notice too, as GameStop announced in late 2009 that they would begin offering digital downloads, which they began testing in early 2010 [Paul 09].

With this shift towards digital distribution, it's not only important to provide a digital download, but it has become increasingly important to provide instant play. OnLive, a streaming game service, mitigates downloads by moving them to a central location: its own servers [OnLive 10]. There are inherently difficult problems that OnLive has had to solve and continues to address in order to provide that service to gamers, namely, overall bandwidth and latency. For the rest of game developers who are not building their games this way, streaming game assets to the client is *de rigueur*.

Some games on Steam are developed in such a way that players can begin playing the game before it finishes downloading. However, streaming has yet to get the same widespread attention in a game production as memory budgets, poly counts, textures limits, and bone counts. If that were not the case, then more of our games would be instantly playable. Just as with traditional categories for optimization, attempting to correct some of the areas mentioned at the end of a game production can very well capsize the project. A game designed from the outset with streaming as a focus can drive load times close to the zero horizon and provide for an overall better player experience.

Solving the streaming equation involves collaboration from both technology and design. On the technology side, you will need to have a flexible system to bundle assets into separate packages. Final assets that appear in a game will most likely have to be reconstructed from disparate bundles, some of which make use of temporary assets as placeholders. To maintain good performance, threads or coroutines should be used for requesting asset bundles asynchronously. Finally, bandwidth simulation should be enforced throughout development so that the development team is always aware of load times. On the game design side, designers must be actively involved in designing the flow of the game with asset sizes in mind. Rigorous monitoring of load times at different stages of the game and setting up encounters or events to hide downloads are critical. Finally, determining which assets are required and which can appear when available is necessary for prioritization. Having the right tools in place can make this process much easier for everyone.

2.1.1   Game Asset Streaming Explored

To fully understand how to set up your asset pipeline to prepare for streaming, first we'll explore streaming itself and define a simplistic calculus in the process. Let's assume for now that there is a static set of assets, S, for the game and that the game is deterministic in how those assets are loaded over time. At any specific time, t, new assets may be requested. For this exploration, time will be handled discretely. Let's declare a function $S(t)$ that produces a set S_t that contains all the assets that are currently loaded at time t. So, initially, $S(0)$ produces the empty set

$$S_0 = \emptyset.$$

If time t_f is the time when all game assets are loaded, then

$$S(t_f) = S_{t_f} = S = \{a_0...a_n\}.$$

When an asset, a, is requested, a check is made to see if it is already loaded in memory. Let's define a set R_t that includes the assets being requested at time t. If the assets are not in memory, then they need to be loaded from a disk store. Now, let's define a function $L(t)$, which produces a set of what assets need to be loaded at time t:

$$R_t = \{a_i, ...\} \text{ where } a_i \in S,$$

$$L(t) = R_t \setminus S_t.$$

In the case where R_t is a subset of S, then $L(t) = \emptyset$ because the assets have already been loaded. Let's declare a function $T(L)$ that gives us the time it takes to complete a load request:

$$T(L) = \alpha \quad \forall L \neq \emptyset,$$
$$T(\emptyset) = 0.$$

Now, we can create our first metric, which is a cost/benefit ratio between how long it takes a set of assets to load and at what time the assets were requested:

$$\omega_t = \frac{T(L(t))}{t}.$$

This metric is useful because it tells us potentially whether these assets could be preloaded by the time they are needed. Any ω greater than 1 is a failure in an instant-play scenario. Furthermore, we have an overall metric for our game streaming, which is whether all load requests can be satisfied within a specific amount of time:

$$\Omega_t = \frac{\sum_{i=0}^{t} T(L(i))}{t}.$$

Any Ω greater than 1 is also a failure in an instant-play scenario. As a game designer, you are looking for every optimal time t to introduce assets into gameplay. As an artist, you are focusing on how to reduce $T(L(t))$ in order to have an $\omega \leq 1$. As a tools engineer, you are providing tools to help both parties, as the two are interrelated.

The final load order for this deterministic scenario, after any necessary changes by the game designers and artists, will result in an optimal sequence for assets to be loaded sequentially:

$$\mathbb{S} = \{a_i, a_j, ..., a_n\}$$

2.1.2 Practicum

Now that asset streaming has been defined in simple terms, let's consider the more difficult parts that were purposefully left out. The first is the issue of loading itself, which involves a chain of slower and slower access times. Even when assets are in memory, the question exists of whether those assets are in one of the multilevel caches between the CPU and the memory store. Accessing memory isn't free; however, in the context of streaming assets over a network, it is insignificant. Next, there is disk access, which can be optical (e.g., DVD), magnetic (e.g., HD), or solid-state (e.g., flash drive). There are different characteristics for each storage device [Carter 04] that need to be taken into account in the timing function, $T(L)$, that was defined above. Finally, we'll introduce network streaming as a backing store for disk storage, which can be potentially many times slower than local disk access. Since network streaming is the slowest access time, $T(L)$ should properly represent the time to load an asset based on specific bandwidth capabilities.

Second is the time, t, at which assets are requested. Time was loosely defined above because gameplay time can vary by the type of gamer. In practice, you might want to average the gameplay time by taking a sample from your testers and excluding the outliers. With this average time determined, the game designer and artists can tune the game to try and achieve a no-wait, instant-play scenario. It might be difficult to tune the game load times to a player who has the lowest gameplay time. However, if assets are cached on disk locally after being streamed, then it might be possible to allow for instant play on subsequent plays even for the best of gamers.

Third is the actual assets themselves. Not all games are deterministic, so the time at which an asset is needed varies based on a specific play-through of the game [Thall 09]. One approach to this situation is to average the times at which an asset has been requested over cumulative play sessions during the development of the game. Another approach is to have a completely different load sequence based on characteristics of a play-through (e.g. starting location, player experience level, etc.). A third approach is the combination of the first two approaches, which is to have different load sequences that are based on an average of similar play-throughs. Finally, if there were a completely alternate set of assets depending on the graphics capabilities of the client machine, then that needs to be treated as a separate case.

Fourth is the granularity of the assets themselves. While it might be possible to package each asset individually for transfer over the network, there can be inherent overhead with that approach. For this reason, assets are usually grouped into bundles. What assets are bundled together depends upon the game being made. Sometimes, it makes sense to group assets by type, such as having multiple textures grouped together into one bundle. Other times, it may be more efficient to group bundles based upon their usage in the game, such as having all assets for a character bundled together. In general you want to pack as many assets as necessary inside each bundle to minimize the overhead with each asset bundle and its associated request.

The final consideration is the need for asynchronous requests. If requests were completed synchronously, then the game would halt every time an asset was requested. Any game that wants to achieve instant play needs to hide asset requests asynchronously [Kreigshauser 10]. So, instead of game code like this:

```
Texture2D albedo = AssetManager.LoadAsset("character/tex/albedo");
//Do something with albedo
```

you want to have code more like this:

```
AssetManager.LoadBundle("character/tex", OnAlbedoLoaded);
...

void OnAlbedoLoaded(AssetBundle bundle)
{
    Texture2D albedo = (Texture2D)bundle.Load("albedo");
    //Do something with albedo
}
```

2.1.3   Asset Requests

In general, asset download requests can be divided into four categories: blocking requests, active requests, queued requests, and passive requests.

Blocking requests. Blocking requests are requests for assets which are necessary for the game to proceed and therefore take the highest priority. While a blocking request is being processed, the player is looking at a loading screen. An example of a blocking request would be if the player clicked an option in a menu and the graphics for the next menu have not been loaded yet. The next menu cannot be displayed until those assets have been downloaded. Subsequent download requests are therefore blocked until the blocking request has finished.

Active requests. Active requests are requests for assets which have a high priority, but the absence of these assets is not impeding the game's progress. For example, in a game lobby with 3D avatars walking around and chatting, the assets for the players' avatars would be downloaded through active requests. The avatars are important to this area of the game, but the absence of the avatar assets does not stop the players from being able to chat while the avatars are downloaded. If an active download request is made and there are no blocking requests currently being processed, then the active requests can begin. It's up to the developer whether to submit all requests simultaneously or to issue them sequentially.

Queued requests. Queued requests are requests for low-priority assets. Queued requests are often used for loading superfluous props or effects. As the name suggests, queued requests are stored inside of a queue while any active requests are being processed. Once all active requests have completed, then the asset manager begins processing the queue.

Passive requests. Passive requests are downloads for assets that have not yet been requested by the game code. Passive requests are initiated whenever the asset manager is sitting idle. Any time that the game is not actively downloading assets is wasted time, which may show up in a loading screen later, so, until all assets have been downloaded, the asset manager should be constantly downloading. While passive requests are not controlled by game code, giving designers the ability to control the order in which passive requests are made can lead to a significant improvement in player experience.

Some considerations to keep in mind when building your asset manager is to determine whether you can pause active downloads. There are times where requests with lower priority (e.g., passive or queued) need to be overridden by higher-priority requests (e.g., active or blocking requests). Bandwidth is limited, so it may not make sense for a lower-priority request to continue. In those cases, you would either want to pause an active download or cancel it altogether and resume it at a later time.

2.2   Integrating Streaming from Day One

Download time is one of the most critical aspects to player experience in a streamed game, and therefore asset streaming is one of the first areas that should be approached in the development of a game. The developers need to have an environment in which they can experience download times and visualize what is going on in the asset manager. If the engine allows for play-testing inside the editor, then the download simulation can be done inside the editor. Otherwise, the final game should have an option to simulate a download when pulling assets from the hard drive. During the simulation process, a visual display of what the asset manager is currently doing should be displayed on screen so that trouble areas with asset downloads can be isolated and fixed. A simple display of progress bars with an asset's name, size, and request type is often sufficient to show developers all the information necessary to assess the current state of a level's asset streaming. Additionally, you might also want to write a log with this information.

In order for developers to be able to get up and running quickly, the bundle process needs to be set up so that the download simulation is pulling from real-world data: actual asset bundles, as opposed to the original source assets. The simplest way to get the bundling process up and running is to use the directory structure of the project source to generate bundles. Bundle creation is then the process of packaging all files under each source directory excluding its subdirectories. This automatically enforces that each asset exists in only one bundle. It also allows you to organize your asset bundles in a logical structure: placing the base assets for a character inside a directory named `bundles/characters` and placing that character's animations inside the directory `bundles/characters/animations`. This structure groups the files logically but still generates two asset bundles that can be downloaded separately. While managing a bundle creation with the directory structure is easy for artists and game designers to use, it can have usability issues when working with very large numbers of assets. If you are expecting to have a large number of assets that would make directory traversal slow, then you might opt for a more formal approach to asset bundle creation that involves manifests and explicit asset-bundle creation.

2.3   Passive Requests: The Art of Asset Streaming

For the most part, blocking, active, and queued asset requests are fairly obvious to implement. The biggest challenge is knowing which request type to use on a given asset. All of these requests, however, are made by specific gameplay code, which means that the game already has a specific need for the asset. Passive requests are an area where you can reduce load times and waiting for assets immensely. If you can accurately predict what the game is going to do in the near future, then you can preload assets and avoid the download time when the asset is requested by gameplay code. Most of the tools used for setting up asset streaming are merely to aid developers by helping them watch what is going on inside the asset manager, but the passive request manager is where a designer can take that information and use it to improve load times.

Setting up the passive request order begins in the build process. When the build process creates asset bundles, it generates an asset manifest file which contains information about all of the bundles that the game can download. It's possible to add ordering to the list of asset bundles in the manifest so that the passive request manager loads by priority. The first step in setting up the passive requests queue is an automated process that tracks when an asset is first requested. In a linear game, the assets can be organized by the level where they first appear; in an open-world game, they can be sorted by location; but in other games such as multiplayer shooters, there's no easy way to predict this, because the player can jump to any level right from the beginning.

While having an automated process that generates the passive request queue automatically is a good start, much better download times can be gained by giving designers the ability to re-sort the queue. This way you can predict what the player might do during a typical play session and adjust accordingly. To gain this type of control, the passive request queue is converted to a priority queue. Designers are provided with the ability to supply priority deltas to certain events, which causes assets to change their priority and therefore their position in the queue. For example, if a player enters the game and loads a saved game at level three, then the assets for levels one and two should drop to the bottom of the queue. Subsequently, the assets for levels three and four would be promoted to the top of the queue.

The passive request manager allows a developer to string together events in a diagram in which they can look at the position of assets in the queue after certain events. By stringing together events and looking at the order of the queue after those events occur, it becomes much easier to know what values to put in the priority deltas. Multiple scenarios can be tested quickly without having to actually play the game. This way is much faster and efficient in setting up the order of the priority queue and can result in a much more fluid and speedy load in the subsequent play tests.

2.4   Bluer Skies

The system described above has been battle tested with projects that each of us have worked on. Let us now entertain how the whole process can be improved. Going back to the first section, the simple calculus introduced can actually be integrated into the tool chain. There can be two different modes of loading assets in the game, one which loads all assets at startup and one that simulates streaming loads. The first, which loads all assets, can be used for data collection during game play-throughs. A table is kept of what assets are requested and at what time they are requested. Furthermore, each table has metadata to describe the player location, level being played, and other characteristic features that allow these reports to be grouped appropriately. Group data can then be analyzed for patterns and graphed for review by the development team. Based on a target bandwidth, the data can help pinpoint problem areas using our ω and Ω metrics. A game designer can adjust the length of certain gameplay situations to offset when other assets are introduced. Alternatively, proxy assets or a lower level-of-detail for assets can be used in place of assets that take longer to load. The group data can be averaged to generate an optimal load scheme that answers both which assets should be bundled together and when a bundle should be loaded. Asset bundles no longer need to be explicitly created, and, instead, a manifest is generated that maps assets to the asset bundles that contain them. Gameplay engineers are relieved from having to know which bundles to request to load a specific asset. Finally, these optimal load schemes are fed back into the game, allowing for a proper load scheme to be picked based on the current characteristics of the play session. All of these improvements mean that over time the game can approach zero load times in a streamlined fashion.

2.5   Conclusion

Digital distribution is still a fairly recent development in the game industry, and although it has gained a great deal of momentum, its true potential has yet to be realized. Preloading a portion of a game to allow a player to start playing early is a good start; however, instant play should be the ultimate goal. To advance progress towards this goal and have online game load times approach zero, asset streaming must become a chief game design concern and one that is included at the very beginning of production. Tools for visualizing the asset download process and managing grouping and order of assets and possibly a whole integrated tool chain that refines this process over time is necessary to allow developers to create the great online games of the future.

Bibliography

[Carter 04] Ben Carter. *The Game Asset Pipeline*. Hingham, MA: Charles River Media, 2004.

[Kreigshauser 10] Joshua Kreigshauser. "Evolution of a Streaming Client." Available online (http://kriegshauser.blogspot.com/2010/02/evolution-of-streaming-client.html), 2010 [cited October 9, 2010].

[O'Connor 10] Alice O'Connor. "Valve Boasts of 205% Steam Sales Increase in 2009." Available online (http://www.shacknews.com/featuredarticle.x?id=1271), 2010 [cited October 9, 2010].

[OnLive 10] OnLive. "Wikipedia: OnLive." Available online (http://en.wikipedia.org/wiki/OnLive), 2010 [cited October 9, 2010].

[Paul 09] Franklin Paul. "GameStop to Sell Digital Game Downloads." Available online (http://www.reuters.com/article/idUSN1245868320091112), 2009 [cited October 9, 2010].

[Riley 10] David Riley. "PC Full-Game Digital Downloads Surpass Retail Unit Sales." Available online (http://www.npd.com/press/releases/press_100920.html), 2010 [cited October 9, 2010].

[Steam 10] Steam. "Wikipedia: List of Steam Titles." Available online (http://en.wikipedia.org/wiki/List_of_Steam_titles), 2010 [cited October 9, 2010].

[Thall 09] David Thall. "Next-Gen Asset Streaming Using Runtime Statistics." In *Game Developers Conference*, pp. 7–8. San Francisco, CA: GDC, 2009.

3

Workflow Improvement via Automatic Asset Tracking

Matt Greene and William Smith

3.1 Introduction

Volition, Inc., is the developer of recent titles *Saints Row 2* and *Red Faction: Guerrilla* for Microsoft Xbox 360, Sony PlayStation 3, and PC platforms. Volition employs over a hundred full-time developers to generate unique content for each of its simultaneous game projects. Keeping track of game art content for projects at Volition is an organizationally daunting task. This article describes how Volition's technical artists built an automated solution to the general problem of asset tracking for the upcoming cross-platform development project, *Red Faction: Armageddon*. This chapter details how the task was researched, developed, and how updates and maintenance were designed to ensure that the system was optimally useful.

3.2 Historical Drawbacks of Manual Asset Tracking

Assets produced at Volition were traditionally tracked by manually cataloging every object, item, and resource using off-the-shelf spreadsheet solutions such as Microsoft Excel. As the scope of Volition's game projects expanded, this method of asset tracking became increasingly time consuming and inefficient. In order to determine a better method for asset tracking, our first step was to identify all drawbacks of the existing manual method. This exercise would assist in building a set of feature expectations for an as-yet hypothetical automated solution.

Lack of overall speed was the first obvious negative aspect of manual asset tracking. In the past, assets were added to the catalogue slowly or inconsistently and information was difficult to quickly retrieve. Additionally, it was difficult to track metadata information such as polygon count, texture information, material properties, or memory footprint. It was nearly impossible to perform a specific search

based on any of these properties. The library of available assets was rarely updated, making the information it contained potentially out-of-date and unreliable.
The tech art team at Volition determined that at minimum, an updated solution
would require the following fundamental feature criteria:

- A new in-house tool was required, built specifically for asset tracking.

- This tool had to automatically catalogue and update asset information.

- All metadata needed automated recording and perpetual updating.

- Full search and retrieval implementation for users was required.

- Unforeseen feature additions were expected; therefore, the tool set had to be
  capable of rapid, modular development and iteration.

3.3 Automatically Building an Asset Database Using the Xbox 360

First, some up-front explanation: all Volition game assets are exported from
content-creation applications (such as 3ds Max) into a proprietary cross-platform
XML format and then optimized down into platform-specific binary formats. This
process is required in order to author platform-independent tools that operate at
the XML level. A typical asset begins it lifecycle in the content-creation application, is exported to cross-platform proprietary XML, and then optimized into
platform-specific binary data and loaded by the game. We decided to incorporate
an additional step into this process in order to automate submission of asset information into a MySQL database that was set aside especially for tracking assets as
soon as they were produced. This step would typically occur after the optimization
step, when the content creator submits the source files, cross-platform XML, and
platform-specific binary files into source control.

This worked as follows: when an asset was added or even modified within Perforce (our source-control software), a PC functioning as a dedicated asset-tracking
machine detected the addition or alteration. This PC immediately queued the asset
to be copied to a local networked Xbox 360 running a lightweight version of the
game's rendering engine as a separate executable. This program, called the Asset
Viewer, displayed the asset on the screen in isolation. Simultaneously, the Asset
Viewer collected technical metadata, including an average of the asset's rendering
expense, its final post-optimization polygon count and memory footprint, material
information such as texture resolution and shader usage, and if any errors were
detected at any point while attempting to gather these values. Running the Asset Viewer application on an actual Xbox 360 console ensured that collected data
would be as accurate as possible, having been derived from the physical console
CPU and GPU. If the process completed without errors, the Xbox 360 returned

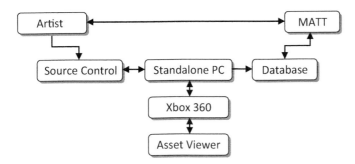

Figure 3.1. Relationships in automated asset metric gathering.

those values along with a screenshot of the asset to the stand-alone PC. The screenshot showed the asset at the identity orientation at the origin of the scene, zoomed in to accommodate variable asset size. The asset-tracking machine then submited the screenshot and all associated data directly to the database. If there was an error, the machine did not submit the asset and instead emailed a description of the error to the asset creator.

Even with this system in place, we had no existing method to easily interpret the database information we were automatically gathering. While the Asset Viewer and asset-tracking PC were being set up, we began work on a tool to cleanly present the contents of the database to an end user. This database viewing tool was our first step toward implementation of an actual asset-tracking interface and was called the Mega Asset Tracking Tool, or MATT. Written in Python, MATT communicated with the database and display information such as an asset's source file of origin and any data recorded by the Asset Viewer. We incorporated into it the ability to search for specific assets and browse the asset screenshots that were taken by the Asset Viewer. The intent was to provide easy access to the database without negatively impacting the workflow of artists, outsourcers, or coordinators. By writing our own interface, we maintained full control over how our end users would experience and interact with the asset tracking system we had constructed (see Figure 3.1).

3.4   Rapid Development of the MATT Tool Using Python

The MATT tool immediately accomplished the initial goal criteria that had been established during the problem analysis phase, but we understood and expected that additional unforeseen features would eventually be requested and incorporated well after the planning stage. For this reason we chose to write the majority of the user interface using wxPython. This turned out to be a wise decision and allowed us to combine partial or existing stand-alone Python tools into the MATT tool

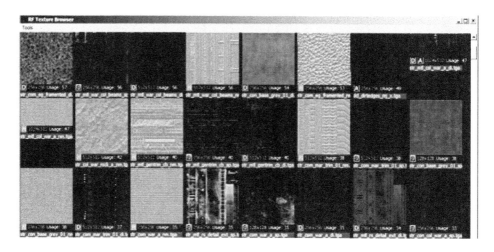

Figure 3.2. Visualizing texture statistics using MATT texture browser module. Textures are annotated with category information, resolution, usage statistics, and shape-recognition for duplication prevention. (See Color Plate II.)

with relative ease. The MATT tool eventually became an elaborate container for a variety of previously existing stand-alone asset-tracking tools. This greatly assisted rapid development of the tool, because Python modules could be written in isolation or even ported from pre-existing Python tools, and then added as a module simply by importing the Python script in the MATT tool.

One specific feature that took advantage of Python's flexibility was a system for visualizing texture usage statistics that was initially written as a separate Python script. As artists became accustomed to using the MATT tool for viewing the project asset library, they began to request access to more data, such as material information or one-click shortcuts to source art files. The Python texture browser was imported into the MATT tool with only a few lines of script, and soon the tool encompassed not only asset tracking after asset submission but also assisted during content creation. Now users could perform traditional texture optimization tasks such as wavelet comparisons or resolution standardization using the same tool they used for browsing the asset library (see Figure 3.2).

The texture browser leveraged the Python Imaging Library (PIL) to interpret raw TGA images before they were optimized into platform-specific binary data (see Figure 3.3). The PIL provided a powerful image manipulation API, which allowed us to perform automated image comparison operations by combining PIL functions. For example, one problem was unintentional artist duplication of imported texture data, which we solved with the texture browser by routinely comparing every TGA image to every other TGA image and generating a hue/saturation/-color and resolution-independent percentage of pixel similarity. Duplicate textures

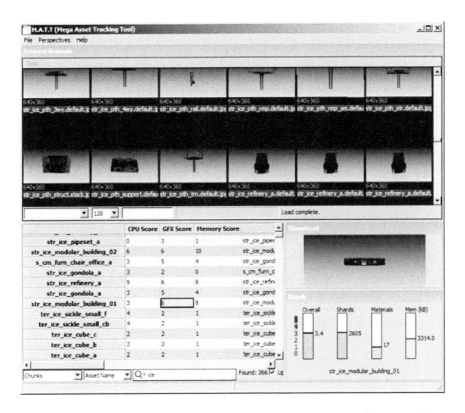

Figure 3.3. MATT tool user interface with module integration. The texture browser interface is included in the top panel and is currently displaying asset screenshots from the Asset Viewer.

were automatically detected and discarded, even at different resolutions or with other aberrations such as hue or tint shifting. This process typically took under ten minutes to run a full comparison of all TGA image data.

As different disciplines requested more features, we simply added more modules to the MATT tool that met these ongoing requirements. Advanced user interface (AUI) support in wxPython allowed for custom configurations of any of MATT tool's expanding range of module windows without having to explicitly and manually manage the windows ourselves. AUI simply acted as a container for existing wxPython panels with no modification.

Part way through the project, another stand-alone application was written in Python to visualize asset-data information as a GPU-accelerated heat map over a top-down image of the entire game world. To do this, the tool parsed the game world XML data for position information and then rendered this information onto a single image. Even though this module used nonstandard Python libraries such as

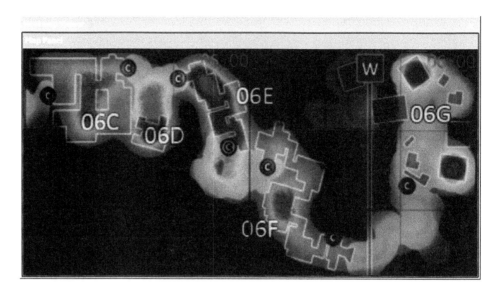

Figure 3.4. Visualizing in-game asset density using MATT heat map module.

pyOpenGL for optimal speed, it was incorporated into the MATT tool painlessly, bringing even more analysis information together underneath one unified tool.

In order to effectively tie the operation of the separate modules together, each module drew from a shared library of internal functions. These functions parsed every element of the game world XML as separate hierarchical objects with as fine granularity as possible. While the MATT tool interface remained the same, internally it was reconfigured to consider traditional assets as conglomerations of subassets, such as mesh data, materials, and textures (see Figure 3.4).

In short, rapid application development in Python allowed us the necessary speed and flexibility to accommodate a far wider range of features and functionalities than we initially anticipated. Multiple tech artists worked on individual MATT features simultaneously, and the amount of time spent building the MATT tool and associated infrastructure ended up amounting to a few months, compared to ongoing years of maintenance using the manual method on previous Volition projects. We surpassed the capabilities of a traditional project asset tracking system almost immediately and were soon able to dedicate all our time towards specific module optimizations and features. Within a year, *Red Faction: Armageddon* had entered post-production and the MATT tool had expanded to govern material library standardization, texture usage and optimization, and the high-poly source art library; supported instant drag-and-drop into 3dS Max; to graph arbitrary asset data in heat maps; and to parse the entirety of the game asset tree in a hierarchical treeview.

3.5 Automating In-Game Search with the BugViewer

As production on *Red Faction: Armageddon* continued, the need arose to extend the MATT tool's capability to instantly search all asset data outside the game-content hierarchy, specifically by cataloging assets and locations in the game world itself. The need for this functionality was twofold: artists, directors, leads, and producers needed a way to rapidly search, locate, and associate metadata with assets at their in-game locations as well as in isolation. The quality-assurance team needed to efficiently test the game during all stages of production and expressed interest in similar functionality. Initially, the capability to perform a search through the game level data for specific asset information such as location or density was planned as an extension of already existing MATT modules. However, upon investigation, we soon discovered that for this specific request, incorporation into the full MATT tool developer feature set was not ideal. We had no need to expose all the content creation and alteration features of the MATT tool to the quality-assurance team, so the BugViewer remained a stand-alone utility, used by both the quality-assurance and the development team.

We remained with Python as the development scripting language of choice, and built a prototype tool called the BugViewer (see Figure 3.5). This stand-alone

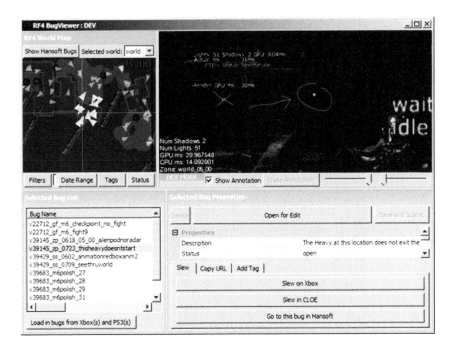

Figure 3.5. In-game location search and annotation using the BugViewer.

wxPython application served a variety of purposes that assisted the MATT tool during everyday development, while also being available to the quality-assurance team with no developer modification.

A growing concern was tool-overload; that the sheer number and complexity of development tools would itself become a detriment to productivity. In order to preemptively combat this issue, we registered a custom hyperlink protocol (bugviewer://) within Windows that would provide one-click connections between each of the interrelated applications that now constituted our asset tracking suite. The BugViewer could generate a hyperlink that users could share that would immediately return whoever followed it back to the in-game location entry in the BugViewer interface, which could then in turn automatically teleport the user to that same location in the level editor or game.

Once this hyperlink system was complete, we had effectively removed the need for anyone to manually look for anything in the game or in the asset library that had already been located by someone else. Users could play the game on their Xbox 360 consoles and execute a command at any time that would save a screenshot, position information and debugging values to an XML file on the Xbox 360 hard drive. This allowed users to tag' game locations with metadata directly on their development consoles, with or without a connected PC. The BugViewer could later retrieve these files from any networked Xbox 360 consoles and submit them along with any associated annotations to a shared repository in Perforce. This would automatically maintain all location information in a machine-readable and searchable format. The BugViewer also provided users with an interactive map to browse and search all the communal "tags" that were ever made. Users could click a single button to instantly teleport the game camera or level editor camera to revisit that exact location to see what that location currently looked like in the game.

One unexpected result of this system was that developers began using the BugViewer for more than just calling out problematic locations in the game. For example, art directors sent hyperlinks to annotated game locations via email to describe revision and iteration requests, while others saved local hyperlinks to common locations purely for convenience. Clicking a hyperlink would immediately open the relevant location in the BugViewer, which acted as a hub with one-click options to instantly teleport the user to that same location in the level editor, the actual game, or to any scheduled tasks related to that location in Hansoft (our schedule management software). Any asset in question was also immediately available for scrutiny in the MATT tool, which still ran separately.

3.6   Lessons Learned

At the time of writing, post-production of Volition's *Red Faction: Armageddon* is underway, and the asset-tracking tools described in this article are still being maintained, updated, and planned for future revision. However it is quite possible to derive a set of overall lessons learned from our approach to automated asset tracking.

The success of our suite of asset-tracking applications was primarily due to a core set of development criteria, specifically,

- programmatic automation wherever possible;

- rapid plug-and-play tool development accommodated by using Python;

- relevant content-specific display of meaningful information;

- efficient search and retrieval of assets and asset-specific metadata;

- simple interfaces built on top of powerful, flexible and modular underlying tools.

In conclusion, our investigation and subsequent automation of the majority of our asset-tracking system turned out to be a significant return on investment at Volition, both in terms of development time saved and asset iteration and optimization time made available as a result. By building a custom modular workflow of interconnected automated systems designed to provide usable information derived from tracking all game assets, we were able to place more finite control in the hands of every member of our development team and thereby improve the technical quality of our product.

4

Continuous Integration for Games

Steven Ramirez

4.1 Introduction

Video games are made up of complex systems that form a cohesive, high-performance application. Content creation for those systems involves using external tools, such as Maya and Photoshop, to take an asset from concept to running in-engine. Developers establish asset pipelines to streamline that process. While each team has their own demands that need to be met, there are requirements that overlap for all teams. This can include automation of unit/build testing, asset generation, build creation, and notification of build errors. CruiseControl.NET (CCNet) is a free, open-source suite of applications by ThoughtWorks that provides the functionality for the above tasks through XML configuration files and the integration server. This chapter explaains how to use the CruiseControl.NET server and provides a framework for you to use.

4.2 Build Pipelines: How Do They Work?

The process of taking source code and assets from their original format to the final, playable game format is called the build pipeline. Build pipelines can provide you with essential information you need in real time. This information can be the current state of the build, unit test failures, and asset changes. Here, we will discuss parts of the build pipeline.

4.2.1 What is CruiseControl.NET?

CCNet is a suite of applications created for the purpose of managing and automating the build pipeline. There are three parts to CCNet: the automated integration server, a web interface called the Web Dashboard and the notification tool called CCTray.

```
<triggers>
    <scheduleTrigger time="00:00" buildCondition="ForceBuild"
            name="Scheduled">
    <weekDays>
    <weekDay>Monday</weekDay>
    <weekDay>Tuesday</weekDay>
    <weekDay>Wednesday</weekDay>
    <weekDay>Thursday</weekDay>
    <weekDay>Friday</weekDay>
    </weekDays>
    </scheduleTrigger>
</triggers>


<sourcecontrol type="p4">
    <view>//depot/MyProject/...</view>
    <executable>C:\Program Files\Perforce\p4.exe</executable>
    <client>MyServerWorkspace</client>
    <user>JohnSmith</user>
    <password>SuperSecretPassword1234</password>
    <port>YourSourceControlMachine:1666</port>
    <timeZoneOffset>0</timeZoneOffset>
    <autoGetSource>true</autoGetSource>
    <forceSync>false</forceSync>
</sourcecontrol>
```

Listing 4.1. A snippet of a typical CCNet config file.

The heart of CCNet is the automated integration server. The server is configured through an XML interface. It defines what tasks to do when there are updates to your source control project. Listing 4.1 shows a snippet of the server XML configuration.

The Web Dashboard is a website that the server can host and from which relevant information can be relayed. Clients can also trigger builds through the website interface. Moreover, the server can display statistics of build results. In

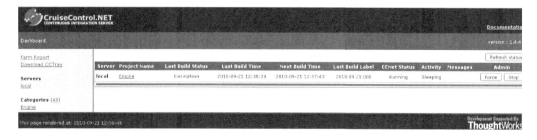

Figure 4.1. The Web Dashboard in action.

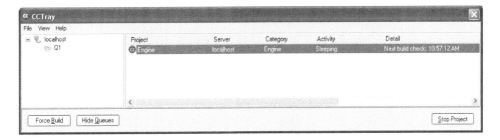

Figure 4.2. The CCTray user interface.

the CCNet server XML file, we could use the `<statistics>` tag to generate the build failure rate over time. Figure 4.1 shows what the website looks like.

CCTray is an optional tool that runs in the Windows System Tray. It provides feedback of the build progress as well as gives the ability to kick off builds on the CCNet server. Moreover, users can volunteer to fix builds and have their username show up in other CCTray clients as the person fixing the build. Figure 4.2 shows what CCTray looks like.

4.2.2 Things to Know Before Getting Started

What your team needs to know and what can be automated can be broken down to the following three tasks: build status notification, asset/build generation, statistics and unit/build/regression testing. First, build status notification allows the team to keep a constant eye on the state of the build. As soon as someone checks in code that prevents the project from compiling, the team can find out how it broke through the change log in the Web Dashboard. The change log is pulled down from the source control project specified in the CCNet XML configuration file. CCNet provides support for multiple source control applications including Perforce, Subversion, Alienbrain, and Git. An example of how to set up Perforce in the server XML file can be found in Section 4.3.2. Notification of changes can be done in the form of an email or in the CCTray.

Asset and build generation involve more work because they involve the compiler-, asset- and content-generation tools. CCNet can break down each step of the build process into CCNet projects that can run individually or can trigger other parts of the pipeline to start. It is up to the build engineer to configure the server to meet the team's needs. An example of how to kick off nightly builds is covered later in Section 4.3.2.

CCNet provides support for NUnit. NUnit is a unit testing framework for all .NET languages written in C#. Its test results can be caught by CCNet and be included in the build results. If there is a task your team needs that is not supported, there is an extendable .NET plug-in framework in CCNet. You can, for example, create a task to update builds to a secured server. Although an example of how to do this is not in this article, the ThoughtWorks CCNet website does provide examples of how to do this. For more information on CCNet or the installer, please go to http://www.ccnet.thoughtworks.com.

4.3 Using CCNet and More!

In this section we will go over installing CCNet and setting up the CCNet integration server. Moreover, we will outline how to put together a CCNet project that will compile Visual Studio projects. Finally, we will go over sending out build status notifications via email as well as setting up CCTray.

4.3.1 Installing and Using the Server

The CCNet installer can be downloaded from the ThoughtWorks website. As of the writing of this article, the latest revision of CCNet is Version 1.5. The CCNet Web Dashboard will be available if IIS (Internet Information Services) is on the server. However, IIS is not needed if you would like to use the server only for .NET remoting and CCTray, since CCTray can use .NET remoting to connect and communicate with the CCNet server.

Please note that if you have installed IIS after installing the .NET framework, you will need to run `aspnet_regiis -i` under the .NET framework install directory to have .NET register with IIS. Otherwise, the Web Dashboard will give a "Do not have access to database" error when trying to connect to the CCNet server. This tool can be found under the .NET 2.0 framework installation directory: `C:\Windows\Microsoft.NET\Framework\v2.0.50727`.

In your CCNet installation directory (this is typically `C:\Program Files \CruiseControl.NET`), a `ccnet.config` file is in the same directory as the server executable. This is the file that we are editing for use in the sample project. If you just run the CCNet executable without any arguments, it will try to run a project config file from its local directory. You can specify what config file to use with the `--config:file` argument. It is worth mentioning that CCNet provides a way to validate the XML config file and check for any errors. You can use the `-validate` command line argument with the CCNet executable or run the CruiseControl.NET-Validator that comes with the CCNet tools installation. Once you have CCNet installed and running, you are ready to run your first project.

4.3.2 Starting Up the Project

A CCNet project is a set of tasks that the server will run once a set of criteria has been met. The CCNet project may be started when there are changes in source control, a team member requests a build, another project starts it, or it is scheduled to run at certain times of the day. Your project will initially look like Listing 4.2.

```
<cruisecontrol xmlns:cb="urn:ccnet.config.builder">
   <project name="MyFirstProject">
   </project>
</cruisecontrol>
```

Listing 4.2. Starting the CCNet project.

The `<cruisecontrol>` element is the header that starts each CCNet XML server config file. For each build project that you want to add to the server, you must add `<project>` blocks. These blocks encapsulate tasks, triggers, publishers, and source control settings. Tasks run when the project starts. Triggers are actions that can kick-start the project. Publishers are post-build events that can happen after a build failure or state change depending on your settings.

Next we want to add the working directory, XML build log directory, project category, and modification-checking frequency. They are all part of the project settings. Listing 4.3 shows how we will set up the CCNet project settings.

```
<cruisecontrol xmlns:cb="urn:ccnet.config.builder">
   <queue name="Q1" duplicates="ApplyForceBuildsReAdd"/>
   <project name="MyFirstProject">

<workingDirectory>C:\WorkingDir</workingDirectory>
<artifactDirectory>C:\WorkingDir\CCNetArtifacts</artifactDirectory>
<category>Super Awesome Game</category>
<webURL>http://192.168.7.216:8080/ViewFarmReport.aspx</webURL>
<modificationDelaySeconds>100</modificationDelaySeconds>

   </project>
</cruisecontrol>
```

Listing 4.3. The project settings.

The project settings are made up of the following blocks:

- `<workingdirectory>`,
- `<artifactdirectory>`,
- `<category>`,
- `<webURL>`,
- `<modificationDelaySeconds>`.

The `<workingdirectory>` block specifies where on the local hard drive the project directory is found. The "name" attribute is the project name that will show up on the CCNet website. The server will generate XML logs whenever a build is started. You tell it where to put those logs with the `<artifactDirectory>` block. They can be cleaned up using the artifact clean-up publisher that is covered later. The `<category>` tag can be used to organize projects. For example, if two projects are building the same game but for different platforms, similarly named categories can help group these projects. The `<webURL>` is the reporting URL for the project. It is used by the email publisher and CCTray to link clients to the server website [Roberts and Willems 10]. The `<modificationDelaySeconds>` block is used to specify the time delay in seconds before checking the source control for changes. Typically, this setting should be more than a minute to avoid flooding the source control server with traffic.

The next thing that we want to add is a schedule trigger. Schedule triggers are not necessary for a CCNet project, but they are useful if you want, for example, nightly builds of your game. Listing 4.4 shows the schedule trigger settings.

The `<scheduleTrigger>` is set so that the CCNet project runs on the days specified in the `<weekDay>` block. The trigger In Listing 4.4 has the CCNet project

```
<cruisecontrol xmlns:cb="urn:ccnet.config.builder">
   <queue name="Q1" duplicates="ApplyForceBuildsReAdd"/>
   <project name="MyFirstProject">

<workingDirectory>C:\WorkingDir</workingDirectory>
<artifactDirectory>C:\WorkingDir\CCNetArtifacts</artifactDirectory>
<category>Super Awesome Game</category>
<webURL>http://192.168.7.216:8080/ViewFarmReport.aspx</webURL>
<modificationDelaySeconds>100</modificationDelaySeconds>

      <triggers>
      <scheduleTrigger time="00:00" buildCondition="ForceBuild"
           name="Scheduled">
      <weekDays>
      <weekDay>Monday</weekDay>
      <weekDay>Tuesday</weekDay>
      <weekDay>Wednesday</weekDay>
      <weekDay>Thursday</weekDay>
      <weekDay>Friday</weekDay>
      </weekDays>
      </scheduleTrigger>
      </triggers>

   </project>
</cruisecontrol>
```

Listing 4.4. Adding in a schedule trigger.

run at midnight. You can change the time to run with the "time" attribute (you have to specify military time). The "buildCondition" attribute modifies when the CCNet project will build. If you specify "ForceBuild", then the project will always run even if there are no changes noted in source control. You can also set the "buildCondition" attribute to "IfModificationExists" which will make the project run only if there are changes.

A source control tag is used to let the server know what type of source control application you are using. CCNet has support for many types of source control, including AlienBrain, Perforce, and Subversion. CCNet uses this tag to connect to your source control and sync the directories you specify. In this way, CCNet can operate the tasks on the latest files and work as a continuous integration server. In our example, we set up the source control tag to use Perforce (see Listing 4.5).

```
<cruisecontrol xmlns:cb="urn:ccnet.config.builder">
   <queue name="Q1" duplicates="ApplyForceBuildsReAdd"/>
   <project name="MyFirstProject">

<workingDirectory>C:\WorkingDir</workingDirectory>
<artifactDirectory>C:\WorkingDir\CCNetArtifacts</artifactDirectory>
<category>Super Awesome Game</category>
<webURL>http://192.168.7.216:8080/ViewFarmReport.aspx</webURL>
<modificationDelaySeconds>100</modificationDelaySeconds>

       <triggers>
       <scheduleTrigger time="00:00" buildCondition="ForceBuild"
           name="Scheduled">
       <weekDays>
       <weekDay>Monday</weekDay>
       <weekDay>Tuesday</weekDay>
       <weekDay>Wednesday</weekDay>
       <weekDay>Thursday</weekDay>
       <weekDay>Friday</weekDay>
       </weekDays>
       </scheduleTrigger>
       </triggers>

       <sourcecontrol type="p4">
       <view>//depot/MyProject/...</view>
       <executable>C:\Program Files\Perforce\p4.exe</executable>
       <client>MyServerWorkspace</client>
       <user>JohnSmith</user>
       <password>SuperSecretPassword1234</password>
       <port>YourSourceControlMachine:1666</port>
       <timeZoneOffset>0</timeZoneOffset>
       <autoGetSource>true</autoGetSource>
       <forceSync>false</forceSync>
       </sourcecontrol>

   </project>
</cruisecontrol>
```

Listing 4.5. Setting up the Perforce source control tag.

The source control type is specified in the "type" attribute of the
`<sourcecontrol>` tag. To let CCNet know that we are using Perforce, we set
the value to "p4." In general, CCNet will do a sync to the latest changes by default. The `<autoGetSource>` tag can be set to "false" if you want CCNet to run
the build tasks without syncing. It is worth noting that it will normally only sync
file changes just as Perforce would do when going through the Perforce client. To
change this behavior, you can set the `<forceSync>` tag to "true" to have it force
update every file in the Perforce view. It is important to note that the `<client>`
tag is the server's Perforce workspace. CCNet will only check the `<view>` directory
for changes; however, it will update the entire depot during a sync. Thus, the
`<client>` should be a workspace that only has the projects you want to update.
Note that this is a special case for the Perforce source control block. Changelists
are read from the sync and are posted to the Web Dashboard to keep track of what
files where changed, by whom, and any notes from when the changed files were
submitted.

4.3.3 Tasks

You need to provide the CCNet project with a task list before it will do anything.
Note that tasks run in the order that they appear. If a task should fail, CCNet
will move onto the publisher section. There are many types of tasks that CCNet
can handle, including building source projects with Nant and MSBuild. If you find
that you need to run your own tool, then CCNet can run that application through
the Windows command line utility.

One of the tasks that you can perform is using MSBuild to compile your project.
MSBuild is a separate tool that comes with Visual Studio and the .NET Framework
to compile .NET projects and has support for building C/C++ projects with the
Visual Studio compiler. If you were to look at .NET projects, you would see that
they are just MSBuild scripts. MSBuild scripts are XML files that script how a
project should be built. Listing 4.6 shows how the MSBuild task is set up.

```
<cruisecontrol xmlns:cb="urn:ccnet.config.builder">
   <queue name="Q1" duplicates="ApplyForceBuildsReAdd"/>
   <project name="MyFirstProject">

<workingDirectory>C:\WorkingDir</workingDirectory>
<artifactDirectory>C:\WorkingDir\CCNetArtifacts</artifactDirectory>
<category>Super Awesome Game</category>
<webURL>http://192.168.7.216:8080/ViewFarmReport.aspx</webURL>
<modificationDelaySeconds>100</modificationDelaySeconds>

      <triggers>
      <scheduleTrigger time="00:00" buildCondition="ForceBuild"
           name="Scheduled">
      <weekDays>
      <weekDay>Monday</weekDay>
      <weekDay>Tuesday</weekDay>
```

```
                    <weekDay>Wednesday</weekDay>
                    <weekDay>Thursday</weekDay>
                    <weekDay>Friday</weekDay>
                    </weekDays>
                    </scheduleTrigger>
                    </triggers>

                    <sourcecontrol type="p4">
                    <view>//depot/MyProject/...</view>
                    <executable>C:\Program Files\Perforce\p4.exe</executable>
                    <client>MyServerWorkspace</client>
                    <user>JohnSmith</user>
                    <password>SuperSecretPassword1234</password>
                    <port>YourSourceControlMachine:1666</port>
                    <timeZoneOffset>0</timeZoneOffset>
                    <autoGetSource>true</autoGetSource>
                    <forceSync>false</forceSync>
                    </sourcecontrol>

                    <tasks>
                    <msbuild>

                    <executable>C:\WINDOWS\Microsoft.NET\Framework\v2.0.50727
                                    \MSBuild.exe</executable>
                    <workingDirectory>C:\WorkingDir\source</workingDirectory>
                    <projectFile>MyProject.sln</projectFile>
                    <buildArgs>/p:Configuration=Debug</buildArgs>
                    <targets>Build;Test</targets>
                    <timeout>900</timeout>
                    <logger>C:\Program Files\CruiseControl.NET\server\ThoughtWorks
                                .CruiseControl.MsBuild.dll</logger>
                    </msbuild>
                    </tasks>

            </project>
        </cruisecontrol>
```

Listing 4.6. Adding the task section.

All tasks, including <msbuild>, must go inside the <tasks> block. The MSBuild
version that the <executable> tag points to is .NET 2.0. Later versions of the
.NET framework will also have newer versions of MSBuild. You can choose to
use the newer versions by changing the .NET framework version number inside
the executable path. The <workingdirectory> block points to the Visual Studio
solution directory. The <projectFile> block points to the solution we want to
build. The <buildArgs> block has the extra arguments you can pass to MSBuild.
MSBuild allows you to override project level properties with the "/property" or
"/p" arguments.

The <targets> block are the targets that will be compiled (separated by semi-
colons). These are the same targets that are defined in a MSBuild project. The
<timeout> tag can be used to tell CCNet how long to wait before shutting down
the task. If you would like to use your own custom logger, the <logger> tag can
be point to a custom DLL logger. CCNet has a default logger, but it does not

format the output. You can find the custom MSBuild logger through a search of
the ThoughtWorks CruiseControl.NET website [Roberts and Rodemeyer 07].

4.3.4   Publishers

It is common practice for email notifications to be sent when the build is broken.
You can send email notifications to leads, producers, or anyone who would like to be
notified by email. You can also use publishers to clean up build logs and generate
statistics for the project. Listing 4.7 demonstrates how the email publisher is set
up.

```
<cruisecontrol xmlns:cb="urn:ccnet.config.builder">
   <queue name="Q1" duplicates="ApplyForceBuildsReAdd"/>
   <project name="MyFirstProject">

<workingDirectory>C:\WorkingDir</workingDirectory>
<artifactDirectory>C:\WorkingDir\CCNetArtifacts</artifactDirectory>
<category>Super Awesome Game</category>
<webURL>http://192.168.7.216:8080/ViewFarmReport.aspx</webURL>
<modificationDelaySeconds>100</modificationDelaySeconds>

      <triggers>
      <scheduleTrigger time="00:00" buildCondition="ForceBuild"
            name="Scheduled">
      <weekDays>
      <weekDay>Monday</weekDay>
      <weekDay>Tuesday</weekDay>
      <weekDay>Wednesday</weekDay>
      <weekDay>Thursday</weekDay>
      <weekDay>Friday</weekDay>
      </weekDays>
      </scheduleTrigger>
      </triggers>

      <sourcecontrol type="p4">
      <view>//depot/MyProject/...</view>
      <executable>C:\Program Files\Perforce\p4.exe</executable>
      <client>MyServerWorkspace</client>
      <user>JohnSmith</user>
      <password>SuperSecretPassword1234</password>
      <port>YourSourceControlMachine:1666</port>
      <timeZoneOffset>0</timeZoneOffset>
      <autoGetSource>true</autoGetSource>
      <forceSync>false</forceSync>
      </sourcecontrol>

      <tasks>
      <msbuild>

      <executable>C:\WINDOWS\Microsoft.NET\Framework\v2.0.50727
                  \MSBuild.exe</executable>
      <workingDirectory>C:\WorkingDir\source</workingDirectory>
      <projectFile>MyProject.sln</projectFile>
      <buildArgs>/p:Configuration=Debug</buildArgs>
      <targets>Build;Test</targets>
      <timeout>900</timeout>
```

```
<logger>C:\Program Files\CruiseControl.NET\server\ThoughtWorks
            .CruiseControl.MsBuild.dll</logger>
</msbuild>
</tasks>

<publishers>
<statistics />
<xmllogger logDir=".\XMLLogsc"/>
<modificationHistory  onlyLogWhenChangesFound="true" />
<artifactcleanup cleanUpMethod="KeepLastXBuilds"
        cleanUpValue="50" />

<email from="Servername@gmail.com" mailhost=
        "smtp.gmail.com" mailport="587" includeDetails
        ="TRUE"
mailhostUsername="Servername@YourCompany.com"
        mailhostPassword= "AwesomeServer" useSSL="TRUE">

<users>
<user name="Build Master" group="buildmaster" address=
        "BuildMaster@YourCompany.com"/>
<user name="Coder person" group="codeteam" address=
        "CodeTeam@YourCompany.com"/>
</users>

<groups>
<group name="buildmaster" notification="always"/>
<group name="codeteam" notification="change,failed,
        success"/>
</groups>

<modifierNotificationTypes>
<NotificationType>Failed</NotificationType>
<NotificationType>Fixed</NotificationType>
<NotificationType>Always</NotificationType>
<NotificationType>Change</NotificationType>
<NotificationType>Success</NotificationType>
</modifierNotificationTypes>

<attachments>
<file>C:\Data\LogFile.txt</file>
</attachments>

</email>
</publishers>

    </project>
</cruisecontrol>
```

Listing 4.7. The "Email Publisher" allows you to send emails to individuals or specific groups of people.

In order for the Web Dashboard to function properly, we need to define the <xmllogger> tag and specify where to dump the files. The <modificationhistory> tag notes changes between builds and will keep a log of them. We can then specify dumping to only log items when there are changes to save space on the server. The <statistics> tag must come first after the file merges in order to keep track of file merges. It will also generate stats of broken builds versus good builds over time.

Another useful tag is `<artifactcleanup>` which will remove older entries that are no longer valid from the server. Note that the `<xmllogger>` publisher must be defined after any file merges [Rogers and Sutherland 09].

Email publishers support plain-text and HTML formats. It is highly recommended to have at least one person on the team who will always get build result emails. Before being able to submit emails, mailing host username and passwords must be provided to CCNet. In this example, we set up the publisher to send emails via Gmail. The "from" attribute is the email address that emails will be sent from. You must specify mailing port "587" and set the "useSSL" attribute to "true" before being able to use Gmail [Rogers 10].

The `<users>` block is a list of all the possible users that the email publisher can send messages to. After specifying a name and email address, you can assign that user a "group" category. Groups are the set of people that can be emailed depending on the type of notification they are interested in. Notifications can range from "always," which will email that group regardless of the build result, to "change," which will email that group only when the build has changed from a successful build to a failed one and vice versa. You can add additional notification types by using comma-separated values in the "notification" attribute inside the `<group>` element. The `<modifierNotificationTypes>` block is a list of `<notificationType>` elements. Each `<notificationType>` element is a build state for whom CCNet should send messages.

Attachments can be appended to emails with the `<attachments>` tag. This is useful for appending debug logs for when the project runs unit tests or is building assets.

At this point you should have a project that can compile source and email notifications. Team members can also get up-to-date status updates using CCTray to notify and make requests about the project to be built. For reference, Listing 4.7 shows the complete sample project.

4.3.5   CCTray

CCTray can be installed through the CCNet Web Dashboard or from an installer provided by the ThoughtWorks website. Adding the CCNet server is as simple as going to the CCTray settings and adding the server IP address. It also supports connecting to older versions of the CCNet server. Because you will have projects that do entire builds or specific parts of the build pipeline, be sure that team members only watch projects that are related to their discipline. This is done by checking off which projects you want to watch during the connection setup.

CCTray can display balloon pop-ups when builds are finished. In addition to giving the user a heads-up about new builds, the messages that it displays can be changed. If, for example, there is a new build of a tool that everyone should get, then CCTray can display that whenever that CCNet project finishes the new build. Listing 4.8 shows a CCTray config file set-up to watch a level editor project.

```
<Configuration xmlns:xsd="http://www.w3.org/2001/XMLSchema"
    xmlns:xsi="http://www.w3.org/2001/XMLSchema-instance">
  <Projects>
    <Project serverUrl="tcp://YourAwesomeServer:20000
      /CruiseManager.rem"
        projectName="Level Editor" />
  </Projects>
  <PollPeriodSeconds>5</PollPeriodSeconds>
  <BuildTransitionNotification showBalloon="true">
    <Sound />
    <BalloonMessages>
      <BrokenBuildMessage>
        <Caption>Broken build</Caption>
        <Message>The level editor is broken</Message>
      </BrokenBuildMessage>
      <FixedBuildMessage>
        <Caption>Fixed build</Caption>
        <Message>The level editor has been fixed</Message>
      </FixedBuildMessage>
      <StillFailingBuildMessage>
        <Caption>Build still failing</Caption>
        <Message>The level editor is still broken.</Message>
      </StillFailingBuildMessage>
      <StillSuccessfulBuildMessage>
        <Caption>Great work</Caption>
        <Message>The level editor has been updated!
          Please update.</Message>
      </StillSuccessfulBuildMessage>
    </BalloonMessages>
  </BuildTransitionNotification>
  <TrayIconDoubleClickAction>ShowStatusWindow
    </TrayIconDoubleClickAction>
</Configuration>
```

Listing 4.8. CCTray config file.

The tags that we want to modify to make custom messages are the `<project>` and `<BalloonMessage>` tags. The "serverURL" attribute is the TCP connection to the CCNet server. In addition to specifying the server, you have to let CCTray know what project it is watching. The "projectName" attribute handles this. Once that block is finished, we can change the messages for the build status notifications. The messages we can change are

- `<FixedBuildMessage>`,

- `<BrokenBuildMessage>`,

- `<StillBrokenMessage>`,

- `<StillSuccessfulMessage>`.

Each message tag has a `<caption>` and `<message>` tag for the balloon notification that will be displayed. The `<message>` tag is the one to modify if you want to let people know to sync up for a new version of a tool.

4.4   Conclusion

The process discussed in this chapter should be a starting point for your own project. For handling assets, most of the project settings will remain similar. If you are in need of a task or builder that is not provided by CCNet, an extendable framework built in the form of .NET DLL plug-ins can be utilized to provide advanced functionality. The ThoughtWorks website provides a sample on how to get started. If you would like to run CruiseControl.NET on a separate platform such as Linux or Mac, then there is an alternative called simply CruiseControl. It is the predecessor to CruiseControl.NET and provides much of the same functionality. For more information on CruiseControl, please visit http://cruisecontrol.sourceforge.net/.

Once you have the server up and running, be sure that the team has installed and setup CCTray to start getting data from the server. A quick tutorial by the build engineer should be provided to make sure everyone understands how to use CCTray and the Web Dashboard. Changes to the project can be closely monitored and lessen the pain (hopefully) of finding out when the build breaks.

Acknowledgments

I'd like to thank my coworker William Roberts at Schell Games for proofreading my article and providing some great feedback. Additionally, a thank you goes to all of the people who contributed to CruiseControl.NET at ThoughtWorks. And finally, thank you to my fiance Chelsea Hardesty for her patience during all my late nights working on this article. If you have any questions or comments, I can be reached at Sramirez@SchellGames.com.

Bibliography

[Roberts and Rodemeyer 07] Mike Roberts and Christian Rodemeyer. "Using CruiseControl.NET with MSBuild." Available at http://confluence.public. thoughtworks.org/display/CCNET/Using+CruiseControl.NET+with+ MSBuild, 2007.

[Roberts and Willems 10] Mike Roberts and Ruben Willems. "Project Configuration Block." Available at http://confluence.public.thoughtworks.org/display/ CCNET/Project+Configuration+Block, 2010.

[Rogers 10] Owen Rogers. "MSBuild Task." Available at http://confluence.public. thoughtworks.org/display/CCNET/MsBuild+Task, 2010.

[Rogers and Sutherland 09] Owen Rogers and Craig Sutherland. "XML Log Publisher." Available at http://confluence.public.thoughtworks.org/display/ CCNET/Xml+Log+Publisher, 2009.

5

Persistence Management of Asset Metadata and Tags

Jaewon Jung

5.1 Introduction

Game development has to deal with a gigantic number of assets; more than ten gigabytes of data are not uncommon. If one considers not-yet-optimized-for-release assets, which are required while developing, it can be even more. Accordingly, tools for game development should also be able to deal with a huge volume of assets effectively and offer developers a way of quickly pinpointing a specific asset they want, by whatever criteria, among this pool of assets.

Each asset can have many associated metadata, for example dimensions, format, and mip count for image and triangle count, and vertex count and LOD information for geometry. Usually, developers want to sort and search assets based on these metadata. The metadata for a huge number of assets can also be quite large, and it requires some time to gather all the metadata for every asset. As the development proceeds, assets are frequently added, removed, and changed. Therefore, persistently keeping the metadata for assets across runs and being able to selectively update them when needed, only for changed assets, become must-have features for a level editor.

A tag-based management of data has many advantages over a traditional hierarchy-based management, which has been extensively used in the folder-based file system and the web browser bookmarks. Tags can also be considered one of metadata for the asset, but it is external data, not intrinsic data embedded in the asset data itself. This method requires a somewhat different approach from other metadata.

In this chapter, I'll describe considerations and issues one encounters while implementing this kind of asset metadata management system. Specifically, I'll focus on how one should design and structure the persistence system of asset metadata in order to minimize blocking the user while dealing with huge assets.

5.2   Usual Metadata

We deal with intrinsic metadata first. Each type of game asset like textures, geometric models, animations, and sounds has its own set of metadata that can be a frequent target of queries during development. All the metadata should be collected and cached the first time the tool is run. This may be time consuming. Once cached, that data should be saved in a persistent format and properly updated when any asset changes. Also, this kind of operation should be fast enough, even with a huge number of assets, so as not to block a developer's workflow. A plain file first comes to a mind as a storage format.

5.2.1   Storage Format to Use

One should first choose whether to use a text or a binary file. Then, the exact file format should be decided upon. Though a binary format can generally be more compact and more efficient to parse, I'll discuss using a text format for the sake of human readability and personal preference (Nonetheless, the overall concept is also applicable to binary formats).

For a file format, I recommend XML [Wiki 11a] or JSON [Wiki 11b] because both are quite flexible, battle-tested formats. Also, there are many public parsers/generators for these formats, and one of them can be easily incorporated into the existing game/engine code; however, any reasonable text format will work. One should keep in mind that the parsing speed should be fast enough for a 10 MB or larger file in order to avoid doing harm to the overall loading time of the editor. This should be considered when choosing between an open-source/commercial parser or implementing your own.

5.2.2   Don't Block the User

Parsing the metadata persistence file and applying the loaded data to the editor may take a few seconds. Also, you should recompute the metadata for changed or newly added assets. Above all, on the first run (meaning no asset metadata has been previously cached), the editor should compute and cache metadata for all assets before this system can be practically used by a level designer. Even for the first time, the system must respond to user inputs like scrolling and then compute metadata for visible assets first in order to be useful as soon as possible.

Thus, background processing or threading must be considered while designing the system. Also, it'll be a great advantage if the underlying engine supports a threaded or background loading of various types of assets. Otherwise, one should resort to a nonideal timer-based approach for loading assets and caching their metadata.

5.2.3 Incremental Update: Main DataBase and Transactions

Let's suppose the system successfully gathered all metadata and saved them to a database file. At the next run of the editor, some asset changes have been detected. In that case, the system should properly update the database. However, naively updating the database in memory and resaving it on each occasion can be very time consuming and block the user.

We adopt the concept of differential backup [Wiki 11c]. Basically, it means that after the initial full gathering, the system saves changes like data update, addition, and deletion as a transaction file separate from the main data base file. The generated transaction files (there can be one transaction file or several for each asset type) in one run are merged at the start of the next run of the editor. Using this approach, the asset management system can append each change instead of saving the whole updated database to a file every time a new metadata is cached.

Let's suppose that we use XML format for the transaction file. When a change should be saved, it doesn't parse the file as an XML file at all. Instead, it just goes to the end of file, deletes some end tags, appends data related to the change, and restores previously deleted end tags. This approach is essential since, in the first run, the transaction file(s) can become quite large (it's the first time, so there is nothing in the main database), and it'll cause a stall if one tries to parse it as XML every time a new asset is cached. See Listing 5.1 for a code sample.

```
FILE *transactionFile = fopen(fullPath.c_str(), "r+t");
if(transactionFile == NULL)
    return false;
const char endTag[] = "</Transactions>";

// To delete the end tag of "</Transactions>"
int result = fseek(transactionFile, -( (long)sizeof( endTag ) )
    + 1, SEEK_END);

if(result != 0)
// It means this is the first transaction saved.
{
    fseek(transactionFile, 0, SEEK_SET);
    fprintf(transactionFile, "<Transactions>\n");
}
fprintf(transactionFile, "%s%s",
                newTransactionNode->getXML().c_str(), endTag);
fclose(transactionFile);
```

Listing 5.1. A code sample of appending new data to the transaction file.

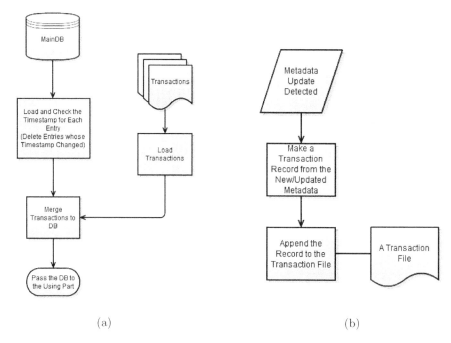

(a)   (b)

Figure 5.1. (a) What happens at loading time; (b) What happens at run time.

At loading time in the next run of the editor, the system reads both the main database file and transaction files and properly merges them before handing them over to a module for use.

Detecting changes. At loading time (see Figure 5.1(a)), the editor will scan the whole asset directory and check if any files were added or deleted. It must also be notified about any changes in the directory at run time. For a Windows platform, you can use a series of API functions starting from FindFirstChangeNotification() for that [MSDNLib 11]. See Figure 5.1(b) for what happens at run time.

5.3 Tags

A traditional hierarchical management of assets is not flexible enough to handle a variety of needs that today's game developments require with the gigantic number of assets. Tags have become a standard approach as an organizational aid that complements the hierarchical grouping.

Tags can be considered metadata, but because of the extrinsic nature of tags and concerns for sharing them, they requires different handling from other metadata.

5.3.1 Tag as a Key

For the intrinsic metadata, the databases are organized by each asset name as a key for an entry (see Listing 5.2). Considering that changes occur per asset and the count and types of intrinsic metadata may be different for each asset type, it's natural to use the asset name or identifier as a key in this case.

In contrast, tags are purely external. For example, in the case of other metadata, an entry should be invalidated if the system finds out its write-access timestamp has changed. However, in the case of tags, it is improper to invalidate all

```xml
<AssetMetaDataFileDB>
 <Models>
  <Model fileName="objects/library/props/cw2_level_specific
     /cw2_liberty_island/cw2_cargo_ship/cw2_cargo_ship.cgf"
     lodCount="3" triangleCount="4856" vertexCount="6147"
     submeshCount="0" nRef="1" physicsTriCount="4"
     physicsSize="1" bSplitLODs="1" textureSize="10"
     tags="" fav="0" timeStamp="129215454816047867">
   <aabb min="-16.224487,-99.513443,-0.26987457" max=
      "15.785674,73.774185,36.674038"/>
   <triCountLOD lod="0" triCount="4856"/>
   <triCountLOD lod="1" triCount="1823"/>
   <triCountLOD lod="2" triCount="874"/>
   <triCountLOD lod="3" triCount="0"/>
   <triCountLOD lod="4" triCount="0"/>
   <triCountLOD lod="5" triCount="0"/>
  </Model>
  <Model fileName="objects/library/props/cw2_level_specific
     /cw2_downtown/signage/cw2_skybridge_signage_lod1.cgf"
     lodCount="0" triangleCount="322" vertexCount="559"
     submeshCount="0" nRef="1" physicsTriCount="0"
     physicsSize="0" bSplitLODs="0" textureSize="10"
     tags="" fav="0" timeStamp="129215454814019945">
   <aabb min="-8.4807739,-0.19953218,-2.540997" max=
      "8.3388901,0.88881469,2.7234063"/>
   <triCountLOD lod="0" triCount="322"/>
   <triCountLOD lod="1" triCount="0"/>
   <triCountLOD lod="2" triCount="0"/>
   <triCountLOD lod="3" triCount="0"/>
   <triCountLOD lod="4" triCount="0"/>
   <triCountLOD lod="5" triCount="0"/>
  </Model>
 <Textures>
  <Texture fileName="levels\wars\cw2_bryant_park
     \cw2_bryant_park.dds"
     nTextureWidth="2048" nTextureHeight="2048"
     nMips="12" format="22" bIsCubemap="0" timeStamp=
     "1275182069"/>
  <Texture fileName="levels\wars\cw2_battery_park\do_not_ship
     \m01_insertion_radar.dds" nTextureWidth="512" nTextureHeight=
     "512" nMips="8" format="24" bIsCubemap="0" timeStamp=
     "1275182068"/>
 </Textures>
</AssetMetaDataFileDB>
```

Listing 5.2. An example of metadata database file in XML.

```
levels/!art/asset_zoo/models/crytek kiev.cgf
levels/!art/asset_zoo/models/doors.cgf
levels/!art/asset_zoo/models/down town.cgf
levels/!art/asset_zoo/models/grand central station.cgf
levels/!art/asset_zoo/models/group_battery_park.cgf
```

Listing 5.3. A tag file example.

associated tags just because of that. Also, tags can be universally applied across all asset types. On the querying side, a tag-key database will be more useful than an asset-key database, in most cases. Furthermore, it is useful to distinguish tags for local use only from shared tags. Therefore, tags will be saved by the tag itself as a key instead of the asset name key, as in the case of intrinsic metadata. Specifically, each tag and its associated asset list will be saved as a separate file (in this case, since just a plain list of assets having that tag is all the information to be saved, no elaborate file format is required) in a designated tag folder (see Listing 5.3).

Considerations for the user interface. In the case of the tag management UI, in accordance with the general scheme above, it's recommended to provide an explicit creation and deletion UI for tags (see Figure 5.2)), rather than an implicit tag management (see Figure 5.3)). Here, I by the implicit way mean, providing a text input UI for tags per each asset and detecting the tag creation/deletion events there from the user input. The explicit way matches better with the internal scheme above and also has advantages in handling shared tags.

Figure 5.2. Explicit tag management UI from Evernote.com.

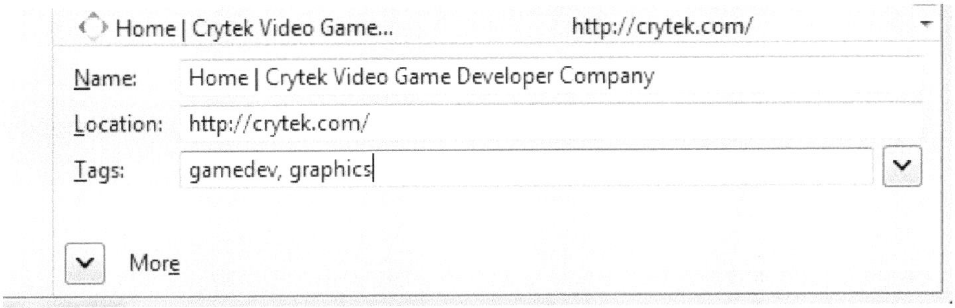

Figure 5.3. Implicit tag management UI from Firefox.

5.3.2 Sharing Tags

There are many ways to share tags, but here we consider only sharing tags by using a version control system (VCS). Implementing tag sharing through a VCS can be especially easy if the editor already supports interactions with the VCS.

There are four essential operations regarding tags as outlined below:

- Create a tag.

- Add assets to a tag.

- Remove assets from a tag.

- Delete a tag.

Tag creation/removal. For shared tags, in addition to the normal task of creating/deleting a tag file, like Listing 5.3, the system should do the corresponding job of updating the VCS repository. For most VCS repositories, this will be a two-step process of marking the file as added/removed and then actually committing that marked change to the repository.

Adding/removing assets. When updating a shared tag, the system will first get the latest version from the VCS and reload the tag file if changed (also lock it if necessary) before doing the actual update. After the update, the change will again be submitted to the repository. This sequence of tasks must be performed by user request through the UI for shared tags.

5.4 Other Considerations

Up to this point, we have discussed some considerations when implementing an asset metadata/tag persistence system. There are some other things which may be worthy of further consideration for a better result.

5.4.1   Use of a Real Database

One possible consideration is using a real database system instead of raw files as a metadata storage. It has some benefits. A database will be generally more reliable and things like differential update can be handled automatically because most databases support the concept of transactions and the differential backup. In the case of tags, by using a database system, sharing can be dealt with naturally without relying on a VCS. It may be slow in overall operations, considering the relative cost of database operations in comparison to the raw file operations. This may be worth pursuing.

5.4.2   Build-Time Generation

In order to minimize the waiting time, asset databases can be generated with each daily build. So, if one gets the latest build, metadata databases will be ready for use and require minimal waiting for gathering only metadata for the users custom assets. Further in this direction, one can even try a submission-time database build. In other words, asset databases are rebuilt every time there is a new data commit to the repository.

5.4.3   Metadata-Aware Format Design.

If you have the luxury of redesigning or changing file formats for each asset type and associated export pipelines, you can make gathering of metadata more efficient. For example, in the header part of each asset file, you can allot a special block that contains metadata for the asset in an optimal layout. Then, without loading an entire asset, the system can collect the metadata very quickly by reading just that header block. To accomplish that, the export pipeline must update that metadata header section properly every time while exporting an asset.

5.4.4   Thumbnails

In relation to the metadata-aware format design, the thumbnail images of assets can also be considered for special treatment. Usually, the assets in the editor are represented by a thumbnail image that describes it properly (see Figure 5.4). For a texture, it'll be the image of the texture itself; for geometry, a rendered shot of it; for a material, a rendered shot of a primitive geometry with that material applied; etc.

Saving these thumbnails in a proper resolution with other metadata won't be feasible in most cases, considering its huge storage consumption. But if you save only the low-res version of it and can devise an efficient storage scheme for them separately from other metadata, storage may become feasible, and then it'll provide the instant (although low-res) display of the thumbnail for all assets instead

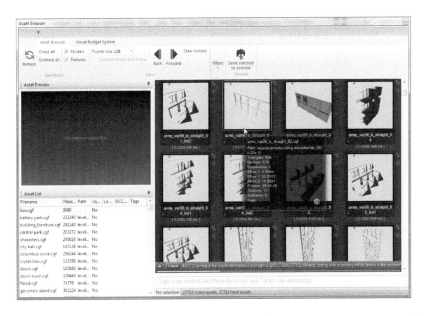

Figure 5.4. Asset browser in sandbox of CryENGINE3. (See Color Plate III.)

of updating thumbnails on demand at run time, which can limit a designer's productivity [Javahawk 09].

5.5 Conclusion

Considering the sky-rocketing cost of game development, creating proper tools for productive development can be even more important than creating the end product itself. Especially for big AAA titles, assets for the game have also become huge, and in order to manage them productively, a dedicated tool like the asset browser in Sandbox is now essential.

In this chapter I have discussed an effective strategy for persistently keeping asset metadata and tags, so as to minimize user waiting or blocking in various asset browsing scenarios.

Bibliography

[Wiki 11a] "XML." *Wikipedia.* Available at http://en.wikipedia.org/wiki/XML, 2011.

[Wiki 11b] "JSON." *Wikipedia.* Available at http://en.wikipedia.org/wiki/JSON, 2011.

[Theodore 09] Steve Theodore. "Check Out That Asset! - A Strategy for Managing Art Files." *Game Developer Magazine* (August 2009), 45–47.

[Wiki 11c] "Incremental Backup." *Wikipedia*. Available at http://en.wikipedia.org/wiki/Incremental_backup, 2011.

[Javahawk 09] "Content Browser Introduction - UDK Tutorials by Javahawk." *YouTube*. Available at http://www.youtube.com/watch?v=EOae7z9jRKU, 2009.

[MSDNLib 11] "FindFirstChangeNotification Function." *MSDN Library*. Available at http://msdn.microsoft.com/en-us/library/aa364417(VS.85).aspx

6

Real-Time Tool Communication
Alan Kimball

6.1 Introduction

When developing a title, game engineers have two major goals. The first is to write a fast, stable game engine. The other goal is to write tools that are highly usable and accessible to content creators. These two goals are often at odds with one another. Highly optimized game code often has significantly different development needs than an extremely customizable code. When developing a game, it is important for the content creators to have as much freedom as possible, but after the game ships, performance and robustness are much more important.

To balance the need for a highly optimized runtime and a robust feedback loop, our team realized that our tool and engine had to be separate, but they needed to communicate very closely. Whenever a tool changed an asset, it was important for the engine copy to be updated in real time. This new requirement for real-time communication between the tools and the engine can add significant overhead to the development of tools. For small, special-purpose tools, adding in real-time communication functionality may increase the development time to an unreasonable level. Instead, building a real-time communication framework on which each tool can be built allows even the smallest change to be updated in real time.

6.2 Integrated Editors

One popular solution to giving immediate feedback to the user is to integrate the engine and the tool code bases. Unfortunately, during development, an engine may not be stable enough to be relied on for content creators' needs. Relying on 100% uptime for the engine may lead to unexpected blockages and confusion if anything goes wrong. Additionally, in some cases, content creators cannot work on the platform on which their assets will finally reside. It would be quite unwieldy to require all content for a console or handheld developer to author all of their assets on the target platform. For these reasons, it is often important to have the tool chain and game engine on completely separate code bases.

6.3   Real-Time Communication

The first step to having a tool chain and engine communicate is the transport layer. Depending on your requirements, there are a number of different options. To maximize our cross-platform abilities, our transport layer was based on top of TCP/IP. By using TCP/IP instead of named pipes, shared files, or any proprietary communication systems, we were able to use the same code to communicate to a wide variety of platforms, including Sony Playstation 3, Microsoft Xbox 360, PC, Sony Playstation Portable, and Nintendo Wii. For platforms that did not have native access to TCP/IP stacks, we were able to use a different transport but keep the rest of the interaction the same. By separating the transportation from the rest of the protocol, we were able to bring new systems online much faster and more robustly.

On top of the communication layer, we needed a protocol to pass the information from the tool to the console. Robustness and the capacity to be debugged are of the utmost importance since this is a developer-only feature. For that reason, along with simplicity, we used a simple string-based protocol. Whenever a field value changed on the tool, the name of the object, the field that was changed, and its new string value were sent to the game.

This concept of sending each individual field change message has a number of major dependencies. First, the engine and the game must be referring to the exact same information. If the tool and the engine do not refer to the exact same data structures, this protocol will send information that is not relevant to the runtime. By using the same object representation, neither the tool nor runtime code need to write special case serialization routines.

6.4   Properties

In some cases, the format of the data file and the in-game representation might not match. One case where this is most prevalent is when the runtime needs to be optimized and change its internal representation of data. For example, at tool time, it may be most convenient to have the tools and data files refer to percentage of the screen instead of depending on the actual resolution of the back buffer. At runtime, it may be important for the actual objects to refer to absolute pixels. It would be counter-productive to force all data files to rely on the implementation of the engine.

For these simple conversions, we can model certain fields after concepts from C#. In C#, most data is set via a property. Functionally, a property is a convention for representing "get" and "set" methods as fields. But by normalizing our data and reflection system to support properties, we were able to abstract out any simple conversions.[1] The data are stored and displayed for the user in a way that is most understandable. At runtime, when the field is set to a value, instead of directly changing a value, a method is called. This method can then modify the input data however is needed and then transform them before setting the internal value at runtime.

Another benefit of this property system is that it decouples the implementation from the interface. If the underlying implementation changes, properties can be used as shims to convert existing data into the new format. These properties can be made without modifying any tool or existing data.

One major issue with properties is that they add unnecessary overhead to load time. An object with only data fields can be loaded with little more than a `memcpy()`, but any properties called at load time would require an extra method call. This can complicate serialization systems and significantly impact load times. However, if properties are only used to transform the internal state of an object, they can be moved into a conditioning step during the build. By moving the work to build time, this system will not add performance impact during the load.

6.5   Robust Data

At load time, it is often easy to verify that data are correct, but once you have data that are being created at runtime, this gets much more difficult. With instantaneous feedback, content creators will feel more comfortable testing the limits of different systems. This type of experimentation should be encouraged, but some experimentation can lead to unexpected edge cases. If a designer has access to a field that may cause memory allocation, the engine must be very careful to fail gracefully. At load time, engines can easily check budgets and fail to load if things do not pass, but during real-time experimentation, a content creator may break a budget. Here, if the system completely shuts down, it would give unwanted negative feedback to the designer. Experimentation is dangerous.

Memory allocation is the simplest example of a failure case, but other cases must be handled similarly. If a field cannot go below or above a certain value, the runtime must be able to handle these changes gracefully instead of shutting down because a user attempted to test the limits of a system.

Allowing the designer to try things is very important. At the same time, if the data work while editing in real time, then it should also work after saving the file. If a content creator has broken a budget or any rule of the system, it must be very obvious that these changes will not work in the long term. The game should not crash, but it should be extremely obvious that the user has made a mistake. In many cases, simply telling the user may not be sufficient. If something seems to

---

[1]These conversions can include converting from degrees to radians or converting from one color space to another. The most important rule is that the conversions must only depend on the input data and not on any other state.

work during the real-time editing, it should work in the shipping game. For these cases, forcing the user to fix the error before moving on will ensure the data are in a coherent state. For example, if a material requires a user to specify a lookup table when it is in a certain mode, the tool should prompt the user for the lookup table if they specify that special mode at runtime.

6.6   Null Checking

Following from above, it is also important that runtime systems are able to handle partially created data. When loading from disk, it is safe to assume that the content is in a valid state, but there is no guarantee for when a tool is editing the data. A designer may, out of curiosity, wonder what happens if they delete a vital field. Or in other cases, they may create a new object but not fill in the important information. In either case, your code will run into a null value. Once again, the game cannot crash; it must deal with the data gracefully.

Unfortunately, littering code with null checks is sometimes not a viable solution. Contracts can keep code robust, but too many null checks can add more noise than is really viable in a game. If the game handles these failures too gracefully, the data are not be fixed, and there may be an abundance of incorrect data that is never fixed.

One option is to incorporate exception handling. The simple case exceptions can catch the most egregious errors, but they also add a large amount of overhead which may not be viable for a game, even during development. Additionally, using exception handling may cause more dangerous errors to be hidden; if an exception is handled too gracefully, it may not be obvious that the data are wrong. does not care about that field in the common case, then the runtime system should handle the null case. If a designer marks a field as null, what they are indicating is that the value is not relevant to them. If the runtime needs that value, it is the responsibility of the runtime to make sure the value is not null.

At load time, it is often easy to validate data. In these cases the validation could be run whenever a field changes. This would catch many possible failures. Much like other data errors, whenever validation fails, the user must be alerted immediately and unignorably. Because changes are being made in real time, the user may know what they have done. If, when making a change, the entire game pauses and alerts the user that something is wrong, the user can immediately look into the change to understand what has been done. In many ways, this immediate feedback will allow the user more opportunities to understand the system. If a user is only told about errors during build, the feedback loop may be too long. If they are told immediately what has gone wrong, it is much easier to understand the rules they need to follow.

6.7   Copying Data

Whenever possible, do not copy memory at runtime. Whenever data is copied, there is a disconnect between the input value and what is actually being used. In some cases, this is necessary, and the runtime system that does the copy will need to keep track of it so it can replicate any changes made by the content creator. However, this can be complicated and error prone. In many cases, the copy can be avoided completely.

6.7.1   Caching

Game developers are obsessed with performance. One way to speed up code is to cache intermediate values. But are these caches necessary? Is it possible to recalculate when needed? Or can a property be made so that the copy occurs whenever the user modifies the data? By utilizing a property system, the data will be recached when needed without having to have a specific caching system.

In some cases, caching on first use is better than caching when set. In these cases, the value may be a true cache with only some of the values cached at a time, so doing this at load time is not viable. In these cases, the cache logic needs to be slightly more robust. Data, which in the past could be assumed immutable, can change at any time. When setting a field of an object during communication, it may be important to also mark that entire object as "dirty." By doing the heavy-handed marking of "dirty," the cache system will have little work to do but will be able to correctly handle the case of data changing in real time without adding a significant overhead to the caching system.

6.7.2   Data Reuse

One important feature of real-time editing may be to set hit points or positions of entities. What should the system do if the runtime needs to edit these fields? An entity may move during the game. The value specified at load and the value while running the game may not match. What should happen if the tool needs to change these values? The object is not in a consistent state anymore. Should the tool reset the value of the entity? Should the value be ignored? These questions depend on the game and the needs of the user.

The easiest way to answer these questions is to clearly separate the starting data from the data that are modified at runtime. At first, this may seem inconvenient and wasteful, but it does have a number of advantages. Most obviously, it removes the question of what should happen. The tool is only modifying the starting position of an entity, not moving the actual position. If the game is actually running, then you wouldn't expect the tool to change these values.

There are also secondary advantages to separating this data. Multithreaded code can be synchronized more easily, and network communication is less heavily taxed when dealing with separate mutable and immutable sections.

6.8 Complicated Assets

In many cases, sending a field-changed message is all that is needed to change an asset. However, in some cases, that protocol would be too slow. Two classic examples of this are texture and model changes. In most cases, assets are represented as large, untyped arrays of data. Adding the overhead required to properly describe all of this information and referring to the values as strings would be wasteful and quite difficult. One option is to implement a real-time model-editing API like Verse.[2] It has some restrictions on the formatting of the data, but passes model information in real time.

Another option is to chunk changes and have a special case for these asset types. For our pipeline, when a texture or model changed, we would recondition the asset and notify the engine to reload the file. This notification followed the same communication pipeline as other real-time changes but utilized special case code to reload the asset at runtime. While not as powerful as real-time editing, avoiding that problem entirely is significantly easier than implementing it inside the relatively simple communication system. This has the added benefit that any image editor can be used. Instead of writing a plugin for each image editor, we wrote a file system level [3] tool that would wait for textures to change and alert the runtime when that happened.

Because we wanted to see real-time editing in our tool, we took a hybrid approach for models. We knew we could not afford the generic reflection-based system, but we also wanted a faster turnaround for large models. Here, we added a binary diff system. Instead of sending the entire changed asset (which for a sufficiently complex model was quite large), we would only send what had changed. This relied on the processing power of our computers, but in this case, the optimization allowed us to have nearly real-time changes for model data. Writing a fast, powerful binary diff system was beyond the scope of the project, so we were able to rely on a known layout of our vertex structure. In general, most of our changes happened in small contiguous memory blocks. The diff would walk the data for the first and last change in the block and only send over those bytes. On the runtime side, it would also take advantage of this diff information to know what part of the GPU representation of the vertices needed to be locked and updated.

6.9 Conclusion

Real-time editing capabilities are incredibly useful for speeding up content-creation time. Once a content creator has experienced this functionality, it is very difficult to return to the normal work-build-test model. It frees them up to do what

---

[2]For more information, see http://www.quelsolaar.com/verse/index.html.

[3]Writing a file system watcher can be implemented with a small number of OS calls. Care must be taken to test on a variety of different image editing suites since many suites have odd I/O behaviors which may leave files in an indeterminate during writing.

they do best: create content. As with all powerful tools, there are a number of significant caveats such as runtime performance versus content iteration speed and simple implementation versus fast user feedback. By following a number of simple rules, real-time communication can be available to content creators without adding significant time to game or tool development.

7

Robust File I/O

Alan Kimball

7.1 Introduction

Reading data from storage is a core feature required in any game engine. Be it a hard drive, a cartridge, a disc, or from the cloud, game data needs to be deserialized quickly. At the same time, during development it is vitally important for game data and formats to be iterated quickly. During much of the development of a game, assets and game systems need to be developed in parallel. The need for efficiency and robustness can lead to many problems during development. By building two compatible but different serialization systems inside an engine, both of these requirements can be handled in a simple and robust manner.

7.2 Existing Technologies

One possible solution to this problem is to rely on existing technologies. Serializing data is not unique to games, and a large number of solutions have been found for reading data. Most high-level languages have multiple solutions to the problem: Java has Hibernate, the .NET runtime has the serialization framework, Python has pickle. All of these solutions are highly optimized and incredibly robust. These solutions also suffer from issues which often make them unappealing in game development.

First and foremost, they may not be accessible on the platform on which your game is running, or on the platform which your game may be ported to in the future. These frameworks are large, and often tightly coupled to their runtime. If a game needs to change platform, porting a complete serialization API is time-consuming and sometimes impossible.

Second, for our purposes, these existing solutions are too complicated. These frameworks are built with robustness, not speed, as the primary goal. When a game is complete, your data have already been tested and verified, so having an error-proof system only adds complexity. Features like extensibility, standards compliance, and readability, which are common features of general-purpose serialization systems, are useless and only increase load times. At the end of the day, all that matters is that the data is loaded, not the standards that were used.

Finally, the solutions are often not built with a focus on the complexity of game data. Formats based on XML or other plain-text representations are overly verbose for describing many forms of data. In many cases, these serialization techniques will rely on binary blobs to avoid these issues. These binary blobs are simply another file format, which defeats the entire purpose of a generic and mutable file format.

7.3   Object Databases

Although most existing technologies do not fit game development directly, their core concepts are sound. Most games are written in an object-oriented language, so storing game objects directly is very appealing. A serialization system should only have two methods:

```
Object *LoadData(string filename);
void SaveData(string filename, Object *value);
```

When loading data from a file, the file needs to completely describe the data. When saving to a file, the data needs to completely describe itself. With high-level languages like Java and .NET, their frameworks facilitate this work automatically. With lower-level languages like C++, this job is left to the programmer.

Writing a metadata system[1] is highly dependent on programming language and platform, but most conform to an API similar to the following code:

```
class MetaObject
{
    static MetaObject *getMetaObject(string name);
    void setByString(Object *object, string field, string value);
    string getByString(Object *object, string field);
    vector<string> getFields();
};

class Object
{
    MetaObject *getMeta();
}
```

---

[1]A metadata system allows programmatic access to information about the layouts of objects. By having this information, runtime code can inspect objects without a direct connection to the object's code.

With this functionality, a simple string-based file format can be created. For our implementation, we used XML:

```
<object name= object0  type= ExampleObject >
  <field name= field0  value= 10 />
  <field name= field1  value= someString />
  <field name= pointer  value= object1 />
</object>
<object name= object1  type= AnotherObject >
</object>
...
```

Names of objects are only required during serialization to resolve pointers. During load these names can either be saved (for debugging or saving purposes) or thrown away after load.

This simple file format is extremely lenient about format changes. Fields can be reordered, removed, or added, and the file will stay backwards compatible. It is easy to debug, can be edited with rudimentary tools, allowing it to be modified and updated without a complex tool chain. It is mergeable with a text merge utility, making it significantly easier for multiple users to edit it simultaneously.

Unfortunately, this format suffers from the same issue as other off-the-shelf solutions: it is not built for speed. The above example may only require a handful of bytes to represent in memory, but the on-disk size may be tens or hundreds of times larger. Fortunately, this format is only used during development time during load, so these trade-offs do not cause lasting issues to the shipping product.

The file API above is completely agnostic to the method of storing the data. By relying on a simple file format, the underlying representation of the data can change.

7.4 Disk Image

The opposite extreme of an XML file is a direct memory image of what will be used in game. By serializing an image of the object layout, data can be read with minimal memory and performance overhead. These files are extremely fragile and need to be matched with an exact build of the game, but they are optimal.

Memory images can also be completely created from the game code and the XML files. As with our iterative file format, all tools and other external customers can rely on the robust, easy-to-parse files, while the final engine can rely on the fast, carefully crafted files (see Listing 7.1).

The three major issues with serializing a memory image are pointers, virtual tables and platform specific issues.

```
for(Object* object : objects)
{
    int size = object->getMeta()->getSize();
    diskOffsets[object] = buffer   start;
    memcpy(buffer, object, size);
    buffer += size;
}
```

Listing 7.1. Creating memory image.

7.4.1   Pointers

For reasonably complex data, pointers are required to connect different objects. In memory, these pointers are direct memory references but on disk this connection is much more difficult.

To solve this problem, after serialization, all pointers need to become offsets. This is most easily done in multiple passes: The first pass is to copy all of the target objects into a separate memory buffer. From here, all of the objects are contiguous in memory and are representative of what will be serialized to disk. Next, a second pass must be made through all of the objects to find all of the internal pointers. These pointers must first be transformed to point at the newly copied data and then be converted into an offset from the beginning of the memory block.

```
// Pointer fixup
for(Object* object : objects)
{
    for(int offset : object->getMeta()->getOffsets())
        {
        void** ptr = diskOffsets[object] + offset;
        *ptr = diskOffsets[*ptr];
        }
}
```

7.4.2   Virtual Tables

The C++ standard does not specify how virtual functions must be defined, but most implementations rely on a pointer to the virtual table. The location of this pointer is implementation-specific, but because this format only has to work for a specific build of a game, that constraint is not a significant problem. There are a number of different ways to find the virtual table inside an object, but the easiest method is to simply allocate a number of different objects and inspect the memory in a debugger to determine where the compiler decided to place the virtual table pointer.

By replacing each virtual table pointer with an ID of the type of object, the loader can walk each loaded object and determine the type required. This solves both the issue with the virtual-table along with any issues without knowing what data have been serialized to the file. On load, a lookup table can be used to convert these IDs back to virtual table pointers.

7.4.3   Platform-Specific Issues

If the tool chain and target platform are not the same, the serialized memory image may not match the target platform. Once again, because data are crafted specifically for the current build on a specific platform, these issues can be handled while saving. Although this may cost performance while saving the file, most transformations on the data will be transparent compared to other operations. Common sources of issues are endian ordering and alignment requirements.

For endian[2] correctness, a second pass can be made on all of the data to switch the endian ordering of each field. Endian ordering is a known value at compile time, so the change should be simple to predict and implement.

To deal with different alignment requirements, the tool must be able to completely mimic the target platform. If the final system requires specific alignment or padding rules, the tool must adhere to the same rules in memory. Any quirk or requirement needed by the compiler on platform must be completely reproduced by the tool-side code. This can be done via compiler directives to ensure that data are in the right place inside an object.

7.4.4   Runtime Functionality

To load up an object in the disk image conversion process, the code for that object needs to be compiled into the tool. In some cases, runtime code cannot be functional in a tool. This may be because the code depends on libraries that are not available at compile time. This can be solved a number of different ways.

From an implementation point of view, the easiest way to solve this problem is to separate data from functionality. Serialized objects should be only represented as plain old data. The objects can contain methods, but those methods should only deal with the internal state of the object and should be cross-platform. For in-game functionality, the code needs to reside in an external object that is not serialized from disk. This significantly simplifies the tool code, and it can also lead to a cleaner, more-understandable code base.

Often, this is not possible. When an object needs to reference code that will not work in the tool, preprocessor macros can be used to form compatible, but different

---

[2]Depending on the platform, the order in which numbers are represented varies. For example, x86 and related platforms are little-endian while PowerPC architectures are big-endian.

objects at tool time. These macros can remove the offending code from the tool but allow the functionality to stay at the runtime.

7.4.5   Constructor

When programming in C++, you have a number of different guarantees. One guarantee is that your constructor will always be called. However, when you serialize your object from data, your constructor is still called, but it is called during the disk-image-conversion step, not on platform. This can make it difficult to handle runtime initialization of information. For example, if a game system needs to request resources from the graphics system, it is not possible to do that during the constructor.

The easiest solution to this is to add a secondary initialize method. Although it adds another pass to the deserialization, it is difficult to completely avoid this issue. By requiring the base object type to have a deserialize method, the load can easily iterate through all loaded objects and call that method to handle any on-load functionality.

7.5   Conclusions

By keeping an extremely simple interface for loading and saving files, the format of the files that are saved and loaded can be kept completely separate from game code. This abstraction allows two drastically different ways of serializing data. Our XML format has minimal requirements on a metadata system but is still extremely flexible and easy to implement. Once data has been created, it can then be converted into a much faster and more optimal format that can be used for final game assets.

Part II

Buildable Tools

Every programmer likes to get in there and build things. Maybe that's what draws us to this field. The prospect of building something (and the lack of heavy lifting) is always a plus.

This part presents a set of tools that you can go off and build for your team, your company, or your next side project. They are offered with enough detail to get you to completion but not with the granularity of line-by-line code listings for the entire app. Let me highlight just a couple of the articles.

We start off Part II with the first article that I wanted for this book, Chapter 8, "Real Time Constructive Solid Geometry." My former colleague and friend, Matt Baranowski, was working with Sander van Rossen on this topic as a side project at the same time as the book idea formed, and it was a perfect match.

This part also contains an article on audio debugging (Chapter 11). Audio is treated very badly by game companies, I'm afraid. Everyone drools over lovely graphics and buzz words like screen space, ambient occlusion, or deferred rendering and forgets that without audio our games are entirely useless or worse... not fun. To me, audio is akin to shadows. If you have a 3D scene with shadows, you might never notice them. Without shadows, however, the scene is just plain wrong. We are very happy we have an excellent article on debugging audio by Simon Franco.

Finally, there is an article on remote version control usage by Mike O'Connor (Chapter 15). Sometimes we forget that a tool isn't just what we build from scratch, but it's also the scripts, apps, and programs that interface with the third-party tools that make our jobs easier. Because more and more game companies have remote offices, Mike's article will certainly be a valuable read.

8

Real-Time Constructive Solid Geometry

Sander van Rossen and
Matthew Baranowski

8.1 Introduction

We present a content generation tool that allows users to specify and manipulate complex volumetric building blocks that are combined by a constructive solid geometry (CSG) algorithm to produce final optimized geometry ready for use in games. Instead of manipulating individual triangles in a final mesh, using this method, the user can interactively edit volumetric objects such as windows, walls and doors while the system takes care of generating a watertight mesh interactively (see Figure 8.1). This method can be used in an editor to enable faster iterative development of game environments. It can also be used to generate well-behaved meshes from user-generated content in a game.

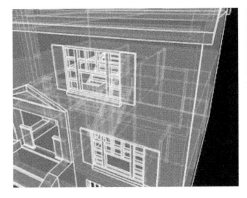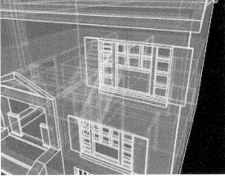

Figure 8.1. Moving a window on a wall interactively. (See Color Plate IV.)

Constructive solid geometry is a well-researched algorithm for generating complex 3D geometry through the composition of solid volumes using Boolean operators such as union, difference, and intersection. For the purposes of real-time games, we are interested in the outer boundary representation of the resulting CSG volume in the form of a triangle mesh optimized for GPU rendering. Our contribution is to present an algorithm that is incremental, can run at interactive rates, and produces well-behaved meshes with optimized triangulation.

This technique has been effectively used in the Id Tech engines, the Source Engine from Valve, and the Unreal Engines from Epic. These engines implemented CSG calculations with the aid of a BSP-tree data structure. This method is described in [Schneider 03]. The BSP tree was also used to accelerate visibility determination when these engines initially used software rasterization and, as a result, generated many more triangle fragments than would otherwise be necessary. This became a disadvantage within modern engines designed for powerful GPUs that, generally speaking, reach their peak performance rendering large batches of large triangles. The global nature of BSP-tree planar splits also meant that a local change in the CSG model specification could modify the entire output mesh. Our system addresses the different optimization priorities of modern game engines as well as the need for quick incremental feedback within game tools.

We present a modernized version of the CSG algorithm that

- does not use BSP trees, although it can be implemented with small BSP trees at the leaves;

- can perform all common CSG operations;

- makes it trivial to perform CSG on multiple brushes in parallel;

- allows for updates to be applied locally and independently from the rest of the model;

- can be updated at interactive rates for local changes;

- produces geometry optimized for modern GPUs;

- produces watertight geometry and is therefore physics-friendly;

- can be extended to produce optimized triangulations without T-junctions.

Furthermore, the combination of these properties makes this CSG implementation useful for use in procedural geometry synthesis. It is possible to create parameterized CSG components that include information on how to first remove a given volume from the world before adding new solid geometry. This makes it possible to, for example, insert predesigned windows and doors onto walls interactively.

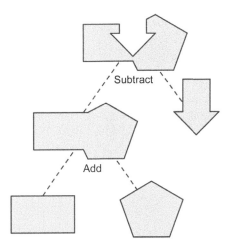

Figure 8.2. An example CSG tree in 2D.

8.2 The CSG Algorithm

In most CSG algorithms, the final geometry is specified by a hierarchy of CSG operations and the volumes that are operated on. Whereas most CSG algorithms use either BSP trees to build their final geometry or rasterization techniques to render their final geometry, our algorithm creates the final geometry separately for each CSG node. This allows the algorithm to maximize parallelization and minimizes the amount of work required when small incremental changes are made to the CSG tree.

For simplicity, we've chosen to use a binary tree of CSG nodes in this implementation, but other hierarchies should work as well. Figure 8.2 shows an example of a CSG tree where every leaf is a volume and every node is a CSG operation combining two volumes. We calculate the final geometry by iteratively categorizing (see Section 8.2.1) all the polygons contained in the branches of each node. Section 8.2.2 describes how each node categorizes each polygon depending on its CSG operation.

The leaves in our implementation are primitive volumes generated from convex polytopes, or brushes, defined as the volume bounded by a series of planes (see Section 8.2.3). Any other geometric representation can also be used as long as it satisfies the following constraints:

- It can be used to determine if a given polygon is inside, outside, or touching it.

- It can be used to split a polygon into separate pieces when it cannot be categorized as being either inside, outside, or touching it.

- It has a geometric representation (preferably this should be watertight to avoid holes in the final geometry). From here on, we will refer to these volumes as brushes following popular convention used in Id Tech and Unreal Engines.

Even though CSG is technically a volumetric representation, like many CSG implementations, this algorithm only computes the outer shell of the volume defined by the CSG tree and rejects fragment polygons based on their final categorization. As a result, the algorithm never needs to create any new polygons; it only needs to split existing geometry and remove all the fragments that are determined to be inside or outside the final CSG volume. Occasionally, polygons need to be inverted by reversing the order of their vertices.

The advantage of using convex polytopes as primitive volumes is that all the splits are done using planes, and the resulting fragments are guaranteed to be convex as well. The resulting output mesh is suitable for a quick preview and many other uses. In Section 8.3, we'll discuss some methods to further optimize and improve the triangulation of the final mesh for production use.

8.2.1   Categorization

To determine the final geometry of the CSG tree, polygons are categorized as being inside, outside, or touching the final CSG volume. When a polygon cannot be categorized as being completely inside, outside, or touching, it is split up into individual fragments that can then be categorized separately. The splitting is performed at the leaf level of the tree and is described in Section 8.2.3, "Cutting and categorizing polygons with a brush."

Polygons that are touching the CSG volume are categorized into two different sub categories; either aligned with the CSG tree or inverse aligned. Aligned touching polygons are a part of the final CSG shell with normals facing in the same direction as the CSG volume. Inversed touching polygons have normals facing in the opposite direction of the CSG volume. It is important to keep track of these categories through the intermediate steps, as some operations will invert the original polygons. It is also required to properly handle the situations where brush faces are overlapping as illustrated in Figure 8.3.

Consider the example of two brushes with overlapping faces that are combined using a union operation. In Figure 8.3(a), one of the brushes is inside the other, and their overlapping polygons are facing the same direction. To avoid duplicate polygons, it is important to have a globally consistent way to decide which brush's polygon to keep and which to reject. A simple way to decide which surface to reject is by comparing the order of the brushes in the tree, keeping the shared area of the brush that has the highest order in the tree, and removing the shared area of the other brush. However, in the situation in Figure 8.3(b), both brushes are adjacent but not intersecting. In this case, the overlapping polygons have opposite normals,

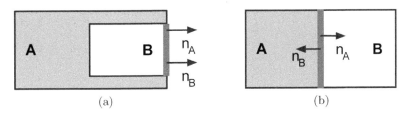

(a)   (b)

Figure 8.3. (a) One brush in another brush with shared polygonal area; both touching surfaces are pointing in the same direction. (b) One brush touching another brush with shared polygonal area, both touching surfaces are pointing in the opposite direction.

and both need to be removed. This shared area can be thought of as being inside both cubes.

As the CSG tree is traversed, each CSG node modifies the categorization of the input polygons according to the specific CSG operation. Finally, at the root node, if categorization of a polygon is inside or outside, we remove it. When it is categorized as touching and inverted, we reverse the order of its vertices. All the polygons that are categorized as touching and aligned do not need any further processing.

Popular Name	Official Name	Logical Operation	Description	Illustration
Addition	Union ($\square$)	A || B or *!(!A && !B)*	Join two brushes together	
Common	Intersection ($\cap$)	A && B or *!(!A || !B)*	Only keep the common area of two brushes	
Subtraction	Difference ($\setminus$ or $-$)	A && !B or *!(!A || B)*	Remove the area of brush B overlapping the area of brush A	

Table 8.1. Overview of the most common CSG operations.

Original Categorization	Inside	Touching Aligned	Touching Inversed	Outside
After "not" Operation	Outside	Touching Inversed	Touching Aligned	Inside

Table 8.2. Logical "not" operation.

8.2.2 CSG Operations

Table 8.1 describes the most common CSG operations and the ones implemented by our algorithm. It is helpful to think of CSG operations in terms of Boolean algebra on sets, specifically sets of points in a 3D volume. By extension, our algorithm performs these logical operations on sets of categorized geometry. In a similar way, the CSG tree can be thought of as analogous to a logical expression tree, and similar transformations can be applied.

The "logical or" operation is a matter of taking the categorization results of the left and right child and using them both to determine new categorization. Table 8.3 shows how to combine the results of the categorizations of the left and right nodes.

For example, as noted in Table 8.1, each CSG operation can be expressed as a combination of the "logical not" (for 0–2 child nodes) and "logical or" operations. To calculate the "logical not," or the inverse of the volume of a CSG tree

		Result of Categorization of Right Child			
		Inside	Touching Aligned	Touching Inversed	Outside
Result of Categorization of Left Child	Inside	Inside	Inside	Inside	Inside
	Touching Aligned	Inside	Touching Aligned	Inside	Touching Aligned
	Touching Inversed	Inside	Inside	Touching Inversed	Touching Inversed
	Outside	Inside	Touching Aligned	Touching Inversed	Outside

Table 8.3. Logical "or" operation.

node, it is simply a matter of reversing the categorization of the node's output polygons. Table 8.2 shows how polygon categorization is changed by the "logical not" operation.

The situation described in Section 8.2 is handled in the "logical or" operation in Table 8.3. If the left and right children have a combination of the "touching aligned" and "touching inversed" categorization, then we have the situation as shown in Figure 8.3(b), and we categorize it as being "inside." On the other hand, if the touching orientation is the same for both children, then we're dealing with the situation as shown in Figure 8.3(a), and we categorize it as either aligned or inversed, depending on the original categorization.

This allows us to implement all CSG operations using a single "logical or" function that can optionally invert the polygon categorization of its children's polygons. If a "logical not" operation needs to be performed on the results of the "logical or" function, we reverse the categorization of the polygons. If the algorithm is implemented by passing a list per category, in which to store the categorized polygons, the "logical not" operation is simply a matter of reversing the order of the parameters of the "logical or" function.

The final categorization method is the one that categorizes and cuts the polygons with a brush at the leaf level and is described in Section 8.2.3.

We should mention that an important optimization of this algorithm is to use a bounding volume hierarchy, which can be used to skip entire branches in the CSG tree when a brush does not intersect with them.

Table 8.4 describes how operations can be simplified, and with it, performance can be improved even further when it's known beforehand if a brush intersects with neither or only one of the child branches.

Operation	Only Intersecting Left Branch	Only Intersecting Right Branch	No Intersection with Branches
Union	Skip current node, jump to left branch	Skip current node, jump to right branch	Categorize everything as outside
Intersection	Categorize everything as outside	Categorize everything as outside	Categorize everything as outside
Difference	Categorize everything as outside	Skip current node, jump to right branch	Categorize everything as outside

Table 8.4. Operation simplifications.

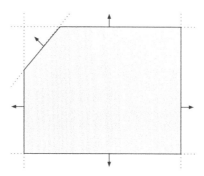

Figure 8.4. A 2D example of a brush, a volume bounded by geometric planes.

8.2.3 Brushes

As mentioned in Section 8.2, our implementation uses brushes, or convex polytopes, as the primitive building blocks for the CSG tree. A brush is defined as the volume bounded by a set of geometric planes, as illustrated in Figure 8.4. We first describe how to create the geometry of a brush from a set of geometric planes, after which we describe how to categorize the polygons of one brush against another brush.

Creating a mesh from a brush. There are several ways to calculate the mesh surface of a brush. One popular method works by projecting a quad, that is axis-aligned with the most major axis of the plane's normal, on each of the brush planes and clipping it by all the remaining planes of the brush. This method is simple to implement and is reasonably fast even for brushes with a large number of planes. It does, however, have some drawbacks in practice:

- It is necessary to choose a maximum size for the initial polygon quad and to ensure that no brush exceeds that size. Otherwise, the brush mesh can contain holes. Unfortunately, the larger the maximum size is, the less accurate the intersections will be, as the accuracy of floating-point numbers decreases as the numbers get bigger.

- The vertices generated by splitting each quad need to be merged to calculate adjacency information.

- Due to floating-point imprecision, there will be a difference between what should logically be the same vertex on different polygons. Increasing the size of the original quad increases this disparity.

Another method of calculating the brush mesh is to first find all valid intersections between the planes of the brush and then to solve the relationship between these points analytically. With this method, floating-point inaccuracies are minimized and have no effect on the validity of the structure of the brush itself. Although

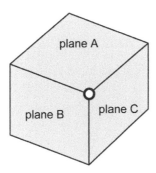

Figure 8.5. A vertex formed by an intersection of plane A, B, and C.

this method is not as fast as the previously mentioned method, it is, however, less likely to create inaccurate geometry. Its speed is less of an issue, however, as there are ways to cache the base geometry of a brush, which is described in Section 8.3.

As shown in Figure 8.5, every 3D intersection must go through at least three planes. All the valid vertices can be found by looping through all the combinations of three planes in our brush and calculating the intersection of those three planes. When the resulting vertex is valid, meaning it has no infinite or NaN values, we then check it against the remaining planes in the brush to ensure that this vertex doesn't lie on the outside of the brush. This can be done by checking if a vertex lies on the positive side of a plane, in which case it's outside and we reject it; otherwise, we store the vertex, including all the planes that intersect with that vertex.

At this point, each vertex has a list of planes associated with them, and unless a plane only goes through a single vertex, these combinations of planes should form edges. As shown in Figure 8.6, each edge is formed by exactly two planes and will have two vertices; one at each end. Our edges can be determined by finding two vertices that share two intersecting planes. Because every plane will have exactly

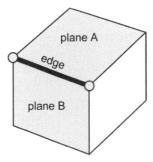

Figure 8.6. An edge formed by plane A and B and its two vertices.

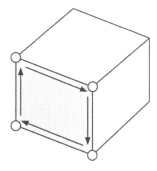

Figure 8.7. Ordering of vertices around a polygon.

one polygon, we can then associate these edges with the planes they lie on and also the polygons these edges are a part of.

All polygons have a consistent ordering of their vertices, and on each polygon each vertex has two edges that touch it; one edge is going towards the vertex, and one edge is leaving the vertex. We can order the edges by iteratively finding the edge that leaves one vertex and then following it to its next vertex and build the polygon in the process (see Figure 8.7).

Cutting and categorizing polygons with a brush. During the processing of each node of the CSG tree, the polygons of each brush will be split by all the other brushes that intersect with them, and the resulting fragments will be categorized as being inside, outside, or touching the intersecting brush it is compared against (see Figure 8.8). A mesh is split by taking each of its polygons and testing them against each of the planes of the other brush. When a polygon is not completely inside or outside, it needs to be split into two polygon fragments.

A polygon is split by first calculating the signed distance between each polygon vertex and the splitting plane. When vertices of an edge fall on the opposite sides of a plane, that edge needs to be split by inserting a new point where the edge intersects the plane. For convex polygons, we can assume that a plane will split two edges at most. Some vertices may lie exactly on the plane, in which case we don't need to split and can use the existing vertex. Each resulting edge is attached to one of the two polygon fragments resulting from the split. Some good references for details of edge-splitting algorithms are [Foley 95] and [Schneider 03].

If the edge is split separately for both polygons, you may end up with slightly different vertex coordinates over the course of many splits on both polygons, due to floating-point imprecision. It is necessary to avoid this to ensure that the resulting mesh is well formed, without T-junctions.

As an edge is split by a plane, it is important that the polygons adjacent to that edge also reflect that split. If the edge is split separately for both polygons, you may end up with slightly different vertex coordinates over the course of many

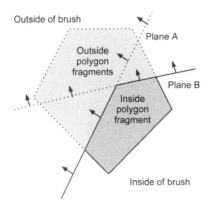

Figure 8.8. Splitting a polygon with the planes of a brush.

splits on both polygons, due to floating-point imprecision. It is necessary to avoid this to ensure that the resulting mesh is well formed, without T-junctions. As shown in Figure 8.9 a T-junction occurs on an edge if only one face is split but the coincident edge of the adjacent face is not. This forms a tiny crack in the mesh that can cause flickering of pixels of the background to show through when rendering due to discrepancies in rasterization of the two faces that use different vertices.

To help avoid T-junctions and ensure a robust mesh representation, polygon edges are represented using the half-edge data structure as described in [Weiler 85]. As shown in Figure 8.10, with the half-edge data structure, all edges are split into two half edges and contain only a single vertex, a pointer to the next half edge on the same polygon and a "twin" pointer that leads to the half edge on the other side of the edge. Using this sparse data structure, it's possible to quickly traverse a mesh in a variety of ways. This is useful, for example, to find both polygons on both sides of an edge or to find all the polygons or edges that are connected to a single vertex.

A T-junction can also occur when separate meshes representing different volumetric primitives are placed adjacent to each other but with coincident edges that have different endpoints. Section 8.3.1 describes a global T-junction detection and elimination algorithm that can be applied as a post-processing step on the global CSG scene.

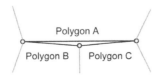

Figure 8.9. A crack in a mesh caused by a T-junction.

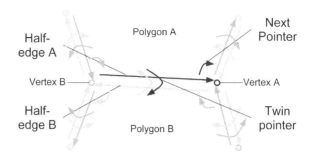

Figure 8.10. The half-edge data structure.

When a plane splits an edge, its twin edge is also automatically split, thus updating the adjacent polygon and ensuring a well-formed mesh.

After the polygon has been split, one part will be in front of the plane (outside), and the other part will be at the back side of the plane (inside). By categorizing the piece of the polygon that is in front of the plane as outside, and continuing to split the remainder by all the remaining planes, we eventually end up with a polygon that completely lies inside, or is touching, the brush. If it's touching, the normal of the plane we're touching needs to be compared to the normal of the polygon to determine if the polygon is inverse aligned or aligned.

In Listing 8.1, we demonstrate the basic algorithm to cut all the polygons by the planes of another brush. Keep in mind, however, that in this example, for the sake of brevity, all polygons are always cut by all planes of the brush even if a polygon actually lies outside that brush. This causes polygons to be split many more times than required and should be avoided in production code. Always remember that the more splits you have, the bigger the floating-point errors become, the more work has to be done for all subsequent brush intersections, and the more work has to be done at the final mesh-optimization stage.

One thing to consider is the necessity of performing the entire categorization process in the local space of the brush whose polygons we're cutting. This can be done by adding transformation data to all brushes and transforming the planes of the brushes with which we split our mesh, with the relative transformation between the mesh and the splitting brush. This gives us the following advantages:

- It keeps the calculations as close to the origin as possible, where floating-point accuracy is highest.

- It makes it possible to cache the mesh we create for each brush before it is cut by other brushes.

- It allows the whole mesh of a CSG branch, with all the brushes already intersected internally, to be cached, allowing us to skip a whole lot of work when translating or rotating a group of brushes.

```
// Check if we're categorizing polygons from the same
// brush that we're using for categorization.
if currentBrush == this.Brush:
  // Set all polygons from this brush to visible,
  // in case they were set invisible before.
  // (this avoids duplicate polygons)
  for polygon in inputPolygons:
    polygon.visible = true

  // Categorize all polygons as touching and return.
  touching.append(inputPolygons)
  return

for inputPolygon in inputPolygons:
  result = this.splitPolygons(inputPolygon,
                              newPolygon, outside)
  if result == Category.aligned:
    // The brush we're touching now is not the brush the
    // polygon belongs to, so it's a duplicate polygon.
    // We only keep the duplicates that belong to the last
    // brush it touches (it can become visible again later).
    touching.append(inputPolygon)
    inputPolygon.visible = False
  else if result == Category.inverseAligned:
    touchingInv.append(inputPolygon)
    // ... same as above ...
    inputPolygon.visible = False
  else if result == Category.inside:
    inside.append(inputPolygon)
  else if result == Category.outside:
    outside.append(inputPolygon)

function splitPolygons(inputPolygons, newPolygons, outside):
  // Loop through all the polygons to split them
  // by the planes of the other brush
  finalResult = Category.inside
    for cuttingPlane in self.Brush.planes:
      result, outsidePolygon = inputPolygon.split(cuttingPlane)
      if result == Category.outside:
        return result;
      elif result in (Category.aligned, Category.inverseAligned):
        // We remember that one of the planes
        // was aligned with our polygon ..
        finalResult = result
      elif result == Category.split:
        // Add the part that was outside to
        // our list of polygons ..
        newPolygons.append(outsidePolygon)
        // .. and add it to the outside category
        outside.append(outsidePolygon)
        // Note: remaining polygons are either
        //       completely inside,
        //       or plane (inverse) aligned
  return finalResult
```

Listing 8.1. The brush categorization and clipping method.

- The above points also make it trivial to implement instancing of groups of brushes.

However, it does put a bigger burden on the final steps, where we have to transform our individual vertices before we can optimize our mesh, as described in Section 8.3, or when we need to render it.

When the shape of a brush is changed, or when it is moved, all the brushes that touched it before and after the modification need to be updated. If a brush is very large, it is more likely to touch more brushes and therefore more likely to take up more processing time. To improve performance, large brushes should automatically be split on each axis if their size passes a certain threshold. The polygons at the intersection between the brushes can be flagged as never being visible and can be skipped from processing entirely.

8.3   Mesh Optimization

The mesh generated by the interactive algorithm is a good representation of the final output and may be used for quick iteration testing of the game environments. However, the generated mesh may contain many extraneous polygon fragments resulting from the brushes splitting process. The geometry may also contain T-junctions, which can cause the rasterization of polygons to be misaligned slightly and create cracks in the final rasterized geometry where the background shows through. The best way to assure that adjacent polygons are rasterized without any gaps is to ensure they use the same exact vertex values. This may require adding additional vertices where polygons meet in a T-Junction.

8.3.1   T-Junction Elimination

Detecting and removing a T-junction involves keeping a table of all unique infinite lines, which contain edges from the unoptimized CSG mesh. An infinite line is defined as an intersection of two planes that are mutually perpendicular to the direction of the line. The entry in the table for a given line also contains an origin point to provide a relative ordering for a list of points that fall on this line. The first step is to add all edges in the unoptimized CSG mesh to a T-junction elimination table. Optionally, the edges can be sorted by length and added longest first to improve the precision of the underlying calculations. When an edge is added, we check if it falls on an existing line by calculating the distance of edge endpoints to the two planes defining each line. If an edge falls on an existing line, its end points are added in order based on the distance from the line origin. Otherwise, a new unique line entry is created. Listing 8.2 shows the details of this process.

The second phase involves asking the T-junction table if any edge of the CSG model contains any other points between its end points. This can be quickly deter-

```
edges = [] // list of all edges
lines = [] // initially empty list of infinite lines
edgeToLineMap = {} // maps from edges to lines the fall on
for edge in edges:
    edgeDirection = edge.start - edge.end
    if edgeDirection.length < epsilon:
        continue // skip degenerate edge
    for line in lines:
        d[0] = line.planeA.distanceToPoint(edge.start)
        d[1] = line.planeB.distanceToPoint(edge.start);
        d[2] = line.planeA.distanceToPoint(edge.end);
        d[3] = line.planeB.distanceToPoint(edge.end);
        for distance in d:
            if abs(distance) > pointOnLineTolerance:
                next line // point does not lie on this line
        line.insertPoints(edge.start, edge.end)

        // insert edge points into ordered list on the line
        for p in (edge.start, edge.end):
            delta = p   line.origin
            t = dotProduct(delta, line.direction)
            for pointOnLine in line.points:
                if pointOnLine == p:
                    break
                if pointOnLine.t < t:
                    line.points.insertBefore(pointOnLine, p)
            else:
                line.points.append(p)

        edgeToLineMap[edge] = line
        return

    // otherwise create a new line based on this edge
    newLine = lines.add()
    newLine.origin = edge.start
    newLine.direction = normalize(edgeDirection)
    normalA, normalB = makePlanesPerpendicularToDirection(
      edge.start, newLine.direction)
    newLine.planeA = Plane(edge.start, normalA)
    newLine.planeB = Plane(edge.start, normalB)
    newLine.insertPoints(edge.start, edge.end)
    edgeToLineMap[edge] = newline
```

Listing 8.2. Inserting edge points into a list of infinite lines.

mined by traversing the ordered list of points on the edge's corresponding line entry in the table. If this is the case, the original edge has to be split and the polygon retriangulated.

8.3.2 Retriangulation

The output of the first stage of the CSG algorithm will contain many convex polygon fragments resulting from plane splits, many more than a skilled modeler would use to create the same mesh. The next optimization phase will attempt to generate a more optimal triangulation. Ideally, we want triangles that define the same outer shell, but are as large as possible but fewer in number for efficient rendering on the GPU. This procedure starts by detecting groups of coplanar polygons that share the same material properties, determining their boundaries and holes, and then supplying this information to a robust triangulation library.

The implementation of a triangulation library is beyond the scope of this article. However, there are several freely available libraries as well as some references if you want to build your own. [Narkhede 95, Schneider 03] The triangulation library must be able to support complex polygons with holes as input. Our system should not produce any self-intersecting polygons however.

The retriangulation phase builds contours of edges that form the boundary of a group of fragment polygons created by the original CSG algorithm. The group of fragment polygons must be coplanar and can be grouped based on material and other user-defined properties. The grouping is done by sorting all the polygon fragments based on their properties and grouping equivalent polygons that are adjacent in the sorted list. The resulting contours are tested to see if they are oriented in the clockwise direction, in which case they are outer boundaries, or in the counterclockwise direction, in which case they are inner boundaries of a polygonal hole. The well-formed nature of input CSG fragments ensures that each inner boundary will be contained within exactly one outer contour. To determine

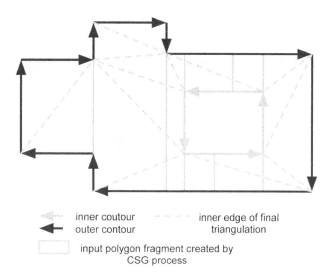

Figure 8.11. Detecting contours form a group of convex brush fragments.

which outer contour a hole belongs to, it is sufficient to test if one of its points falls within an outer boundary using a standard point in a polygon test (see Figure 8.11).

Below is an outline of steps involved in the retriangulation phase:

1. Sort all the polygons produced by the CSG algorithm into groups based on their plane, material ID and other properties.

2. Gather all edges for a group of polygons that share the same plane and material ID.

3. From this, determine the set of closed and connected boundary edges. These are the half edges that don't have a twin edge in the current working set. These edges will form one or more closed contours.

4. For each boundary contour, determine if it is a inner or outer contour. The inner contours will be the holes in the polygon.

5. For all outer contours, determine which inner contours fall within them. Submit the outer contour and list of holes to the triangulation library for processing.

8.4 Conclusions

We presented a new approach to implementing a CSG algorithm and integrating it into a content production pipeline. The core of the CSG algorithm can be made to run interactively in the editor, which is crucial for properly visualizing the effect of subtractive and intersection CSG operations on the primitive volumes. The T-junction elimination and retriangulation phases of the algorithm can be applied when saving or exporting the CSG model to production-ready world geometry.

Constructive solid geometry has been used in several commercial engines with great success, and a variant of this algorithm has been implemented in the Day 1 Studios' Despair Engine tool set. The primary benefit observed in adding CSG to a game production pipeline is that designers can block out game spaces quickly without involving environment artists. Changes can be made iteratively to the layout of game environments while testing game-play ideas. The final CSG model serves as a blue print used to describe the space layout to the environment art staff who uses it as a basis for the final art pass.

We are particularly excited about the future possibilities in content-amplification and procedural geometry generation that this algorithm enables. As a future extension of this work, it is possible to allow designers to specify model components such as doors, windows, and building structures as separate CSG trees. The CSG trees of these structures could first remove geometry before adding new geometry, allowing, for example, dragging and dropping windows on and across walls, automatically creating and updating the hole in the wall where the window is placed. A procedural generator would contain rules on how to combine the individual building components and be able to generate instances of these CSG trees that create a great variety of buildings in a city interactively. The CSG algorithm would be able to produce the final high-quality geometry, while still allowing the user to change high-level parameters interactively.

Bibliography

[Foley 95] J. D. Foley, A. van Dam, S. K. Feiner, and J. H. Hughes. *Computer Graphics: Principles and Practice*, Second Edition. Reading, Massachusetts: Addison-Wesley, 1995.

[Narkhede 95] A. Narkhede and D. Manocha. "Fast Polygon Triangulation based on Seidel's Algorithm." Available at http://www.cs.unc.edu/~dm/CODE/GEM/chapter.html, 1995.

[Schneider 03] P. J. Schneider and D. H. Eberly. *Geometric Tools for Computer Graphics*. San Francisco, California: Morgan Kaufmann, 2003.

[Weiler 85] K. Weiler. "Edge-based Data Structures for Solid Modeling in a Curved Surface Environment." *IEEE Comput. Graph. Appl.* 5:1 (1985), 21–40.

9

A COLLADA Toolbox

Rémi Arnaud

9.1 Introduction

COLLADA was first introduced during SIGGRAPH 2004 [Barnes and Arnaud 04] as a digital asset exchange (.dae) specification. The effort to develop COLLADA started in 2003, involving many companies such as Alias, Discreet, Digital Eclipse, and Electronic Arts, and led to the publication of the version 1.4 specification as an open standard by the Khronos Group [Khronos Group 11a], the same group managing the OpenGL, OpenGL ES, WebGL, and other well-known graphics standard specifications. The 1.4 specification had minor fixes and updates, providing the version 1.4.1 specification, which, at the time of this publication, is the most popular implementation available.

During SIGGRAPH 2008, version 1.5 of the COLLADA specification was introduced [Khronos Group 08], adding features from the CAD and GIS worlds such as inverse kinematics (IK), boundary representations (B-Rep), geographic location, and mathematical representation of constraints using MathML descriptive language [W3C 94a]. Currently, the 1.4.x format is the format supported by most applications, while 1.5 support is limited to applications in the computer-aided design space. Versions 1.4.x and 1.5.x exist and are maintained in parallel. This chapter uses version 1.4.1 of the specification, although everything is applicable to either version of the specification.

Since COLLADA is an open standard, many software vendors have provided implementations. COLLADA was designed from the start to be a lossless intermediate language that applications can export and import. It is important to understand that COLLADA is a language, and in order to be useful, a language needs to be both spoken and understood. But as with every language, it is expected to be used in slightly different ways and to evolve over time. The COLLADA specification aims at formalizing how the COLLADA language can be used, and an application that follows the specification to the letter should be able to cope with all those variations, but in practice, implementations are limited by their underlying infrastructure and limited vocabulary, not to mention short comings that make invalid assumptions.

COLLADA is built upon the XML standard for encoding documents electronically [W3C 08], so all COLLADA documents can be managed by many commercial and freeware XML tools. COLLADA is defined by its human-readable specification as well as with the XML-Schema language [X3C 01] so that the COLLADA documents can be automatically validated, and programming language specific tools can be used to create APIs that help with loading and presenting the documents.

The objective of this chapter is to present a set of tools (aka, a toolbox) that can handle COLLADA documents and provide help in dealing with typical issues encountered. This is by no meanas an exhaustive list of tools, but it includes the fundamental tools to test, edit, and process COLLADA documents. In practice, many issues are easy to deal with, and several easy-to-use free tools and technologies are available.

9.2 Conformance Test

The COLLADA 1.4.x conformance test has been in the works for several years. Completion of the work effort was announced during GDC 2010 [Khronos Group 10] and made publically available during GDC 2011 [Khronos Group 11c]. The Adopters Package contains both conformance testing software and documentation intended to drive rapid evaluation, deployment, and acceptance of the COLLADA specification. Creating a conformance test for a language is a very difficult process in and of itself, and has never attempted by a Khronos working group in the past. All prior work was done to create a conformance test for an API which is easier to design since an API has well defined inputs, outputs, and fits the model of established software testing methodologies.

The goal set for COLLADA conformance testing is to make sure the content is understood, or at least not changed in a destructive way by a given application. One way to test COLLADA is to create a matrix of all the applications to be tested, and make sure that content exported by one application can be loaded by any another application. Testing N applications for M features would involve $N \times (N-1) \times M$ tests, which is not practical. The problem with this methodology is that is does not provide a way to know which application is conformant and which is not. If an application fails to communicate with another, it should be clear which one of the two is at fault. In fact, we need a way to test the conformance of one application independently of the others.

Another difficulty with COLLADA conformance testing is that the COLLADA specification defines the content, but does not define what the application should be doing with it. This is a design strength of COLLADA, as it does not limit its usage to a particular domain of workflow, but this makes it difficult for the conformance test, since unlike a graphics API such as OpenGL, there is no expectation of what an application should display given a COLLADA document. An application can be limited to wireframe, or 2D, or might only visualize the image element or physics elements, or have no graphic display at all and still be a conformant COLLADA application.

Therefore, the conformance test is based on a different principle. The application tested has to load provided COLLADA content and export the content back. It must be possible to compare the two XML documents and search for specific items related to a given test. In addition, applications can be asked to create a rendering from a COLLADA document and then a rendering from another document so that the conformance test can compare the two pictures produced by the same application

The conformance test is a Python-based framework that connects to the application to be tested so that the conformance test framework can start and stop the application, can import and export a COLLADA document, can save and load the application in native format, and can generate images. The conformance test then goes through hundreds of tests, usually overnight, and provides the results in an interactive set of .html pages that make it easy to spot when tests are failing. An application vendor can spend the necessary time fixing the issues and when ready, submit the result of the conformance test to Khronos so it can be judged.

Since there are so many features in COLLADA and it is recognized that some tools do not need to be 100% fluent in the language to be useful, the working group decided to provide three levels of COLLADA compliance: baseline, superior, and exemplary. Baseline conformance establishes the lowest level of interoperability between applications within a tool chain. Superior and exemplary conformance increases the level of interoperability by requiring additional feature support and asset information preservation without transformation. Exemplary software is suitable for the advanced processing and archiving of your valuable 3D assets. Baseline conformance level still guarantees good behavior of the tool and ensures that a baseline tool will not destroy the content that it does not understand.

Now that the COLLADA conformance test is available, Khronos can start enforcing the usage of the COLLADA trademark and restrict its usage to the software that has passed the test. The COLLADA Adopter Program [Khronos Group 10] is very clear about this:

> Any company may freely use the publicly released COLLADA specification to create a product, but implementations of the COLLADA specification must be tested for conformance in the Khronos COLLADA Adopters program before the COLLADA name or logo may be used in association with an implementation of the specification.

At the time this article was written, no applications have been through this process, as the test was just finalized and not enforced, but the expectation is that as more and more applications are going through this process and gaining their conformance qualification from Khronos, there should be a lot fewer issues with using COLLADA content. As more and more applications pass the conformance test, the end users are invited to check the published results to check the result of a specific test that can help track down an issue. Everyone can help by requesting his or her favorite application vendor to submit its COLLADA conformance test to Khronos.

The first thing to do when encountering issues with a COLLADA export is to make sure the correct, up-to-date exporter is used. In particular there are at least three existing COLLADA importer/exporters for Autodesk 3dsMAX and Maya. The basic one is provided by default by Autodesk and does internal conversion between COLLADA and Autodesk proprietary FBX format, which has some limitations; the FCollada [Feeling Software 11] plug-in, which has been used by many developers successfully; and the core of implementations such as Adobe Photoshop. However, FCollada is no longer maintained, and a new faster SAX style plug-in can now be used, known as OpenCOLLADA [NetAllied Systems 09]. Installing a plug-in for COLLADA import/export will require disabling the default FBX COLLADA implementation, but that is definitely the first thing to do when having bugs, or performance or memory issues with COLLADA with 3ds Max or Maya.

9.3 Schema Validation

When tracking down an issue with a COLLADA document, it is always difficult to know if the issue is generated by the application that exported the document, or by the application that is importing the content. The first thing to do is to make sure the document is a valid COLLADA XML document. If an error is reported, then we will know there is a problem application that has exported the document. If this is the case, one should check if a better exporter is available, if a different set of exporter options can be used, or if the content can be modified in the application to avoid the feature causing an issue. In any case, if the document is invalid, the error should be reported to the application vendor. The first test is to check if the COLLADA document validates against the COLLADA schema. A COLLADA document always contains a reference to the COLLADA namespace:

```
<COLLADA xmlns="http://www.collada.org/2005/11
    /COLLADASchema" version="1.4.1">
```

Opening this URL in a web browser brings up the information shown in Figure 9.1. The link to the schema http://www.khronos.org/files/collada_schema_1_4 is provided on this page and can be saved as `collada_schema_1_4.xsd` locally for examinination or faster access.

There are many XML tools that can be used to validate a document against a schema. The method we propose here is to write a simple C# program using the free Express edition of Visual Studio [Microsoft 10]. The code below can easily be extended to create other utilities to examine and manipulate COLLADA files.

COLLADA 1.4 Schema

January 5, 2006
[Updated 26 Jun 2008]

Introduction

This document describes the COLLADA 1.4 Schema namespace. The specifications are designed and develop
creation of open standard APIs for dynamic media. This document also contains a directory of links to these s

COLLADA Schema

An XML Schema document for COLLADA 1.4 documents.

For more information about XML, please refer to the Extensible Markup Language (XML) 1.0 specification.
For more information about XML namespaces, please refer to the Namespaces in XML 1.0 specification.

Normative References

1. COLLADA 1.4.1 Specification
2. COLLADA 1.4.1 Release Notes
3. XML Schema Part 1: Structures Second Edition

Figure 9.1. Display of website:http://www.collada.org/2005/11/COLLADASchema.

Using Microsoft C# 2008 or 2010 (.NET 2.0), let's create a Console application, displayed in Listing 9.1.

```
using System;
using System.Collections.Generic;
using System.Linq;
using System.Text;

using System.Xml;


namespace ValidateXml
{
  class Program
  {
    private static bool isValid = true;
```

```csharp
static void Main(string[] args)
{
 if (args.GetLength(0) == 0)
 {
  Console.WriteLine("Usage XmlValidate document.dae");
  return;
 }
 XmlReaderSettings settings = new XmlReaderSettings();

 settings.ConformanceLevel = ConformanceLevel.Document;
 settings.ValidationType = ValidationType.Schema;
 settings.Schemas.Add(
      "http://www.w3.org/XML/1998/namespace",
      "http://www.w3.org/2001/xml.xsd");
 settings.Schemas.Add(
   "http://www.collada.org/2005/11/COLLADASchema",
   "http://www.khronos.org/files/collada_schema_1_4");

 settings.IgnoreWhitespace = true;
 settings.IgnoreComments = true;

 try
 {
  XmlReader reader = XmlReader.Create(args[0], settings);
  while (reader.Read())
   {
    // Can add code here to process the content.
   }
  reader.Close();
 }
 catch (System.IO.FileNotFoundException e)
 {
  Console.WriteLine("\n[File Not Found] {0}", args[0]);
  return;
 }
 catch (System.Xml.XmlException e)
 {
  Console.WriteLine("[XML error] {0}", e.Message);
  isValid = false;
 }
 catch (System.Xml.Schema.XmlSchemaValidationException e)
 {
   Console.WriteLine("[Validation error] {0}", e.Message);
   isValid = false;
 }
 // Check whether the document is valid or invalid.
 if (isValid)
  Console.WriteLine("\nDocument is valid");
 else
  Console.WriteLine("\nDocument is invalid");
 }
 }
 }
}
```

Listing 9.1. An XML COLLADA validation tool in C#.

Once compiled, the executable can be invoked using the command line (cmd):

```
>ValidateXml.exe
Usage XmlValidate document.dae
>ValidateXml.exe duck.dae
Document is valid
```

Let's test the validator, first, by making the document invalid for basic XML parsing. The document duck-err1.dae has a missing > at the end of the <COLLADA definition

```
<COLLADA xmlns="http://www.collada.org/2005/11/COLLADASchema"
    version="1.4.1"
```

Let's run the validator on this file:

```
>ValidateXml.exe duck-err1.dae
[XML error] Name cannot begin with the '<' character,
    hexadecimal value 0x3C. Line 3, position 5.
Document is invalid
```

Then let's check if the validator can detect COLLADA schema issues in a valid XML document. For example, the document duck-err2.dae is using cam instead of camera. The COLLADA schema says that only camera and asset child elements can be used at this position in the object hierarchy, as a child element of library_cameras. The document is a valid XML document, but it does not respect the rules that make it a COLLADA document:

```
>ValidateXml.exe duck-err2.dae
[Validation error] The element 'library_cameras' in namespace
   'http://www.collada.org/2005/11/COLLADASchema' has invalid child
   element 'cam' in namespace
   'http://www.collada.org/2005/11/COLLADASchema'.
   List of possible elements expected:'asset, camera' in namespace
   'http://www.collada.org/2005/11/COLLADASchema'.

Document is invalid
```

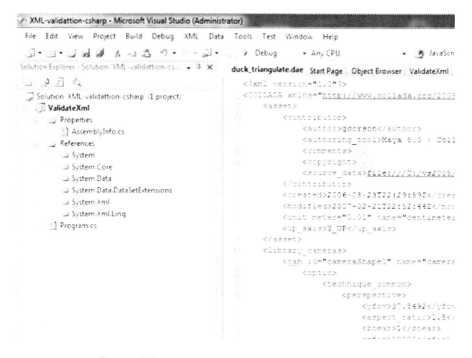

Figure 9.2. Visual Studio can edit .dae documents.

9.4   Editing a COLLADA Document

Now that we are equipped with a validation tool, we need to be able to edit the
COLLADA document, locate the error and fix it. As XML is basically text, any
text-editing tool (Notepad, Vi) would do. Most text editing tools provide syntax
highlighting. We can also use Visual Studio to edit the COLLADA document as
seen in Figure 9.2.

One issue with XML validation is that it often does not return a line number.
This is because carriage return and any number of tabs or white spaces have the
same meaning in XML. In fact, a lot of applications do not even bother with new
lines, as these are useful only for humans, so the entire document can be stored in
a single line of text, which most text editors can't handle.

Going back to the error found by the validator, the first thing to do is to search
for the issue in the file. Standard text editors provide basic search function that can
be used for that purpose. The validator told us we are looking for a `cam` element,
so, for example, let's use Visual Studio to search for the child element `cam`, which
can be found by looking for `<cam`, as shown in Figure 9.3.

The validator also told us that a valid element should be either `camera` or `asset`,
so we can replace `cam` with `camera`, save the file, and make sure it is valid.

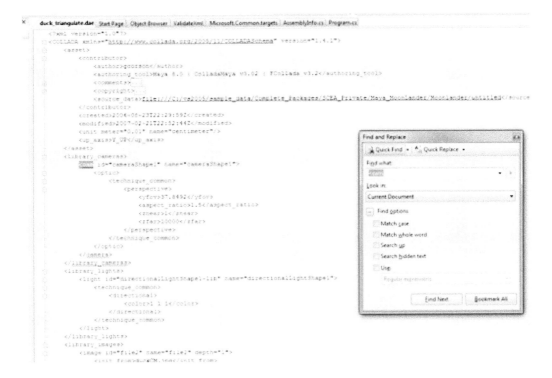

Figure 9.3. Visual Studio can search .dae documents.

COLLADA documents can be very large. It is not rare to have .dae files that are 50 MB or larger, which would be impossible to manipulate if edited as a single line of text, so we are going to need more specialized editing tools. There are several XML editors, most of them commercial tools such as Altova XMLSpy and Oxygen XML Editor, which are two of the best available XML tools, but are probably too sophisticated and expensive for our current purpose.

One free option free is an open source tool from Microsoft, XML Notepad [Microsoft 07a]. Let's install it (Microsoft) and open the `duck-err2.dae` file as shown in Figure 9.4.

We are immediately presented with a very different interface. The left side of the editor represents the tree hierarchy of the COLLADA document, the right side shows the content of the corresponding element in the left side. This XML editor is also very good at dealing with large XML documents. It will open a 50 MB document in a few seconds.

The validator told us that we have an invalid `cam` child element of the `library_cameras` element. So we simply can expand the `library_cameras` element in the hierarchy, and we should find the faulty `cam` element. Navigating

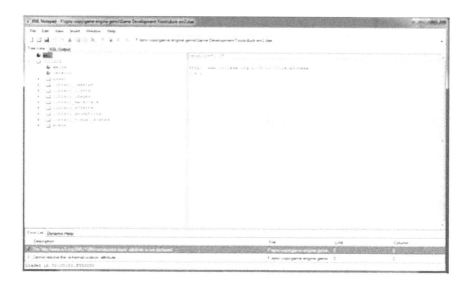

Figure 9.4. XML Notepad editor.

through the hierarchy of the XML document is much more natural and enables finding the issues returned by the validator without the need to find a specific line number or search for strings that could be repeated at several places in the document until we find the one that has to be edited. Right click on the element to change its name to camera (see Figure 9.5).

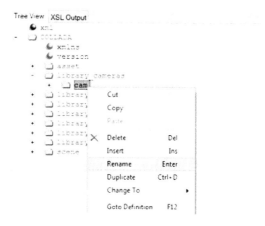

Figure 9.5. Renaming an element in XML Notepad.

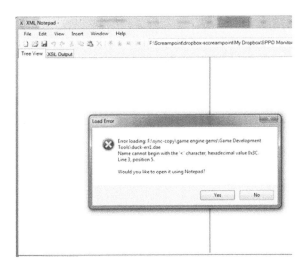

Figure 9.6. XML Notepad won't load invalid XML documents.

Save the file, and make sure it now passes the validation. An XML editor will always export valid XML documents, so it will make sure that the <camera is matched with the corresponding camera/> end tag automatically. This alone makes an XML editors a better tool to edit COLLADA documents.

XML notepad will refuse to open nonvalid XML documents. Let's try to open the duck-err1.dae document; it throws an error, the same error reported by our validator, and proposes to edit the file with the default notepad, which is not recommended in general. Editing nonvalid XML documents is best done with Visual Studio or Vi. In practice, applications export valid XML documents that may or may not be valid COLLADA documents, so this should not be a common problem to deal.

9.5 Coherency Test

The coherency test is a more advanced COLLADA document validation software. Not only does it test the document for a match with the COLLADA schema, but it also implements a set of rules that the schema alone cannot detect. For example, the coherency test will make sure that all the elements referenced can be found in the document. The coherency test is available in source code or precompiled for Windows, Linux, and Mac OS on Sourceforge at http://sourceforge.net/projects/colladarefinery/files/(COL1).

For convenience let's download the executable, rename it to coherencytest.exe, and put it in a directory already in the path so we can invoke it from any directory under the cmd prompt. On Windows, I recommend creating a bin directory under

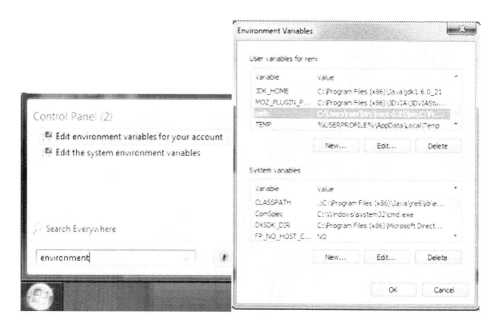

Figure 9.7. Add coherency test to your path.

/Users/yourname/bin, add the directory to the path using the environment control panel. Copy the XmlValidator.exe to the bin directory as well (see Figure 9.7).

Run the coherency test on the duck-err1.dae and duck-err2.dae and look at the returned errors in Listing 9.2. The coherency test on `duck-err1.dae` returns a document object nodel (DOM) error, as the file is not a valid XML document. Note that the C# validator returns the line number for this error, but the coherency test provides a much better explanation asto what the error is: "Couldn't find end of Start Tag COLLADA."

The coherency test on `duck-err2.dae` returns the issue regarding the `cam` child element, telling us that it is unexpected but should be either `camera` or an `asset`, but it does not tell us that the parent element is `library_cameras`. It does provide a line number [41], but it is approximate. Combining the output of the coherency test and our XmlValidator can help to locate the errors.

More importantly, the coherency test can detect more errors than our simple XML validator. The second and third reported errors are basically the same, telling us that we cannot resolve the element #cameraShape1. The coherency test checks every reference to elements in the document and verifies they exist. Searching for all the `cameraShape1` content in XML Notepad returns three instances (see Figure 9.8).

```
>coherencytest duck-err1.dae
ERROR: DOM Error Handler msg=error parsing attribute name
ERROR: DOM Error Handler msg=attributes construct error
ERROR: DOM Error Handler msg=Could not find end of Start Tag COLLADA
ERROR: DOM Error Handler msg=Error parsing XML in
      daeLIBXMLPlugin::read
ERROR: DOM Error Handler msg=Failed to load file:
    /F:/.../duck-err1.dae
DOM Load error = -3
filename = duck-err1.dae

>coherencytest duck-err2.dae
WARNING: DOM Warning Handler msg=The DOM was unable to create an
      element named cam at line 41. Probably a schema violation.
ERROR: CHECK_schema Error   msg=Element '{http://www.collada.org
/2005/11/COLLADASchema}cam': This element is not expected.
    Expected is one of ( {http://www.collada.org/2005/11
    /COLLADASchema}asset, {http://www.collada.org/2005/11
    /COLLADASchema}camera ).

ERROR: DOM Error Handler msg=daeStandardURIResolver::resolveElement()
      - Failed to resolve file:/F:/.../duck-err2.dae#cameraShape1
ERROR: CHECK_uri Failed uri=file:/F:/.../duck-err2.dae#cameraShape1
      not resolved
ERROR: CHECK_file failed, file:/F:/.../ducky.tga not found
```

Listing 9.2. Coherency test example.

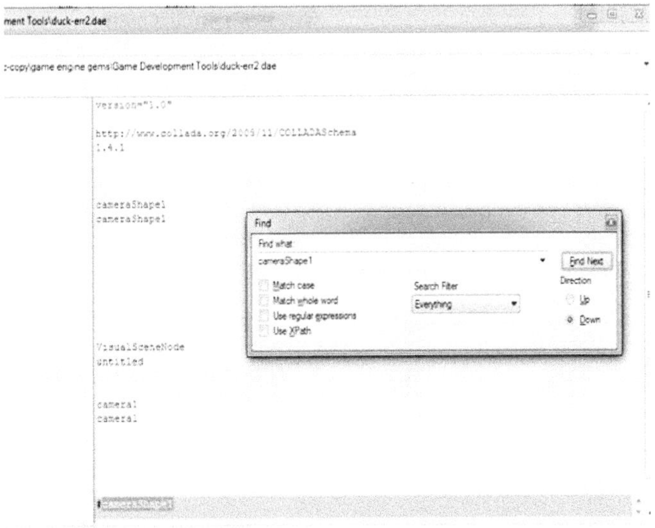

Figure 9.8. Searching in XML Notepad.

The error is now clear, the `instance_camera` element is referencing (using #) the `cameraShape1` element. An element with the id="cameraShape1" is found, but it is `cam`, and not `camera`. The coherency test verifies that an element with the right id exists, and also that it is of the right type where it is referenced in the document. Renaming the element from `cam` to `camera` will simultaneously fix the two first errors returned by the coherency test.

The last error returned by the coherency test on the `duck-err2.dae` is related to external references. It is telling us that it cannot find the ducky.tga image used for a texture.

9.6   Patching XML Notepad

Microsoft XML implementation has a well-known bug that at the time of this writing has not been fixed [Microsoft 07b]. Basically the schema validation does not implement the `<xs:import` statement as used by the COLLADA schema. This error is specific to .NET, other XML implementations don't seem to have this problem.

Here is an extract from `collada_schema_1_4.xsd`:

```
<!-- import needed for xml:base attribute-->
<xs:import namespace="http://www.w3.org/XML/1998/namespace"
  schemaLocation= "http://www.w3.org/2001/03/xml.xsd"/>
```

As a result, XML Notepad fails to validate the COLLADA document, even though the http://www.khronos.org/files/collada_schema_1_4 is entered in the schema's list (see Figure 9.9).

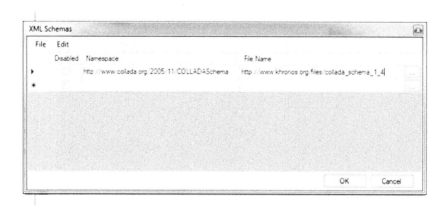

Figure 9.9. Setting XML namespace in XML Notepad.

The error message that will be found in the status bar at the bottom is that the "namespace:base" attribute is not declared.

XML Notepad source code is available at http://xmlnotepad.codeplex.com and can be downloaded using anonymous login with an SVN client such as tortoiseSVN [Collabnet 01]. The project settings are for Visual Studio 2005, so the solution file `xmlnotepad/xmlnotepad.sln` will be automatically converted if opened with a more recent version. The only issue I had recompiling was that I had to disable all the signing options for all the subprojects; otherwise the application refuses to launch, as it cannot find the proper XML Notepad component.

Then the XML Notepad can be hacked to force the loading of the missing schema by adding one line in the Checker.cs, in ValideContext(), just before the call to `Load Schemas()`:

```
foreach (XmlSchema s in doc.Schemas.Schemas()) {
   sc.Add(s);
}
// hack for collada schema
set.Add("http://www.w3.org/XML/1998/namespace",
   "http://www.w3.org/2001/xml.xsd");

if (LoadSchemas(doc, set, resolver)) {
   set.ValidationEventHandler += handler;
   set.Compile();
}
```

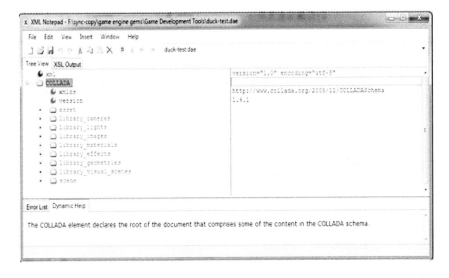

Figure 9.10. XML Notepad modified to use COLLADA schema.

This modified version of XML Notepad can now validate .dae documents, and provide dynamic help in the status bar that displays the comment in the COLLADA schema corresponding to the element selected in the tree view; see Figure 9.10.

Alternatively, the `xml.xsd` schema can be saved locally, so XML Notepad will not require an internet connection to execute. We can further modify the code to automatically load both the XSD and COLLADA schema to turn XML Notepad into a COLLADA editing/validation tool that can execute without an internet connection:

```
// hack to force application to validate with local copy
// of COLLADA schema
try
{
    string appPath = Directory.GetCurrentDirectory();
    set.Add("http://www.w3.org/XML/1998/namespace",
        appPath + "/xml.xsd");
    set.Add("http://www.collada.org/2005/11/COLLADASchema",
        appPath + "/collada_schema_1_4.xsd");
} catch
{
    Console.WriteLine("Cannot find xml.xmd or
        collada_schema_1_4.xsd" );
}
```

9.7 Unique ID, Name versus ID

The ID of an element in a COLLADA document has to be unique, as this is the information that is used to precisely identity an element in the document. A COLLADA document that contains several elements with the same ID can cause all kinds of problems, including application crashes. Note that the ID uniqueness is only requested within one document, as it is easy to create a unique ID outside of a document by appending the document name to the element ID (e.g., `duck.dae#cameraShape1` and `pig.dae#cameraShape1` are two unique IDs). The coherency test checks for uniqueness of IDs, and it is recommended to always fix unique ID issues before going further in investigating issues with a COLLADA document.

For example, here's an issue reported by the coherency test related to unique IDs:

```
>coherencytest Xintiandi.dae
ERROR: Unique ID conflict id=_301_HB05_02_jpg ,
    docURI=file:/F:/..../ Xintiandi.dae
ERROR: Unique ID conflict ....
```

We need to search for the `_301_HB05_02_jpg` ID conflict. We can do that with the XML editor; for a simple text-string search, we can also use command line string search (find, greg..), for instance using Windows `cmd`:

```
>find /N "_401_HB05_02_jpg" Xintiandi.dae

---------- XINTIANDI.DAE
[18730] <newparam sid="_401_HB05_02_jpg-surface">
[18732] <init_from>_401_HB05_02_jpg</init_from>
[18735] <newparam sid="_401_HB05_02_jpg-sampler">
[18737] <source>_401_HB05_02_jpg-surface</source>
[18759] <texture texture="_401_HB05_02_jpg-sampler"
            texcoord="CHANNEL1"/>
[38858] <newparam sid="_401_HB05_02_jpg-surface">
[38860] <init_from>_401_HB05_02_jpg</init_from>
[38863] <newparam sid="_401_HB05_02_jpg-sampler">
[38865] <source>_401_HB05_02_jpg-surface</source>
[38887] <texture texture="_401_HB05_02_jpg-sampler"
            texcoord="CHANNEL1"/>
[182858] <image id="_401_HB05_02_jpg">
[184307] <image id="_401_HB05_02_jpg">
```

The /N option returns the line number. It took about two seconds for this command to find all instances of the search string in a 32 MB COLLADA document. We could have searched for the string `id="_401_HB05_02_jpg` instead, which returns only where the conflicting ID is declared. This search string includes the " character, which requires double quoting to pass to the find:

```
>find /N "id=_401_HB05_02_jpg" Xintiandi.dae

---------- XINTIANDI.DAE
[182858] <image id="_401_HB05_02_jpg">
[184307] <image id="_401_HB05_02_jpg">

Looking into the COLLADA document the culprits are

    <image id="_401_HB05_02_jpg">
      <init_from>file:///C:/.../images/0401_HB05_02.jpg</init_from>
.....
    <image id="_401_HB05_02_jpg">
      <init_from>file:///C:/.../images/1401_HB05_02.jpg</init_from>
```

From this we can deduce that there is a problem with the exporter. It is creating an `id` for images from the name of the image, but has a size limitation that makes the generated ID for `0401_HB05_02.jpg` and `1401_HB05_02.jpg` collide. The bug was reported, and as it is getting fixed, one can apply an easy workaround ; rename the image files with shorter names and re-export.

One very common mistake made by COLLADA importers and exporters is to rely on the name attribute of elements rather than on the `id` attribute. This is because a lot of applications are internally using a *name* as the unique identifier for an object, but COLLADA does not attach any convention to the name attribute; the `name` is optional and contains human-readable information, whereas the `id` is the only attribute that is guaranteed to be unique within a document, and used to reference an element from another element. In COLLADA the `name` attribute should be considered as additional metadata that can be attached to an element. Although the specification provides the `<extra>` child element to add additional information, most implementations do not understand or carry over the information stored in the `<extra>` element. It turns out that most applications load and save back the string stored in the name attribute, so several implementations have been done using this container to carry special information between components of their content pipeline.

For example, Crytek is using the `name` to carry engine-specific data between the modeler and the engine [Crytex 10], which will be used as a parameter to how the COLLADA content should be consumed by the engine. For example the name `CryExportNode_example-CGF-example-DoExport-MergeNodes` carries the information that this node is a static geometry (CGF), and can be merged (simplified hierarchy) by the loader. Other parameters such as level of detail (LOD), and physics parameters are transported in the `name` as described in the XSI CryEngine2 documentation.

This example is a practical use of `name` and demonstrates the difference between `id` and `name` in COLLADA, but it is a bit of an extreme usage—using `name` does not provide the capability of correctly defining and exposing extension to COLLADA. It is recommended instead to use the built-in concept of `<extra>` elements and to use the published extension repository to document extensions so that other tool vendors or COLLADA users can take advantage of those extensions. It is also recommended to check the already published extensions before creating your own: https://collada.org/mediawiki/index.php/Portal:Extensions_directory

9.8 XPath

The XML Path Language (XPath) is a query language for selecting nodes from an XML document. In addition, XPath may be used to compute values (e.g., strings, numbers, or Boolean values) from the content of an XML document. An easy-to-follow tutorial is provided on the web by W3Schools [W3Schools 11a]. There is a large choice of implementations available. One common usage of XPath is to use it as a query mechanism for XML databases [Bourret 11]. Using a database to store COLLADA documents is a powerful idea, one that can be used as a mechanism for content repository and collaborative development, version management and archival. Using XPath, a simple query can be sent to a database or used

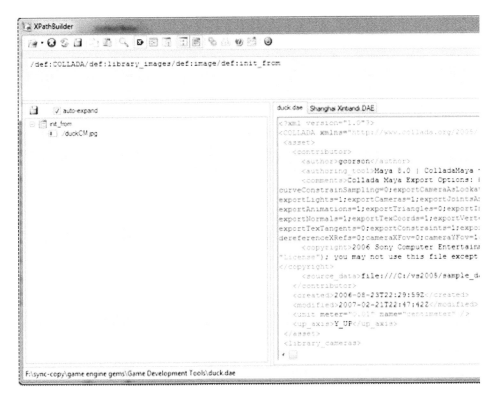

Figure 9.11. Using Xpath in XPathBuilder.

against a specific COLLADA document to return specific nodes in the document. XPath is also available as a query mechanism for many DOM implementations, such as the .NET implementation used by the XML validator and XML Notepad applications.

Let's add XPathBuilder [Bubasoft 11] to our toolbox. For example, let's say that we want to get a list of all the external files used for texturing in a COLLADA document. The XPath query is constructed to follow the hierarchy and return all the corresponding elements, which in our specific example is /COLLADA/ library_images /image/init_from (see Figure 9.11).

XPathBuilder can be used as an inspection tool or to create queries that then can be used in a utility application. For instance, using the query from this example, a small program or script (as most scripting languages have support for XPath) can be written to create an archive containing a COLLADA document and all its associated image files.

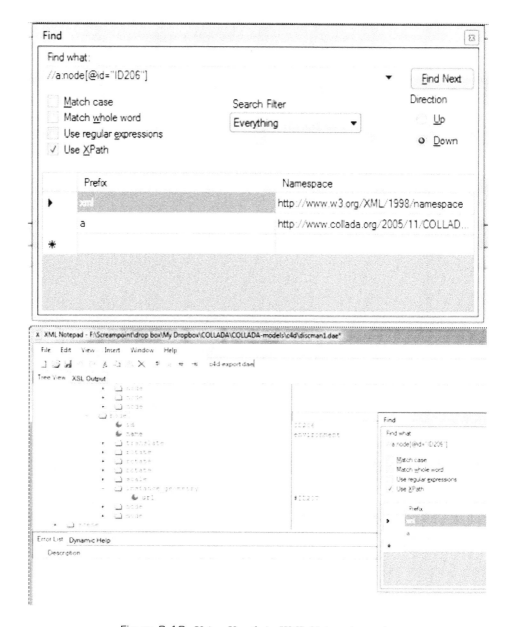

Figure 9.12. Using Xpath in XML Notepad search.

Here are a few examples of useful queries:

- `node`—list all the `<node>` elements in the document;
- `node[@id]`—list all the `<node>` elements in the document that have an `id`;
- `def:node[@id="camera1"]`—find the `<node>` element with a specific `id`;
- `def:node[@id="camera1"]/..`—find the parent element for the `<node>` element with a specific `id`

Here's another example from checking an issue with a C4D COLLADA export. The coherency test reports `ERROR: (type=node,id=ID206) bind_material does not exist`. Let's use those parameters in an XPath query. As this is a standard query language let's use XML Notepad this time (see Figure 9.12).

The query looks for any element named `node` with a parameter `id` equal to "ID206." The "a:" prefix is used to refer to the COLLADA schema as indicated in the search box. This shows that the node "ID206" has an instance of geometry "ID207," but no material binding as returned by the coherency test. Selecting another node shows how `bind_material` should be a child of `instance_geometry`, which is indeed an error. Continuing our investigation, we can search for the geometry with an `id` equal to "ID207" `//a:geometry[@id=''ID207'']` which shows a geometry whose mesh contains sources and vertices but no triangles or other form of geometry. So, now we can report the issue as a C4D exporter bug, and without waiting for this bug to be fixed, we can simply delete the bogus geometry and the corresponding `instance_geometry` (the geometry from the faulty document).

9.9 Absolute versus Relative Paths

A very common issue with COLLADA content is related to missing or misplaced external content referenced by the document. It is a very common issue to forget to configure the exporter to use a relative path when exporting the content, or for an exporter to not provide that option. If the content is exported using the relative path, the external references such as images will be found in a location relative to the position of the .dae document, so that it is possible to copy all the files together, in a zip archive, for example, when the creator needs to send the exported document to someone else.

Typically, a COLLADA document will load just fine, but no texture will be displayed. Let's use our XPath tool to query the location of external referenced images in a large COLLADA document using `//def:init_from`. If the results look like `file:///C:/MyProject/Collada-Models/images/HMN09_st06_02.jpg` then we know the exporter has been using an absolute path, and if the images are not in exactly the same location, they cannot be found.

Note that exporting with an absolute path is not necessarily a bad thing; some teams have decided that all computers will have a special mounted drive to share resources without having to make several copies of the same file. Also, even with relative-path exports, the images may have been saved in a different location than referenced by the relative path in the COLLADA document. Fixing this problem can be either be done by exporting again with relative paths, moving the images where they are referenced, or editing the document and changing the path, which can be done using XML Notepad or another editor.

9.10 Refinery

COLLADA refinery is an open-source content pipeline tool for COLLADA. It can run in interactive mode or in batch mode. A content pipeline is made up of conditioners, small C++ functions interfacing with the COLLADA-DOM. One of the conditioners provided is the —emphcoherency check, which we have already added to our toolbox.

A COLLADA conditioner is a module component in COLLADA refinery. Each conditioner can take a COLLADA document, perform a specific operation on the document, and pass the resulting document to the next conditioner. A series of conditioners is a pipeline that transforms COLLADA documents.

This tool was released in March 2007. In fact, it can be used as-is, or as a source code starting point to add more and more tools to a toolbox. Refinery was created in C++ using the C++ DOM library for performance and cross-platform goals, but one can take the idea and use the XML validate source and copy or create new conditioners using C# and the .NET built in DOM, which is, in my opinion, a much easier environment to use for creating COLLADA tools. Refinery is available in source code or precompiled for Windows, Linux, and Mac OS on Sourceforge at http://sourceforge.net/projects/colladarefinery/files/ [COLLADA 10].

When started, the refinery user interface shows two (green) triangles that can be moved on the surface, one representing the input COLLADA document, one representing the output. On the left side, there is a list of conditioners that can be selected and pasted onto the surface and connected to the input, output, or other conditioners on the surface. For this example let's say that we have a COLLADA document that we want to process in order to replace the absolute path with relative paths, so we select the "filename" (not the best naming convention for this conditioner), add it to the refinery content pipeline, and connect it to the input and output (green) triangles. Connecting two elements is easy: simply click on one element connection point and drag the mouse to the other element connection point (see Figure 9.13).

Now we can set the parameters for this pipeline. Right click on the input triangle, select property, and select the document to process. Select the output triangle and select the destination. Open the properties for the filename conditioner, toggle "Modify Image element" to yes, and type the new prefix to be used before the image filename in the COLLADA document. For example, enter ./images/ if

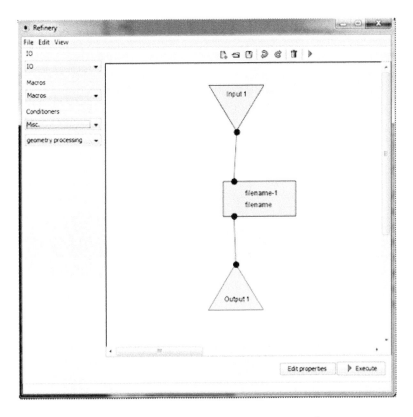

Figure 9.13. COLLADA Refinery user interface.

the images are all stored in a directory ./images relative to the .dae document. Run the script using the "Execute" command. Now you can open the resulting .dae document and check if the filenames are correct; you already have many tools in your toolbox to do exactly that.

The nice thing about this tool is that it can save the conditioning pipeline we just created into a .pip file that can then be used as a batch process on all the COLLADA documents you have, or with future documents. This is always a good idea.

Here's an example posted on the web on how to use Refinery to prepare a COL-LADA export for easy OpenGL ES visualization on an iPhone [Stephen 09]. This is the right idea: transforming a COLLADA document into another COLLADA document in the content pipeline, and using a set of such tools from your toolbox is the perfect use of COLLADA and your toolbox.

Refinery includes manyt more conditioners that can be very useful. More information can be found in the conditioners director [COLLADA 09].

- *axisconverter*: 3D modelers use a different convention for which axis is representing UP and which axis is to the right. COLLADA supports only three axis conventions (`X_UP`, `Y_UP`, and `Z_UP`) which cover most needs, and modelers need to do the proper conversion when loading a COLLADA document that is not using the same convention. Most of the time, when exporting the content back, the axis convention will change to what the modeler default is, which may be problematic for an application that can only work in a fixed convention. It is not the simplest thing to do to change the coordinate system, considering animations, skinning, and so forth. This conditioner should do the work for you.

- *bindmaterialfixer*: some implementations do not correctly use material binding. This conditioner is attempting to create the `bind_material` elements based on the information available.

- *copyrighter*: COLLADA documents contain a copyright notice, which should be filled in before releasing assets. This conditioner simplifies the task when applied in a batch mode.

- *deindexer*: COLLADA can store multiple indexes per vertex, which is very convenient and can save space, but the GPU does not like having more than one index. This conditioner will create a single array (one index) with all the values for each pixel, resulting in duplicated data, but preparing the data for GPU consumption. This is one of the most common tasks that has to be done between the modeler and the application.

- *filename*: this conditioner is used to change the location of externally referenced data (as demonstrated above)

- *imageConv*: This conditioner will apply a format-conversion tool on all the images externally referenced and change the name in the COLLADA document. This is very useful, as applications have a limited choice of image formats. This can be used to convert images into a format that is closer to the GPU, such as DDS, including mipmaps.

- *kmzcleanup*: This conditioner was created to specifically fix the buggy COLLADA documents exported by SketchUp and available on Wharehouse. The conditioner is no longer needed, as Google has fixed SketchUp, but this is a good example of a conditioner that can be applied as an example to create a conditioner to fix a specific tool. For instance, such a conditioner to prepare the data for PaperVision 3D would be a good thing to add [Papervision 10].

- *optimizer*: This conditioner will reorder the triangles based on a cost function, whose goal is to optimize the GPU cache to provide better performance when drawing the meshes.

- *packager*: This conditioner parses all the external references, and all their internal references, in order to create a package that contains all the files that are needed for a given COLLADA document. This is useful when preparing a package to be sent via email, for example.

- *CgToGLSL*: This conditioner is not included in Refinery. This is an example of a conditioner delivered as a separate project (see http://sourceforge. net/projects/collada-cg2glsl/ as a standalone or a Refinery conditioner. This conditioner will take a COLLADA document that has shader code for the Cg language and automatically convert the shader into the OPen GL shading language (GLSL). This conditioner can be really useful to convert Cg shaders for WebGL.

Refinery does not need to be recompiled to add new conditioners; the application written in Java will parse the .dll available and provide the available conditioners in the user interface. In other words, it is possible to add more conditioner tools to the toolbox by providing an extra .dll to Refinery. CgToGLSL is a good example for adding a conditioner to Refinery.

Writing the equivalent conditioner in C# inside the one-page XML validate application (where it says "add code here to process the content") or even adding functionality to XML Notepad may be a less-involved and easier road if portability is not a primary issue (although Mono may provide enough portability [Novell 11]).

9.11 XSLT

XSL stands for EXtensible Stylesheet Language, and is a style-sheet language for XML documents. Its usage can be compared to using CSS with HTML. XSLT stands for XSL transformations. XSLT is a very useful tool to add to our toolbox: it can transform a COLLADA document into another or transform a document into an XHTML page. A lot of information can be found about XSL, as it is a W3C standard [W3Schools 99], (see W3Schools tutorial [W3Schools 11b] that offers an online editor and XSLT test tool). Listing 9.3 shows sample code (list-images.xslt):

Because COLLADA is using a namespace definition, we need to declare it at the beginning of the XSLT file, and we give it the shortname "a" that will be used in the rest of the script when referencing COLLADA elements, such as a:COLLADA or a:images.

The script is simple to follow:

- First it finds the COLLADA root element using `xsl:template match="/a:COLLADA"`.

- Then it loops for all the image elements using `xsl:for-each select=' a:library_images/a:image"`.

```
<xsl:stylesheet version = '1.0'
    xmlns:xsl='http://www.w3.org/1999/XSL/Transform'
    xmlns:a='http://www.collada.org/2005/11/COLLADASchema'>

<xsl:template match="/a:COLLADA">
 <html>
  <body>
   <h2>External references</h2>
   <table border="1">
    <tr bgcolor="#9acd32">
      <th>id</th>
      <th>url</th>
    </tr>
    <xsl:for-each select="a:library_images/a:image">
      <tr>
        <td><xsl:value-of select="@id"/></td>
        <td><xsl:value-of select="a:init_from"/></td>
      </tr>
    </xsl:for-each>
   </table>
  </body>
 </html>
</xsl:template>
</xsl:stylesheet>
```

Listing 9.3. An XSL template (program) to list all external image files.

- It prints out the value of the element `init_from` using `xsl:value-of`
  'select='a:init_from" as well as the value of the image parameter `id` using
  `xsl:value-of select="@id."`
- The HTML tags that format the page are simply inserted in the XLST script
  when they need to appear.

Running this script on duck.dae returns the XHTML document shown in Listing 9.4.

```
<html xmlns:a="http://www.collada.org/2005/11/COLLADASchema">
  <body>
    <h2>External references</h2>
    <table border="1">
      <tr bgcolor="#9acd32">
        <th>id</th>
        <th>url</th>
      </tr>
      <tr>
        <td>file2</td>
        <td>./duckCM.jpg</td>
      </tr>
    </table>
  </body>
</html>
```

Listing 9.4. An HTML page created by an XSL program.

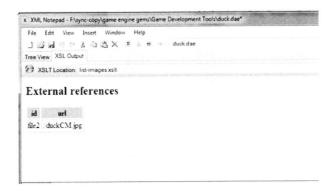

Figure 9.14. Result of XSL (HTML) view XML Notepad.

Let's use XML Notepad, load duck.dae, and then on the XSL Output tab load the above XSLT and execute it (see Figure 9.14). You have built yourself quite a powerful tool to build HTML pages that can be modified to provide any information extracted from a COLLADA document.

It is also possible to add the reference to the XLST directly in the COLLADA document, which will have no impact on the content and how it is loaded by applications, but it will be used by web browsers to display the processed document rather than the raw XML data when opening a COLLADA document with a web browser. Simply add the line `<?xml-stylesheet type="text/xsl" href="list-images.xslt"?>` right after the `{<?xml version="1.0"?>`verb line in a COLLADA document, and it will show the XSL output in Mozilla[1], just like an HTML page will be reformatted by CSS in a web browser (see Figure 9.15).

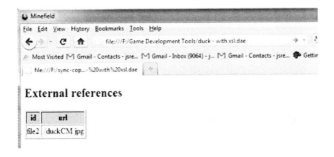

Figure 9.15. Associate XSL to .dae to allow automatic processing when opened in a web browser.

---

[1]Some browsers such as Internet Explorer may not accept the .dae extension and will require the file to be renamed .xml.

XSLT can be used to create XML documents, so it can be used to reformat COLLADA documents; for example, it is quite easy to filter a document to only the elements that are necessary for the next stage of the content pipeline. If your application has no use for some of the information, then there is no need to carry all this information down to the final user, which would only make his loading time longer for no reason.

For more advanced users, there is a scripting language dedicated to processing XML documents and returning either XML or XHTML or JSon, that can be executed by a database server or by the client application. For more information see the XQuery language, [W3C 94b].

9.12 Conclusion

This article demonstrated the power of XML and the many free available tools that can be used with COLLADA. In fact, those tools are commonly available and quite easy to use, as they are the core of data technology for pretty much all the documents we are using on a daily basis (try to rename a Microsoft Word .docx into .zip, and look inside! Try with Powerpoint and Excel too).

COLLADA's strength lies in the fact that it is an open standard, built with open standards, and with the right toolbox, offers everyone the capability to manage, transform, and investigate its data. This article should give programmers the confidence that it easy to open the hood and look inside a COLLADA document, no matter its size or where it came from. More tools can be added when needed to this toolbox in order to help tracking problems or to process the content as part of the pipeline. Maybe this chapter will energize a small group of people to create a C# cross-platform COLLADA toolbox application based on all the information provided and the existing implementations. The author can be contacted at remi@acm.org.

Bibliography

[Barnes and Arnaud 04] Mark Barnes and Rémi Arnaud. "SIGGRAPH 2004 COLLADA Tech Talk." Available at http://www.collada.org/public_forum/files/COLLADASigGraphTechTalkWebQuality.pdf, 2004.

[Bourret 11] Ronald Bourret. "XML Database Products: Native XML Databases." *XML and Databases*. Available at http://www.rpbourret.com/xml/ProdsNative.htm, 2010.

[Bubasoft 11] Buba Software. "XPath Builder that Enables You to Evaluate an XPath Expression." Available at http://www.bubasoft.net/xpathbuilder/Xpathbuilder2.aspx, 2011.

[Collabnet 01] CollabNet Tortoise SVN. "A Subversion Client, Implemented as a Windows Shell Extension." *CollabNet Enterprise Edition*. Available at http://tortoisesvn.tigris.org/, 2001.

[COLLADA 09] Collada.org. "Conditioners Directory." *Wiki Pages*. Available at http://www.collada.org/mediawiki/index.php/Portal:Conditioners_directory, 2009.

[COLLADA 10] Sourcefore.net. "COLLADA Refinery and Coherency Test." *Sourceforge: Find and Develop Open Source Software*. Available at http://sourceforge.net/projects/colladarefinery/files/, 2010.

[Crytex 10] Crytek. "Asset Creation: XSICryExporter." Available at http://wiki.crymod.com/index.php/AssetCreation_XSICryExporter, 2010.

[Feeling Software 11] Feeling Software. "Feeling Software COLLADA Plugin for 3ds Max and Maya." Available at http://sourceforge.net/projects/colladamaya/, 2011.

[Khronos Group 08] The Khronos Group. "Khronos Releases COLLADA 1.5.0 Specification with New Automation Kinematics, and Geospatial Functionality." Available at http://www.khronos.org/news/press/releases/khronos_releases_collada_150_specification_with_new_automation_kinematics_a/, 2008.

[Khronos Group 10] The Khronos Group. "Khronos Group Delivers COLLADA Adopters Package & Conformance Tests." Available at http://www.khronos.org/news/press/releases/khronos-group-delivers-collada-adopters-package-conformance-tests, 2010.

[Khronos Group 11a] The Khronos Group. "COLLADA—3D Asset Exchange Schema." *COLLADA Overview*. Available at http://www.khronos.org/collada/, 2011.

[Khrons Group 11b] The Khronos Group. "COLLADA Adopters Overview." Available at http://www.khronos.org/collada/adopters/, 2011.

[Khronos Group 11c] The Khronos Group. "Khronos Group Releases Free COLLADA Conformance Test Suite." *Khronos Press releases*. Available at http://www.khronos.org/news/press/releases/khronos-group-releases-free-collada-conformance-test-suite/, 2011.

[Microsoft 07a] Microsoft Corporation. "XML Notepad 2007." *Microsoft Download Center*. Available at http://www.microsoft.com/downloads/details.aspx?familyid=72d6aa49-787d-4118-ba5f-4f30fe913628&displaylang=en, 2007.

[Microsoft 07b] Microsoft Corporation. "Microsoft xsd.exe Fails with COL-LADA Schema." *Microsoft Connect: Your Fedback Improving Microsoft Products.* Available at https://connect.microsoft.com/VisualStudio/feedback/ViewFeedback.aspx?FeedbackID=289668, 2007.

[Microsoft 10] Microsoft Corporation. "Microsoft Visual Studio 2010." *Microsoft Express.* Available at http://www.microsoft.com/express/downloads/, 2010.

[NetAllied Systems 09] NetAllied Systems GmbH. "OpenCOLLADA Plugins for 3dsMax and Maya." Available at http://opencollada.org/download.html, 2009.

[Novell 11] Novell. "Mono." Available at http://www.mono-project.com/Main_Page, 2011.

[Papervision 10] "Papervision 3D Training in the UK." *Papervision3D Blog.* Available at http://blog.papervision3d.org, 2010.

[Stephen 09] Stephen Jayna. "Tipu's iTiger: LightWave, COLLADA & OpenGL ES on the iPhone." Availabkle at http://www.everita.com/lightwave-collada-and-opengles-on-the-iphone, 2009.

[W3C 08] W3C. "Extensible Markup Language (XML) 1.0 (Fifth Edition)." Available at http://www.w3.org/TR/REC-xml/, 2008.

[W3C 94a] W3C. "W3C Math Home." Available at http://www.w3.org/Math/, 1994.

[W3C 94b] W3C. "XQuery 1.0: An XML Query Language." Available at http://www.w3.org/TR/xquery/, 1994.

[W3Schools 99] W3Schools.com. "W3C XSL Transformations (XSLT) Version 1.0." *W3Schools.com: The World's Largest Web Development Site, Educate Yourself!* Available at http://www.w3schools.com/xsl/xsl_languages.asp, 1999.

[W3Schools 11a] W3Schools.com. "XPath Syntax -(XPath Tutorial)." *W3Schools.com: The World's Largest Web Development Site, Educate Yourself!,* 2011.

[W3Schools 11b] W3schools.com. "XQuery Tutorial." *W3Schools.com: The World's Largest Web Development Site, Educate Yourself!,* 2011.

[X3C 01] W3schools.com. "The W3C XML Schema." Available at http://www.w3.org/XML/Schema, 2001.

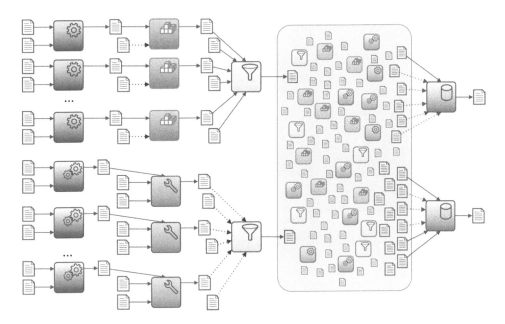

Plate I. Diagram showing an imaginary dependency graph. Compilers are displayed as rounded boxes, with a different color representing alternative transformation steps. Dependencies connect compilers, input files, and output files. Explicit and implicit dependencies are drawn as solid and dotted lines respectively. (See Figure 1.2.)

Plate II. Visualizing texture statistics using MATT texture browser module. Textures are annotated with category information, resolution, usage statistics, and shape-recognition for duplication prevention. (See Figure 3.2.)

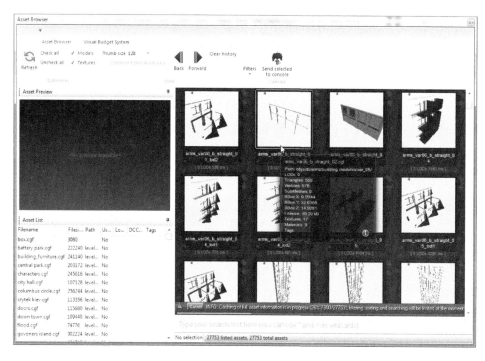

Plate III. Asset browser in sandbox of CryENGINE3. (See Figure 5.4.)

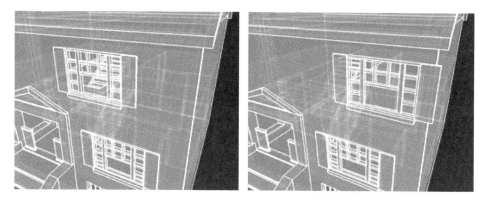

Plate IV. Moving a window on a wall interactively. (See Figure 8.1.)

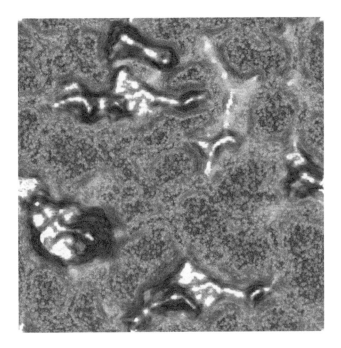

Plate V. Sample data for the terrain. (See Figure 10.5 (b).)

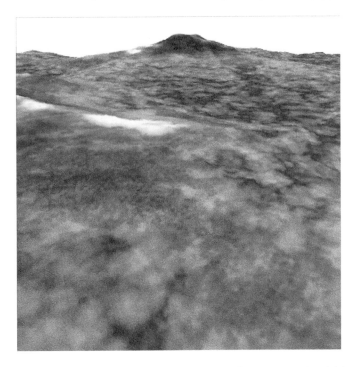

Plate VI. The final results for comparison. (See Figure 10.7 (a).)

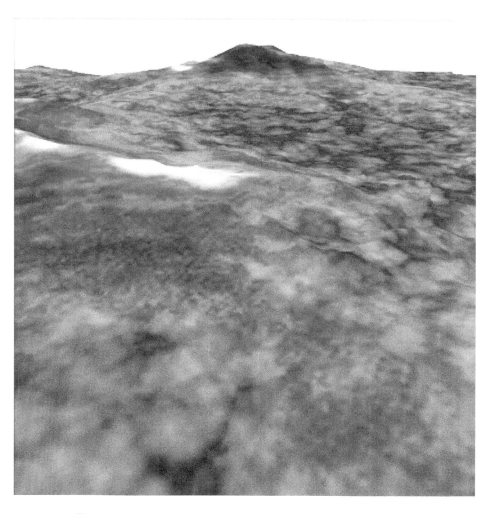

Plate VII. The final results for comparison. (See Figure 10.7 (c).)

Plate VIII. Screenshot of *Minimaxima*. (See Chapter 12.)

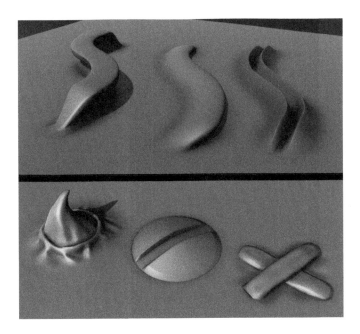

Plate IX. Vector displacement stamps used as custom tools (top) and repeatable details (bottom). (See Figure 16.2.)

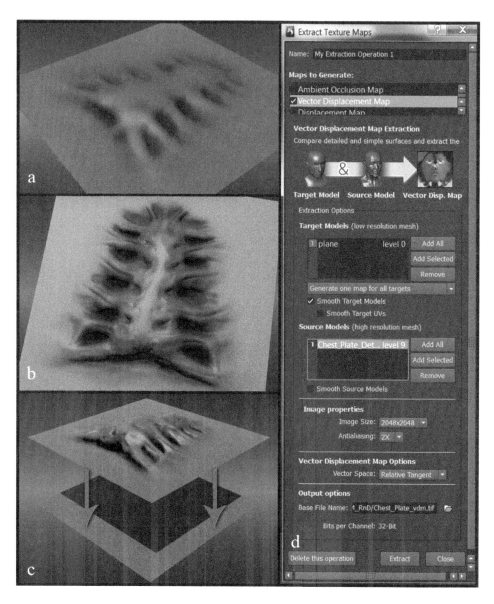

Plate X. The basic sculpting process for sculpting details and extracting a vector displacement map in Mudbox. (a) early sculpt; (b) final detail sculpt; (c) illustration of detail as the source and a base plane as the target; (d) map extraction menu in Mudbox 2011. (See Figure 16.4.)

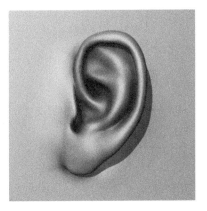

Plate XI. Vector displacement applied as a stencil to achieve complex details such as this ear map. (See Figure 16.3.)

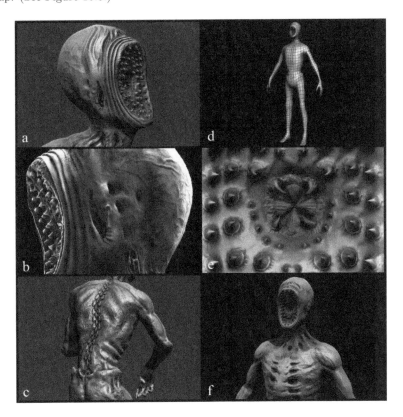

Plate XII. (a) VDM stamps applied for repeating teeth; (b) VDM stamps for gill-like structures; (c) VDM stamps used to repeat and overlap along spine; (d) the base mesh; (e) VDM stencil applied for throat-iris detail; (f) VDM stencil placed for chest detail. (See Figure 16.5.)

Plate XIII. A sculpt of an organic structure (left) at 1.6 million polygons and a file size of 200 MB (.obj format) compared to the same structure stored as a (.tif) vector displacement map (right) at 1024 × 1024 resolution and a file size of 17 MB. (VDM exposure adjusted in Mudbox Image Browser). (See Figure 16.6.)

Plate XIV. Aaaaa! offers a vibrant, stylized vision of the future. (See Figure 18.1.)

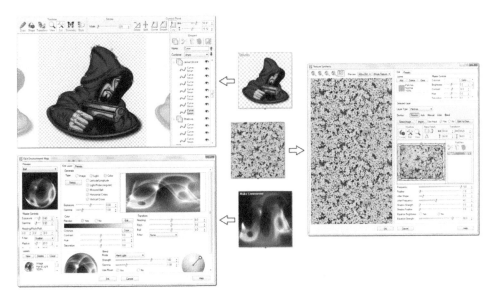

Plate XV. Some nodes, such as Canvas, Synthesis, and Make Environment, reveal entire mini-applications when double-clicked. (See Figure 18.5.)

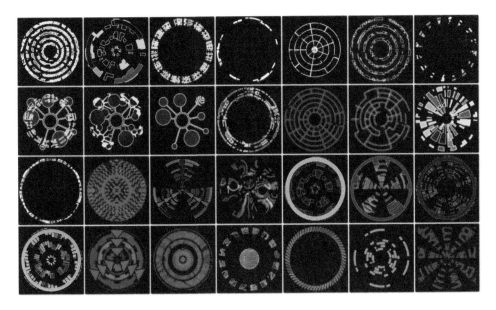

Plate XVI. A sampling of dozens of light ring variations created for *Aaaaa!* (See Figure 18.8.)

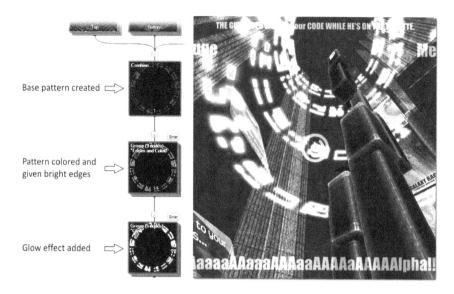

Base pattern created ⇨

Pattern colored and given bright edges ⇨

Glow effect added ⇨

Plate XVII. A light ring created in Genetica (left), and shown in-game (right). The node groups forming this texture were reused for the creation of multiple assets. (See Figure 18.9.)

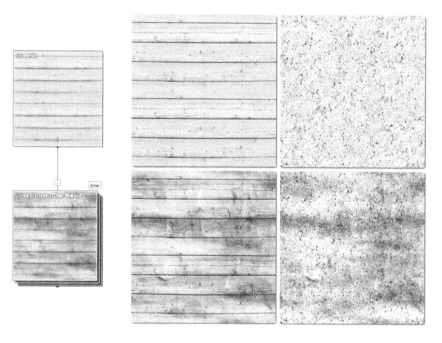

Plate XVIII. Node groups can be reused to perform just about any job. In this case, a group has been created (left) that will batter and smudge any input image (center and right). (See Figure 18.10.)

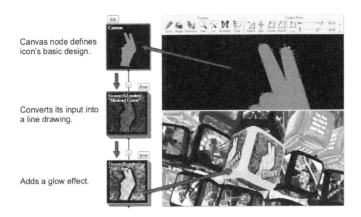

Canvas node defines
icon's basic design.

Converts its input into
a line drawing.

Adds a glow effect.

Plate XIX. The "Flip-It Glove" icon created in Genetica (upper right and left). The icon appearing in *Aaaaa!*'s extensive menu of unlockable content (lower right). (See Figure 18.11.)

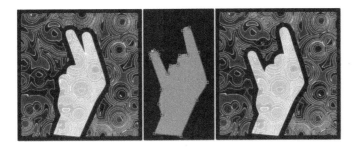

Plate XX. The icon as it appeared in *Aaaaa!* (left). Modifying the shape drawn in the Canvas node (center) will automatically propagate down to the final result (right). (See Figure 18.12.)

Plate XXI. Cube, normal, and opacity maps created in Genetica (left) form convincing compact discs in a game engine when applied to a standard reflection shader. (See Figure 18.15.)

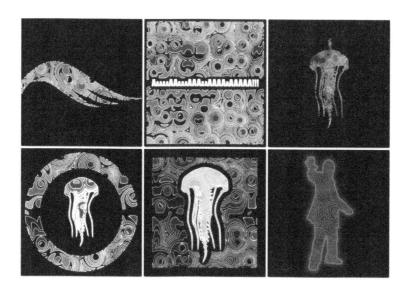

Plate XXII. Avoiding fixed designs allowed numerous icon variations to be created for *Aaaaa!* with exceptional speed. (See Figure 18.13.)

Plate XXIII. Genetica is able to bake a variety of lighting effects into cube maps. The left cube map is unfiltered, while the right one has been modified to create the impression of polished bronze. (See Figure 18.16.)

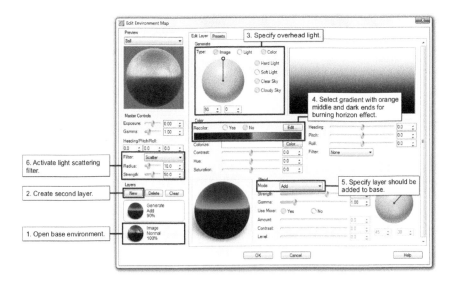

Plate XXIV. The polished bronze effect can be baked into a cube map using the Edit Environment Map dialog, found by clicking the Render Environment Map button in Genetica's main button bar. (See Figure 18.17.)

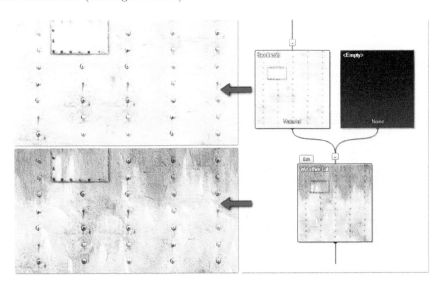

Plate XXV. In this example a seamless texture for a ship hull was created from a photograph (top). A more aged surface was desired, so it was weathered procedurally (bottom). (See Figure 18.20.)

Plate XXVI. Scrubbing in the HUD. (See Figure 21.2.)

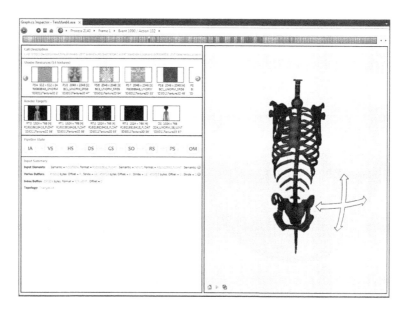

Plate XXVII. The Draw Call Page. (See Figure 21.4.)

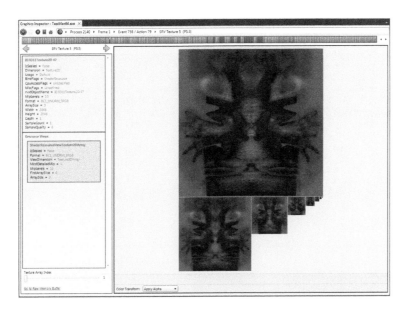

Plate XXVIII. The Texture Page. (See Figure 21.5.)

Plate XXIX. The Graphics Debug Focus. (See Figure 21.8.)

Plate XXX. The HUD showing performance graphs. (See Figure 21.9.)

10

Shape-Preserving Terrain Decimation and Associated Tools

David Eberly

10.1   Introduction

I worked on a truck-racing game with large terrains, each level approximately 3 miles by 3 miles in size.[1] The game shipped on Xbox 360 and Playstation 3. Level artists initially created each terrain as a height field by painting a 2K-by-2K, 16-bit TIFF image, each texel value representing the terrain height. A regular tessellation of the grid using two triangles per texel produces 8M triangles, which is too many triangles to draw per frame. We wanted a decimation algorithm that would give us a greatly reduced number of triangles yet still preserve the general shape of the terrain. Our target was 2.5 percent of the full count, which is approximately 200K triangles. The first portion of this article is a discussion about the algorithm I developed to solve this problem. The shape-preserving heuristic was a good one, although we settled for a slightly larger percent, and the algorithm was not too complicated.

The level artists created lofted roads (the racing tracks) using a plugin for 3D Studio Max and stitched them into the terrain mesh. Each lofted road was itself a height field—a quad strip with two triangles per quad. When stitched into the terrain, the road was required to conform to the shape of the terrain. This meant that any terrain vertices covered by a road needed to be inherited by the road geometry, and the texture coordinates for the lofted road had to be interpolated to generate texture coordinates for the inherited vertices. This process is tedious and time consuming, especially given that the artists iterated frequently, making modifications to the decimated terrain and to the roads. We wanted a tool that would automate this process. The second portion of this article is a discussion about the tools to support the automation. They involve constrained Delaunay triangulation for the automated stitching and some detailed programming to handle

---

[1] *Baja: Edge of Control*, by 2XL Games Inc, THQ publisher (2008)

the inheritance of vertices and texture coordinate generation. As always, technical problems occurred during the development, and artists are fond of requesting new features. The article contains some discussion about these problems and features. For a good survey of decimation algorithms, including those useful for level of detail, see [Luebke et al. 03]. Methods for decimating terrain may be found at The Virtual Terrain Project [Collaborators 10].

10.2   The Decimation Algorithm

The level artists, of course, had full control over the painting of the 2K-by-2K TIFF image. In addition, they specified parameters that would control the decimation. These included a vertex budget, which by default was approximately 100K (to produce approximately 200K triangles), and the width and height of a texel, which were each approximately 8 feet. The vertex budget included road vertices as well as any terrain vertices, so if a level had a large number of roads, the budget was usually chosen to be larger than the default.

10.2.1   Initial Vertex Selection

The terrain tool maintained a set of vertices to be used for a triangle mesh representing the terrain plus roads. All the road vertices were inserted first because, as in all racing games, the roads are what the player sees the most, and you want all the detail you can get for them. However, our game had a free-roaming mode that allowed players to explore the level, so the terrain needed reasonable detail even in regions far from the roads.

The pseudocode assumes two data structures, `Vertex2` which represents a pair of `float` coordinates, and `Edge2` which contains a pair of `Vertex2` objects. The vertex coordinates are in units of image indices (from 0 to 2048). Each road consists of an array of `Edge2` objects that delimit its boundaries. Listing 10.1 contains the pseudocode for inserting the road vertices into the set of vertices that will be used for the final terrain mesh.

Pseudocode for the initial vertex selection from the height field is given in Listing 10.2. The first two inputs are the number of columns of the height image and the number of rows of the height image. The height image values are stored as a two-dimensional array. The next two parameters are the width and height of the initial blocks (in units of number of texels). The last parameter is the set of vertices to be used in the final triangle mesh. The set of vertices is nonempty on input because it contains all the road vertices that are required to be in the final mesh. The incoming height field is of size $2^n \times 2^m$ rather than $(2^n + 1) \times (2^m + 1)$, so the x-maximum and y-maximum vertices must be handled separately. This requires using one less than the `hxSize` and `hySize` values for the coordinate values. The element `InitialHeightVertices` chooses a low-resolution regular grid of vertices

```
void InsertRoadVertices (vector<vector<Edge2>>& roads,
  set<Vertex2>& vertices)
{
  for (int r = 0; r < roads.size(); ++r) {
    const vector<Edge2>& edges = roads[r];
    for (int e = 0; e < edges.size(); ++e) {
      vertices.insert(edges[e].GetVertex(0));
      vertices.insert(edges[e].GetVertex(1));
    }
  }
}
```

Listing 10.1. The road vertices are always in the triangle mesh.

```
void InitialHeightVertices (int hxSize, int hySize,
    int dx, int dy, set<Vertex2>& vertices)
{
  for (int y = 0; y < hySize; y += dy) {
    for (int x = 0; x < hxSize; x += dx) {
      vertices.insert(Vertex2(x,y));
    }
    vertices.insert(Vertex2(hxSize-1,y));
  }
  for (int x = 0; x < hxSize; x += dx) {
    vertices.insert(Vertex2(x,hySize-1));
  }
  vertices.insert(Vertex2(hxSize-1,hySize-1));
}
```

Listing 10.2. Initial vertex selection for the height field.

to guarantee that the final terrain mesh has some uniformity to it and that the xy-domain is rectangular.

10.2.2 Adaptive Quadtree Decomposition

The vertex selection for the terrain is based on an adaptive quadtree decomposition in order to preserve the shape of the terrain as much as possible. The idea is easily illustrated in the one-dimensional setting, where the height field is the graph of a function. Figure 10.1 shows a decomposition of the domain of a curve to obtain an approximation that preserves the shape of the curve.

Figure 10.1(a) shows the domain as a set of four blocks of vertices, each block containing five vertices with adjacent blocks sharing a vertex. A linear interpola-

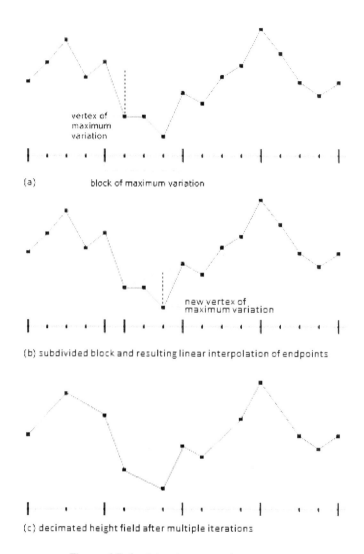

Figure 10.1. Adaptive curve decomposition.

tion of the graph endpoints for each block is shown; the figure has four gray line
segments representing these. The blocks are stored in a max-heap that is sorted
by the maximum vertical distance between curve samples and the interpolation
line segments. The second block in Figure 10.1(a) contains the maximum-distance
vertex, so it is at the root of the max-heap.

The maximum-distance vertex of the block at the root of the max-heap is selected to be in the final terrain mesh. That block is subdivided at the vertex location into two subblocks, the maximum-vertex distances are computed, and the subblocks are inserted into the max-heap. Because the set of blocks has changed, the linear interpolation of the graph endpoints must change. Figure 10.1(b) illustrates this step. Observe that the subblock, whose endpoints are two adjacent vertices, produces exactly a segment of the interpolation—the graph and linear interpolation of endpoints are the same for this subblock. After the subdivision, the figure shows the next root block on the heap and the correspnding vertex of maximum variation. This process is iterated until the vertex budget has been met. Figure 10.1(c) shows a decimated height field for the curve of Figure 10.1(a) after several such iterations.

In essence, the vertices that deviate the most from low-frequency approximations of the height values in the blocks are the ones selected for the final triangle mesh. The large deviations are what our visual systems perceive as contributing to the "shape" of the height field. Naturally, there is a trade-off between a good-quality shape and the vertex budget. The artists want more vertices for better visual quality, but the graphics programmers want fewer vertices for high-performance rendering.

The adaptive decomposition for the two-dimensional height fields is similar to that for curves. For each rectangular block of vertices, a bilinear interpolation of the four corner vertices is used as a low-frequency approximation to the height field of that block. The maximum vertical distance between height field values and the bilinear interpolation is computed. A max-heap of blocks sorted by the maximum

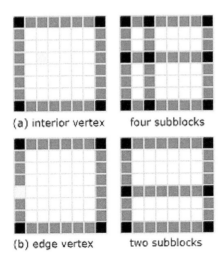

(a) interior vertex   four subblocks

(b) edge vertex   two subblocks

Figure 10.2. Block decomposition for a height field.

vertical distance is maintained. The block at the root of the max-heap is processed, selecting the maximum-distance vertex for the final triangle mesh and subdividing the block into four subblocks (if the vertex is interior) or into two subblocks (if the vertex is on a block edge). Figure 10.2 shows the typical block decompositions for a height field representing a surface.

The block of height-field information is a structure shown in Listing 10.3. The block stores the bounding x- and y-values and the location and variation of the maximum-variation vertex for that block. The constructor is passed the bounds of the block and the height field so that bilinear interpolation may be used to compute variation.

Assuming a data structure `MaxHeap<Block*,float>` for the max-heap, pseudocode for the adaptive subdivision is shown in Listing 10.4. The max-heap structure supports an insertion and removal of blocks from the heap. Although the variation is stored by `Block`, the max-heap knows nothing about `Block`, so the variation is duplicated.

```
class Block
{
public:
  Block (int hxSize, int hySize, int** heights,
    int x0, int x1, int y0, int y1)
    :
    mX0(x0), mX1(x1), mY0(y0), mY1(y1),
    mXMax(-1), mYMax(-1), mVariation(-1.0f)
  {
    float h00 = (float)heights[mY0][mX0];
    float h10 = (float)heights[mY0][mX1];
    float h01 = (float)heights[mY1][mX0];
    float h11 = (float)heights[mY1][mX1];
    float invDx = 1.0f/(mX1 - mX0), invDy = 1.0f/(mY1 - mY0);
    for (int y = mY0; y <= mY1; ++y) {
      float dy = invDy*(y - mY0), omdy = 1.0f - dy;
      for (int x = mX0; x <= mX1; ++x) {
        float dx = invDx*(x - mX0), omdx = 1.0f - dx;
        float z = omdx*(omdy*h00+dy*h01)+dx*(omdy*h10+dy*h11);
        float var = fabs(z - (float)heights[y][x]);
        if (var > mVariation) {
          mXMax = x;  mYMax = y;  mVariation = var;
        }
      }
    }
  }
  // Block is (x,y) with x0 <= x <= x1 and y0 <= y <= y1.
  int mX0, mX1, mY0, mY1;
  // Maximum-variation vertex is at (xmax,ymax;variation).
  int mXMax, mYMax;
  float mVariation;
};
```

Listing 10.3. The Block data structure.

```
void AdaptiveQuadtreeDecomposition (int hxSize, int hySize,
  int** heights, int dx, int dy, int vertexBudget,
  set<Vertex2>& vertices)
{
  MaxHeap<Block*,float> heap;
  Block* b;
  int x, y;
  for (y = 0; y < hySize - dy; y += dy) {
    for (x = 0; x < hxSize - dx; x += dx) {
      b = new Block(hxSize,hySize,heights,x,x+dx,y,y+dy);
      heap.Insert(b,b->mVariation);
    }
    b = new Block(hxSize,hySize,heights,x,x+dx-1,y,y+dy);
    heap.Insert(b,b->mVariation);
  }
  for (x = 0; x < hxSize - dx; x += dx) {
    b = new Block(hxSize,hySize,heights,x,x+dx,y,y+dy-1);
    heap.Insert(b,b->mVariation);
  }
  b = new Block(hxSize,hySize,heights,x,x+dx-1,y,y+dy-1);
  heap.Insert(b,b->mVariation);

  while (vertices.size() < vertexBudget && heap.size() > 0) {
    heap.Remove(b);
    int x0 = b->mX0, x1 = b->mX1, y0 = b->mY0, y1 = b->mY1;
    int xmax = b->mXMax, ymax = b->mYMax;
    delete b;
    vertices.insert(Vertex2(xmax,ymax));
    if (x1 - x0 > 1 && y1 - y0 > 1) {
      b = new Block(hxSize,hySize,heights,x0,xmax,y0,ymax);
      heap.Insert(b, b->mVariation);
      b = new Block(hxSize,hySize,heights,x0,xmax,ymax,y1);
      heap.Insert(b, b->mVariation);
      b = new Block(hxSize,hySize,heights,xmax,x1,y0,ymax);
      heap.Insert(b, b->mVariation);
      b = new Block(hxSize,hySize,heights,xmax,x1,ymax,y1);
      heap.Insert(b, b->mVariation);
    }
  }
  while (heap.size() > 0) { heap.Remove(b); delete b; }
};
```

Listing 10.4. The adaptive quadtree decomposition.

10.2.3 Partitioning Vertices

A Delaunay triangulation may be applied directly to the set of vertices obtained from the functions InsertRoadVertices, InitialHeightVertices, and AdaptiveQuadtreeDecomposition. However, even at the targeted 200K triangles, the number of triangles is large enough that the Delaunay triangulation is quite slow. The performance was improved by partitioning the vertices into small subsets, applying a Delaunay triangulation to each subset, and then stitching the

```
void PartitionVertices (const set<Vertex2>& vertices,
  int hxSize, int hySize, vector<vector<Vertex2>>& tiles)
{
  int numXTiles = hxSize/256, numYTiles = hySize/256;
  int numTiles = numXTiles*numYTiles;
  tiles.resize(numTiles);
  set<Vertex2>::iterator iter = vertices.begin();
  set<Vertex2>::iterator end = vertices.end();
  for (/**/; iter != end; ++iter) {
    Vertex2 v = *iter;
    float xNT = v[0]*numXTiles, yNT = v[1]*numYTiles;
    float xFTile = xNT/hxSize, yFTile = yNT/hySize;
    int xITile = (int)xFTile, yITile = (int)yFTile;
    int i = xITile + numXTiles*yITile;
    bool onXEdge = (xFTile-xITile == 0.0f) && xITile > 0;
    bool onYEdge = (yFTile-yITile == 0.0f) && yITile > 0;
    bool onBoth = (onXEdge & onYEdge);
    tiles[i].push_back(v);
    if (onXEdge) { tiles[i-1].push_back(v); }
    if (onYEdge) { tiles[i-numXTiles].push_back(v); }
    if (onBoth)  { tiles[i-1-numXTiles].push_back(v); }
  }
}
```

Listing 10.5. Partition the vertices to prepare for fast Delaunay triangulation

results together. The final triangulation is not necessarily the Delaunay triangulation of the original set of vertices, but the quality was sufficient for the game application.

Experimentation showed that the performance was reasonable when the domain of the height field was divided by 256 in each dimension; that is, the array of tiles had `hxSize/256` columns and `hySize/256` rows. The pseudocode for the partitioning is shown in Listing 10.5. The `if`-tests ensure that vertices on the boundaries of the tiles are inserted into all the vertex arrays that share those boundaries.

10.2.4 Processing Tiles

Delaunay triangulation must be applied to each tile, followed by stitching together all the triangulations. High-level pseudocode for this is contained in Listing 10.6.

The input to `ProcessTiles` is the set of vertices (road and height field) and the array of tiles. The output is an array of unique terrain vertices, `terrVertices`. The array `terrIndices` contains triples of indices into `terrVertices`. If there are T triangles in the mesh, `terrIndices` has $3 \times T$ indices. For such an index t, the triangle's two-dimensional vertices are given by `terrVertices[terrIndices[3*t+j]` for $0 \leq j \leq 2$. The output array `terrAdjacencies` contains triples of triangle indices. Triangle t has up to three edge-adjacent neighbors. If there is a neighbor

```
void ProcessTiles (const set<Vertex2>& vertices,
  const vector<vector<Vertex2>>& tiles,
  vector<Vertex2>& terrVertices, vector<int>& terrIndices,
  vector<int>& terrAdjacencies)
{
  map<Vertex2,int> vtxMap;
  CreateVertexMap(vertices,vtxMap,terrVertices);
  for (i = 0; i < tiles.size(); ++i) {
    Triangulate(tiles[i],vtxMap,terrIndices,terrAdjacencies);
  }
  Stitch(terrVertices,terrIndices,terrAdjacencies);
}
```

Listing 10.6. High-level processing of tiles.

adjacent to edge $\langle 3t + 0, 3t + 1 \rangle$, then let a_0 be its (nonnegative) triangle index. If there is no neighbor to this edge, the convention is to set $a_0 = -1$. Similarly, a_1 is the triangle index associated with a neighbor of edge $\langle 3t + 1, 3t + 2 \rangle$ and a_2 is the triangle index associated with a neighbor of edge $\langle 3t + 2, 3t + 0 \rangle$.

In Listing 10.6, the vertex map **vtxMap** stores a unique index per vertex, and the unique vertices themselves are copied in order to **terrVertices**. Listing 10.7 is the simple pseudocode for this process.

The Delaunay triangulation is encapsulated by **Triangulate**, as shown in Listing 10.8. This function also has the responsibility for updating the index and adjacency arrays for the terrain. The pseudocode assumes the existence of a class **Delaunay2** that implements incremental Delaunay triangulation and that allows you to read back the indices and adjacencies. The block of code at the end of the function remaps the triangle indices to use the unique vertex indexing and to

```
void CreateVertexMap (const set<Vertex2>& vertices,
  map<Vertex2,int>& vtxMap, vector<Vertex2>& terrVertices)
{
  terrVertices.resize(vertices.size());
  set<Vertex2>::iterator iter = vertices.begin();
  set<Vertex2>::iterator end = vertices.end();
  for (int i = 0;; iter != end; ++iter++, ++i) {
    terrVertices[i] = *iter;  vtxMap[*iter] = i;
  }
}
```

Listing 10.7. Creating the vertex map.

```
void Triangulate (const vector<Vertex2>& vertexArray,
  const map<Vertex2,int>& vertexMap
  vector<int>& terrIndices, vector<int>& terrAdjacencies)
{
  Delaunay2 triangulation(vertexArray);
  vector<int> indices = triangulation.GetIndices();
  vector<int> adjacencies = triangulation.GetAdjacencies();
  int size = terrIndices.size(), deltaSize = indices.size();
  terrIndices.resize(size + deltaSize);
  terrAdjacencies.resize(size + deltaSize);
  for (int j0 = size, j1 = 0; j1 < deltaSize; ++j0, ++j1) {
    int j2 = indices[j1];
    terrIndices[j0] = vertexMap[vertexArray[j2]];
    j2 = adjacencies[j1];
    terrAdjacencies[j0] = (j2 >= 0 ? j2 + size/3 : -1);
  }
}
```

Listing 10.8. The Delaunay triangulation of a tile.

```
void Stitch (const vector<Vertex2>& verts, vector<int>& inds,
  vector<int>& adjs)
{
  typedef map<Edge2,pair<int,int>> SharedMap;
  SharedMap shared;
  int numTriangles = indices.size()/3;
  for (int t0 = 0; t0 < numTriangles; ++t0) {
    for (int j0 = 0, b0 = 3*t0; j0 < 3; ++j0) {
      if (terrAdjacencies[b0 + j0] == -1) {
        int i0 = inds[b0 + j0], i1 = inds[b0 + ((j0+1)%3)];
        Vertex2 v0 = verts[i0], v1 = verts[i1];
        SharedMap::iterator itr = shared.find(Edge2(v0,v1));
        if (itr != shared.end()) {  // update the adjacencies
          itr->second.second = t0;  int t1 = itr->second.first;
          for (int j1 = 0, b1 = 3*t1; j1 < 3; ++j1) {
            int i2 = inds[b1 + j1];  Vertex2 v2 = verts[i2];
            if (v2 != v0 && v2 != v1) {
              j1 = (j1 + 1) % 3;
              adjs[b1 + j1] = t0;  adjs[b0 + j0] = t1;
              break;
            }
          }
        }
        else { // shared edge encountered first time
          shared[edge] = make_pair(t0,-1);
        }
      }
    }
  }
}
```

Listing 10.9. Delaunay triangulation of tiles followed by stitching.

```
void CreateTerrain (int hxSize, int hySize, int** heights,
    int dx, int dy, int vertexBudget,
    const vector<vector<Edge2>>& roads,
    vector<Vertex2>& terrVertices, vector<int>& terrIndices,
    vector<int>& terrAdjacencies)
{
    set<Vertex2> vertices;
    vector<vector<Vertex2>> tiles;

    InsertRoads(roads,vertices);
    InitialHeightVertices(hxSize,hySize,dx,dy,vertices);
    AdaptiveQuadtreeDecomposition(hxSize,hySize,heights,dx,dy,
        vertexBudget,vertices);
    PartitionVertices(vertices,hxSize,hySize,tiles);
    ProcessTiles(vertices,tiles,terrVertices,terrIndices,
        terrAdjacencies);
}
```

Listing 10.10. Top-level call for decimation and triangulation to produce the terrain mesh.

append the triangle indices into a single-index array. It also adjusts the adjacency information to use the new triangle indexing.

The stitching of the triangulations of the tiles is shown in Listing 10.9. The tiles are stitched by storing the shared edges and the triangle sharing them, followed by a lot of typical mesh bookkeeping. The top-level summary of the algorithm is Listing 10.10.

10.3 Processing the Lofted Roads

After the terrain is generated by the function CreateTerrain, the edges of the road need to be inserted into the triangulation. The algorithm uses a constrained Delaunay triangulation. Because we have already generated a Delaunay triangulation that includes the road-edge vertices, all we need to do now is modify the triangulation one edge at a time.

10.3.1 Inserting Edges into the Triangulation

The basic idea for inserting edges is illustrated in Figure 10.3. The road edge to be inserted is $\langle V_0, V_1 \rangle$, where V_0 and V_1 are vertices that were included in the Delaunay triangulation. The common case is that a unique triangle strip connects V_0 to V_1, where each triangle of the strip is intersected by the road edge, and each such intersection is an interior point of a triangle edge.

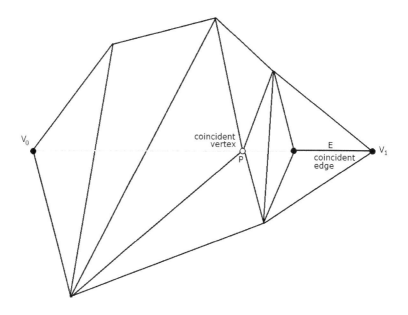

Figure 10.3. Insertion of an edge into the triangulation.

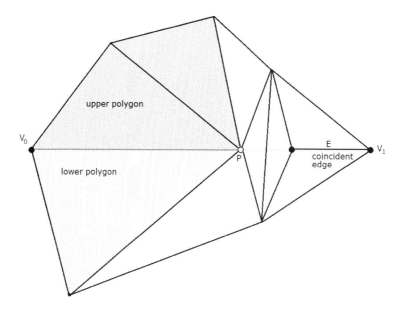

Figure 10.4. Retriangulation of the polygon formed by a 3-triangle strip.

If the road edge had been $\langle V_0, P \rangle$, as illustrated in Figure 10.3, we would have the common case. It suffices to locate the triangle strip, remove its triangles to form a simple polygon, and retriangulate that polygon so that it includes the road edge. Figure 10.4 shows the results when the road edge is $\langle V_0, P \rangle$. The retriangulation generates an upper polygon and a lower polygon, both polygons sharing the edge $\langle V_0, P \rangle$.

In practice, we have no such luck in always having the common case. Sometimes, the road edge contains an interior point that is also a vertex in the Delaunay triangulation, for example, the point P in Figure 10.3. It is even possible that the road edge overlaps an entire edge of the Delaunay triangulation, for example, the edge E in Figure 10.3. Handling these special cases requires quite a large amount of programming.

10.3.2   Inherited Texture Coordinates

The output of the edge-insertion phase is a set of *ordered edges*. Most of these edges are the original road edges, but some of them are road subedges obtained when coincident vertices and coincident edges are encountered during the insertion. The edges are ordered in the following sense. The xy-domain of the road is a simple polygon, which is the union of the triangles that form the road's triangle strip. This polygon is ordered counterclockwise to an observer looking down on the road (in the negative z-direction).

The output edges still form the boundary of a simple polygon with counterclockwise ordering, although the polygon no longer represents a triangle strip. We may iterate over all xy-vertices in the Delaunay triangulation and apply point-in-polygon tests. Any vertices inside the road polygon are "inherited" by the road. The vertex positions remain the same, and the texture coordinates are implicitly the xy-values of the vertex positions (scaled to $[0, 1]^2$). But now, the texture coordinates must be replaced with ones that make sense for the road. Each such terrain vertex that is now a road vertex lives in one of the triangles of the original road's triangle strip. It suffices to locate the triangle of the strip that contains that vertex, compute the barycentric coordinates of the vertex relative to that triangle, and use these coordinates to compute a weighted sum of the texture coordinates that the artists have assigned to the triangle in the strip. As long as the road does not have an extremely large turn, there are no noticeable artifacts from selecting the texture coordinates in this manner.

10.3.3   Dealing with Malformed Roads

Each road was built from a central spline curve. The modeling package provided the artists with the ability to modify the density of the quads along the spline. When the density was larger at spline points of large curvature (at sharp turns in the road) than along relatively straight sections of the curve, sometimes the quads would overlap in the height direction. I watched the artists adjust the density, and it was never apparent that there was overlap. I discovered the overlap only after several assertions in the terrain tool were triggered due to the consequences of overlap.

The amount of overlap was never large, so I modified the terrain tool to preprocess each road, verifying that the quads/triangles formed a height field. They did not when small needle-like triangles were misoriented (normals pointing downward instead of upward). The tool would then slightly perturb vertices of those triangles to undo the overlap.

10.4   Variations in the Content Pipeline

The discussion in this chapter was focused on roads built as quad strips that have the topology of a rectangle—the strip is a sequence of quads, each quad is decomposed into two triangles, and there is a starting edge and a final edge. The actual game had a need for variations in the tool, and the level artists had ways of taking the best-written tool and finding every bug possible.

10.4.1   Iteration of the Tool

Although the original design was to decimate 16-bit height images and stitch in lofted roads, it was only natural that after this first pass the decimated-and-stitched terrain be saved to a file to allow the level artists to load it later and manipulate it. Once happy with the quality of the decimated height field, the level artists would design new roads to be stitched into the terrain. The terrain tool had to be modified to load an already decimated terrain *and* a separate collection of roads to be stitched into that terrain. The bookkeeping is significant, and the addition of new roads kept me busy fixing bugs in the tool, several of them generated by floating-point round-off errors when the new road vertices were significantly close to the vertices of the original decimated terrain.

10.4.2   Closed-Loop Roads

The obvious variation is that many of the racing tracks were closed loops represented as quad strips that have the topology of an annulus. This presents a difficult challenge. The level artists build such roads to have the topology of a rectangle so that texture coordinates may be chosen to obtain a repeating texture along the road with the correct wraparound at the shared edge corresponding to the starting and final edges.

The triangulation is modified to accomodate the starting edge. However, inserting the final edge is a no-operation because it already exists in the modified triangulation. Instead, some bookkeeping was necessary for those vertices and shared edges. Each vertex that is on the boundary between the terrain and road has a texture coordinate for its instance corresponding to the terrain and a texture coordinate for its instance corresponding to the road. For each vertex of a shared edge, a third texture coordinate is needed to represent the wraparound. The complication in the bookkeeping was not the generation of vertex data; rather, a tool already existed for loading vertex buffers corresponding to the terrain and roads. The output of this tool was then decomposed to create vertex buffers that were of an optimal size for the graphics hardware. The terrain tool had to generate its data in a manner that allowed saving it to disk so that the vertex buffer loader could process the additional texture coordinates.

10.4.3 Y-Junction Roads

Another variation that was natural to the game involved support for roads that have a Y-junction (or T-junction, depending on how you want to label the junctions). Because we were on a tight schedule, modifying the terrain tool to support this would have been time consuming. Instead, we asked the level artists to use only linear or looped roads. A Y-junction was built so that an upper arm of the "Y" did not quite meet the branch point. Some high-quality texturing hid the fact that the Y-junction was not technically a "Y".

10.4.4 Placement of World Objects

Manual stitching of the roads into the terrain is very tedious and time consuming, but so is stitching of world objects such as buildings or track-side objects. The terrain tool input-file format was modified to allow the artists to specify whether an object was a road to be stenciled into the terrain, with inheritance of terrain vertices and interpolation of texture coordinates, or a world object to be stitched into the terrain by cutting out that portion of the terrain covered by the object. In the cutout option, terrain vertices were simply discarded, and the terrain vertices on the boundary of the cutout were adjusted to match the base of the world object.

10.4.5 Support for Tweaking the Results

Sometimes the triangles that bordered the boundary between roads and terrains were not quite what the artists wanted. I had discussed options to add support to the terrain tool to allow the artists to tweak the results to their satisfaction and in a manner that matched how artists think (not how programmers think), but the schedule would not support it.

This meant that the level artists needed to avoid tweaking the results during development because the terrain tool could not preserve the intermediate (manual) tweaks for incorporation into the next pass of the tool. Tweaking occurred near shipping time. It is certainly possible to support such a feature, but it requires careful management of the content pipeline to ensure all stages are applied correctly to the content.

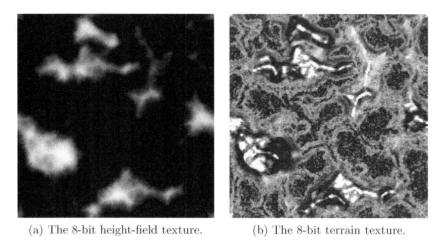

(a) The 8-bit height-field texture.   (b) The 8-bit terrain texture.

Figure 10.5. Sample data for the terrain. (See Color Plate V.)

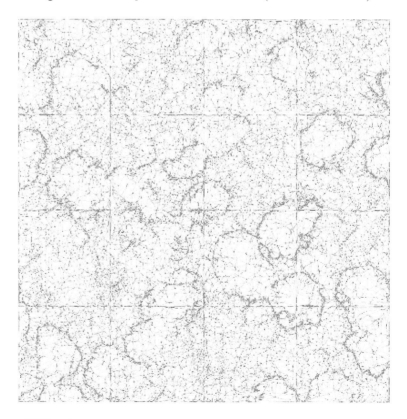

Figure 10.6. The terrain mesh decimated to 2.5 percent of the original height field.

10.5   An Example

I do not own the art content for the actual game, so the example shown here is from the Wild Magic sample graphics application for drawing a large terrain [Eberly 10]. The height field is a 8-bit grayscale bitmapped image rather than a 16-bit TIFF image, but this is irrelevant for the illustration of the concepts. The terrain texture was not designed as a world environment to have roads for racing, but again this is irrelevant for this example. Both textures are 1024×1024 images, shown in Figure 10.5, but the terrain texture is displayed as a grayscale image. See Color Plate V for a larger color version.

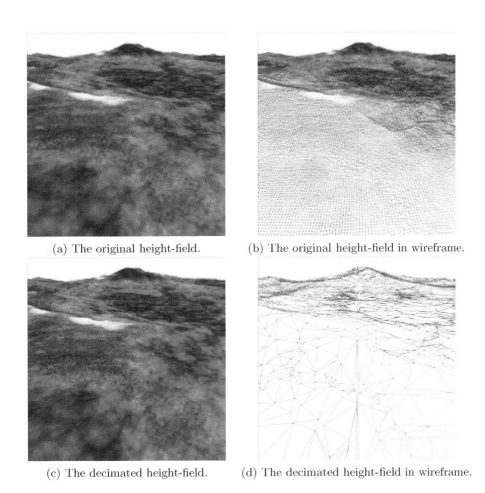

(a) The original height-field.   (b) The original height-field in wireframe.

(c) The decimated height-field.   (d) The decimated height-field in wireframe.

Figure 10.7. The final results for comparison. (See Color Plates VI and VII.)

The terrain tool source code implemented to illustrate the algorithms in this chapter was written to be independent of Wild Magic. I used some Wild Magic classes but stripped out what was not needed and removed the namespace Wm5. However, the test program is a Wild Magic application. The vertex budget was chosen to be 26,214 vertices, which leads to 52,315 triangles in the terrain mesh. This is a reduction to 2.5 percent of the 2,097,152 triangles in the original height field. Figure 10.6 shows a projection of the triangle mesh onto the xy-plane. If you compare this to the height image of Figure 10.5(a), you will see that small triangles occur in regions of high variation and vice versa.

The original height field and the decimated mesh are saved to a format that Wild Magic 5 can load. The terrain viewer allows you to toggle between the two terrains with the camera in the same location and orientation. Figure 10.7 shows screen captures, both as solids and as wireframes. See Color Plates VI and VII for larger color versions of the solid renderings.

Bibliography

[Collaborators 10] VTP Collaborators. "The Virtual Terrain Project Web Site.", 2010. Available online (www.vterrain.org).

[Eberly 10] David Eberly. "Geometric Tools Web Site.", 2010. Available online (www.geometrictools.com).

[Luebke et al. 03] David Luebke, Martin Reddy, Jonathan D. Cohen, Amitabh Varshney, Benjamin Watson, and Robert Huebner. *Level of Detail for 3D Graphics*. San Francisco: Morgan Kaufmann, 2003.

11

In-Game Audio Debugging Tools

Simon Franco

11.1 Introduction

When working on previous generations of gaming hardware, sound designers only had to worry about playing a few sound effects whenever the player did something interesting and otherwise just playing a track of music. In contrast, current gaming hardware now allows our game worlds to be more richly detailed, with potentially hundreds of sound-emitting objects. In addition to this, we also have more complex systems manipulating the game's audio. For example, we may have a context-sensitive music manager. This monitors the game's state and chooses music to match the on-screen action.

In order for sound designers and programmers to maintain control over all of these audio systems, we need to develop more advanced debugging tools. These tools must help both the sound designer and programmer to break down the current soundscape (the combination of all the sounds currently playing) into its component parts. The tools we must develop need to address the most common problems which arise over the course of developing a game's various audio systems. Commonly occurring problems with sound systems include sounds cutting off unexpectedly, sounds failing to play (or unexpectedly playing too loud or too quietly), and the wrong sound playing for a particular event.

11.2 Tools to Debug Sound Systems

This article discusses numerous tools that can be developed and integrated into a game to facilitate the debugging of audio systems. The tools discussed can be developed and integrated separately or can comprise a collection of tools for the sound designer. Each tool provides information about a part of the game's audio playback. When used together, these tools will reduce the amount of time needed by both sound designers and programmers in tracking down issues.

These tools can be developed to work with either a third-party sound engine or an in-house sound engine. They are designed so that they sit above the playback layer, making their addition to your code base as simple as possible. A discussion of each tool along with any implementation notes is presented.

11.2.1   Sound Event Snapshot

Sound events are the high-level objects processed by your audio engine and are used to describe how a sound will be played by the sound engine. Typically they will have a name to identify them: playback settings, such as volume and pitch and one or more associated audio files. As well as their individual settings, they will typically belong to one or more category groups, such as player sounds or music. These sound categories are ways of grouping sounds together and applying modifiers to them, such as volume. Sound events may also have a chain of DSP effects which need to be applied to them while they play. DSP chains may also be dynamically applied to a sound while the game is being played. For example, if a loud sound is being played behind a door of an adjoining large room, then you may have an echo reverb and a low-pass filter applied to the sound.

The sound designer will often want to break down the game's current soundscape into its atomic parts. This is so that they can see which sound events are being played and what their playback settings are. They will also want to control which sounds are allowed to play while the game is running. Examples of common problems which may occur are individual sounds dominating the soundscape, rogue sounds playing out of place, or a sound playing in an odd way, such as at the wrong pitch or volume. The sound designer will need some methods to help them investigate these sounds.

What the tool must provide. For each playing sound event, the tool displays the following information: the name of the sound event, the name of the audio file being played, and the current volume and pitch settings. Figure 11.1 shows an example of how the tool may look.

When an event is selected by the sound designer for further inspection, the tool should display the names and settings of any sound categories the event belongs to and the identity of any controlling game object that owns the instance of this sound event being played. It should show which DSP effects are being applied, if any. If your audio engine supports in-game variables directly affecting a sound's playback, then those variable names and their values should be shown. An example of binding an in-game variable to a sound event would be binding the RPM of the player's car engine to control the pitch and audio file to play for a car engine sound event.

The sound designer must also be able to enable or disable one or more categories of sounds, such as music, within the tool. This allows them to focus on the other sounds being played to make up the soundscape.

EventName	File playing	Volume	Pitch		View packs		Connect to game
GunShot	Weapons\Pistol\GunShot\PistolShot01.wav	0.88	0.07				
Footstep_Pavement	Characters\Footsteps\Footstep_Stone03.wav	0.19	0.06	**Categories:**			
Footstep_Pavement	Characters\Footsteps\Footstep_Stone01.wav	0.41	0.03	Name	Volume Modifier		Enabled
Footstep_Pavement	Characters\Footsteps\Footstep_Stone07.wav	0.49	0.02	MUSIC	1.0		☑
Footstep_Run_Pavement	Characters\Footsteps\Footstep_RunningStone02.wav	0.91	0.04				☐
Footstep_Run_Pavement	Characters\Footsteps\Footstep_RunningStone01.wav	0.89	0.02				
Footstep_Run_Pavement	Characters\Footsteps\Footstep_RunningStone02.wav	0.88	0.0	**DSP Effects applied:**			
IntroSpeechToCityLevel	Speech\CityLevelIntro.wav	1.0	0.0	*None*			
CAR1_CarEngine	Vehicles\CAR1\Engine\EngineSounds01.wav	0.4	0.01				
GangShout	Characters\Vocal\GangMember\GangShout01.wav	0.67	0.0				
CityMusic	Music\Track05.wav	1.0	0.0	**Variables:**			
Wind	Nature\Ambience\Wind01.wav	0.4	0.02	Name		Value	
CivilianChatterAmbience	Characters\Vocal\Ambience\Civilian\Chatter04.wav	0.45	0.00	N/A		0.0	
Footstep_Pavement	Characters\Footsteps\Footstep_Stone09.wav	0.23	0.03				
Footstep_Pavement	Characters\Footsteps\Footstep_Stone2.wav	0.15	0.01	**Object ID:**			
Footstep_Pavement	Characters\Footsteps\Footstep_Stone06.wav	0.45	0.06	732			

Figure 11.1. Sound event snapshot tool.

As well as sound event information, we can show general sound information as part of this tool. For example, we can show which sound packs are loaded. Sound packs are groups of related audio files, such as forest ambience sounds, which have been merged into a single file for ease of loading. As well as showing which packs are loaded, we can show how much memory each sound pack has used. A sample of how this part of the tool may look is shown in Figure 11.2.

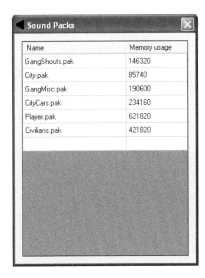

Sound Packs

Name	Memory usage
GangShouts.pak	146320
City.pak	85740
GangMisc.pak	190600
CityCars.pak	234160
Player.pak	621820
Civilians.pak	421820

Figure 11.2. Showing which sound packs are loaded.

Tool design. The tool consists of two main components. One part is integrated into the game and consists of any required functions and data needed to communicate the audio state to our external GUI tool. The other part of the tool is the external GUI tool, which displays the information sent from the game. Information on the game's audio state is sent once per game tick to the GUI tool via a buffer. The GUI tool sends back any commands from the sound designer to the game during this data exchange.

Implementation details. The user-interface portion of the tool should be created as a separate Windows (or other OS) GUI application. This application is run on a PC while the game is running. During this process, it communicates the audio state to the GUI tool via a buffer, which is written to once per frame. This buffer is then sent to the GUI tool via a network connection. The GUI tool can be put into a listen mode, and when the game boots up, it will establish a connection to the tool. It can then proceed to send information on the audio state as the game runs. Similarly, any commands issued by the designer through the tool are sent back to the game along the network connection. This design provides the most flexibility and keeps the game screen clear of obstruction. If the platform running your game cannot communicate via a network to a PC, then the user interface should be built into the game.

The game-side portion should interrogate the sound engine and send updated information on the following to keep the GUI tool up to date:

- which sound events are being played and their settings;

- the names of all sound categories and their settings;

- the names of which sound packs are loaded and what their sizes are.

The hardware platform running your game will have a limit on the number of simultaneous sounds that can be played. Therefore, we are able to make the GUI tool's list of playing sound events a fixed-size array with a matching number of elements. As the number of sound packs and sound categories will be variable, it would be best to have these use a dynamic structure, such as a linked list.

Modifications to the game to support debugging. When we play a sound, we will typically pass the sound event we want to play an instance of into the sound engine, along with any playback parameters, such as the sound's position. We then receive from the sound engine a handle to that instance of the sound event. We will need to make modifications to the play sound function so that only sounds belonging to categories permitted by the designer are allowed to play. This is so the sound designer can enable or disable sound categories in the GUI tool while debugging. We show a sample piece of code in Listing 11.1 that tests if a sound event is allowed to play.

```
// Function called in-game to play a sound. Returns a
// SoundInstance for the game to use.

SoundInstance * SoundSystem::playSound( SoundEvent * event,
                                        Params & params,
                                        unsigned int owner_id )
{
    if ( SnapShot::isAllowedCategory( event->m_category ) )
    {
        SoundInstance * inst = SoundEngine::play( event,
                                                  params,
                                                  owner_id );
        return inst;
    }
    return null;
}
```

Listing 11.1. Modifications to a play sound function to support debugging.

After the audio update has occurred for each frame, we can start to construct our data buffer to be sent over to the GUI tool. This buffer must contain the updated information on the game's audio state to keep the GUI tool up to date. Listing 11.2 shows a sample update function for the game to update the GUI tool. The update function fills in a large buffer, which is sent over to the GUI tool.

```
// Function called once per frame to update UI tool.
void SnapShot::updateGUITool()
{
    Buffer * buf;
    CreateBufferToSendToGUITool(buf);

    SoundInstance *inst = SoundEngine::getFirstActiveInstance();

    for ( ;inst; inst = inst->getNextActiveInstance() )
    {
        // Add all information about an active SoundInstance
        // to the update buffer.
        buff->addSoundInstance(inst->getEvent()->getName(),
                               inst->getWaveFilename(),
                               inst->getVolume(),
                               inst->getPitch(),
                             inst->getEvent()->getCategories(),
                               inst->getDSPChain(),
                               inst->getAnyVariableBindings() );
    }
    // Add the names of loaded sound packs and their memory
    // footprint to the update buffer.
    SoundPack *pack = SoundEngine::getFirstLoadedPack();
    for ( ;pack; pack = pack->getNextLoadedPack() )
    {
        buff->addPackInfo(pack->getName(),pack->getSize());
    }

    // Add our sound categories and their volume settings
```

```
    // to the update buffer.
    SoundCategory *category = SoundEngine::getFirstCategory();
    for ( ;category; category = category->getNextCategory() )
    {
        buff->addCategoryInfo(category->getName(),
                              category->getVolume());
    }

    // Send the buffer over to the GUI Tool!
    SendBufferToGUITool(buff);
}
```

Listing 11.2. Sending the game's audio state to the GUI tool.

As well as sending audio state information, the game-side tool must receive information on which of the sound categories the sound designer wishes to mute. Listing 11.3 shows an example of how we might receive this information from a buffer sent from the GUI tool.

Because the GUI portion of the tool has all audio state information from the game, it can choose how to render that information. This allows us to have the lightweight rendering of the sound instance info, such as the name, and a few parameters. When the event is selected for further investigation from the designer, we can display the full set of information.

```
// Function called once per frame to update UI tool.
void SnapShot::receiveUpdateFromGUITool(Buffer * buff)
{
    // The category info is pulled from the buffer
    // sent over from the GUI tool. We register the category
    // mute state with the game side SnapShot class.
    // This state is tested before playing a sound.
    while ( buff->dataRemaining())
    {
        const char * name = buff->getNextCategoryName();
        bool is_active = buff->getBool();
        SoundCategory * cat = SoundEngine::getCategory(name);
        registerCategoryMuteState( cat, is_active );
    }
}
```

Listing 11.3. Receiving information from the GUI Tool.

11.2.2   Visualizing Sound Data

Another common requirement is for the sound designer to be able to visualize sounds (and sound data) within the game world while the game is running. Although we can create and use the snapshot tool to generate a list of all the sounds currently playing, there are times when we need to see where a sound is in the game world. This allows the sound designer to see exactly which bottle smashing on the floor they just heard, or to see which gunshot animation doesn't have a sound attached to it.

What the tool must provide. Visualizing sound data is not limited only to showing the sounds that are currently playing. We can also use this tool to show sounds that were not able to play. Furthermore, we can show any invisible sound geometry, such as splines used for a controlling a sound's movement, reverb areas, or sound-pack loading zones. With this tool the designer must be able to

- turn the visualization on / off for sounds;

- toggle showing sound event names above these visualizations;

- choose to show or hide invisible sound geometry;

- enable or disable showing invisible geometry names or properties;

- have the option to show the sound properties of a collision polygon being pointed at.

Tool design. The information displayed by the tool should be rendered on the game screen so that the sound designer can move through the game world and see sound data as it relates to game objects. As with the snapshot tool, we can either have the user interface as a separate GUI application, which communicates with the game, or give the designer some simple menu options on the game screen. As there are fewer designer options with this tool, there will be fewer benefits to having a separate GUI application to manage to designer interactions.

Each game object that requires visualization must inherit from a base class called VisualizerObject. Each VisualizerObject has a category and is registered with a global VisualizerManager on construction. The VisualizerManager class is the game-side class that maintains several lists of VisualizerObjects that have been constructed. There is one list per category of VisualizerObject. Once per frame, the VisualizerManager must iterate through each of its categories. If we want to render that category of VisualizerObjects, then we iterate through that category's VisualizerObject list and call the virtual draw method on each VisualizerObject within that list. Care must be taken to ensure that the VisualizerManager is constructed first before any VisualizerObjects are created. Listing 11.4 Shows a sample VizualizerObject base class implementation.

```
enum VO_CATEGORY
{
    VO_SOUND=0,
    VO_REVERB,
    VO_GEOM,
    VO_MAX_CATEGORIES
};
```

```
class VisualizerObject
{
friend class VisualizerManager;
public:

    VisualizerObject(VO_CATEGORY category)
    {
        // Register this object on construction with
        // the VisualiserManager so that it can loop through
        // all its registered objects each frame and call
        // draw as appropriate!
        VisualizerManager::registerObject( this, category );
    }

    virtual ~VisualizerObject() {}


    // Virtual method which will need to be defined by inherited
    // classes.
    virtual void draw() = 0;

protected:

    bool m_active; // Set to true when the object is actively
                   // being processed by the game.
};
```

Listing 11.4. Sample VisualizerObject base class.

Implementation. Visualizations of sound data should keep to a consistent color scheme. The programmer can use, for example, red for inactive objects, green for active objects, and blue for active objects that are unable to perform their actions. For example, a sound that has tried to play but failed would show up as blue in this color scheme.

Active sounds in the game world are rendered by the game as a small piece of colored geometry to show their position. They are colored differently depending on whether they are being played, are unable to play, or are inaudible. The colors they use to represent these states must keep within the previously mentioned color scheme. A circle surrounding them can be optionally rendered to show their audible distance.

```
// Example base class to be inherited by all game objects
// which play a sound. Each one is given its own id.

class SoundObject : public VisualizerObject
{
public:
    SoundObject() : VisualizerObject( VO_SOUND ),
                    m_sound( null ), m_event( null ),
                    m_id( m_shared_id_counter++ ) {}

    virtual ~SoundObject() {}
```

```
    // To be implemented by the class inheriting from this.
    virtual Vector & getPos() = 0;

    // Get this object's ID.
    unsigned int getID() const { return m_id; }

    // Called once per frame by the VisualizerManager.
    virtual void draw()
    {
        // If m_sound is valid then we're playing something!
        if ( m_active && m_sound != null )
        {
            COLOR col = GREEN;

            //Is the sound within audible range?
            if (!SoundSystem::withinEventRange(m_event,getPos()))
            {
                // Change to our out of range color.
                col = BLUE;
            }

            // Draw geometry for the active sound!
            GPU::drawCross( col, getPos() );

            // Render events radius if requested.
            if ( VisualizerManager::doWeShowSoundRadius() )
            {
                // Draw geometry for the active sound!
                float radius = m_event->m_max_audible_distance;
                GPU::drawCircle( radius, getPos() );
            }
        }
        else
        {
            // No sound instance playing.
            GPU::drawCross( RED, getPos() );
        }

        if ( VisualizerManager::doWeShowSoundNames() )
        {
            // Render the text 2 metres above the geometry.

            Vector text_pos = getPos();
            text_pos.y += 2.0f;
            GPU::renderText( m_event->m_name, text_pos() );
        }
    }

protected:
    SoundEvent *        m_event;
    SoundInstance *     m_sound_instance;
    unsigned int        m_id;
    static unsigned int  m_shared_id_counter;
};
```

Listing 11.5. Sample SoundObject base class.

This is done by having game objects that can play a sound inherited from SoundObject. SoundObject itself inherits from VisualizerObject. Listing 11.5 contains a pseudocode listing showing how a sample object is created.

```
class ReverbArea : public VisualizerObject
{
public:
    ReverbArea( ReverbEffect * reverb, const PolyMesh & mesh) :
                VisualizerObject( VO_REVERB ),
                m_active( false ), m_reverb( reverb ),
                m_area( mesh )     {}

    virtual ~ReverbArea() {}

    // Reverb function called once per frame.
    // Looks to see if the listener is inside the
    // reverb area and if so applies the reverb to sounds.
    void update()
    {
        if (m_area.isPointInside(SoundSystem::getListenerPos())
        {
            m_active = true;
            SoundSystem::applyReverb( m_reverb );
        }
        else
        {
            m_active = false;
        }
    }


    // Called once per frame by the VisualizerManager.
    virtual void draw()
    {
        COLOR col = RED;
        if ( m_active )
        {
            col = GREEN;
        }
        GPU::debugDrawAreaMesh( col, m_area );

        // If reverb name rendering is enabled then render
        // the name of the reverb effect in the middle of the
        // area.
        if ( VisualizerManager::renderReverbAreaNames() )
        {
            Vector text_pos = m_area.getCentrePoint();
            GPU::renderText( m_event->m_name, text_pos() );
        }
    }

protected:
    ReverbEffect * m_reverb;
    bool m_active;
    const PolyMesh & m_area;
};
```

Listing 11.6. Sample ReverbArea class.

Classes which manage sound geometry should similarly inherit from VisualizerObject. For example, reverb areas or trigger areas managing the loading and unloading of sound packs. Listing 11.6 shows a pseudocode demonstration of this for reverb areas.

Sound-pack loading zones should similarly be rendered as geometry to show whether the sound pack is loaded or not. They should follow a color scheme to indicate if the sound pack is loaded or not. It should also display the name of its associated sound pack.

The sound properties for surface materials should also be made available for the sound designer to investigate. This can be achieved through the implementation of a simple picking system, whereby the sound designer can use either a mouse (or some other interface) to select a surface in the game's environment and see what sound properties have been assigned to that surface. For example, there may be a wall with a dirt texture, but that material has accidentally been given a metal sound property, so any impacts with that surface will be using their metal variants. To implement this we must perform a ray-cast from the cursor position onscreen into the collision mesh of the world geometry. We then retrieve the collision material belonging to the polygon underneath the cursor and display the sound material parameter on the game's screen.

11.2.3 Playback Logging

This tool is mostly used for tracking bugs occurring within the game's audio system. Sometimes a bug may be difficult to reproduce, as it relies on some subtle interaction between the player and the game environment. An example of this is when a sound does not play. This could be caused by accidentally unloading the sound pack holding the audio data used by that sound event.

What the tool must provide. A solution to this problem is to construct a replay log of all sound commands that were executed by the sound engine over the course of a play session. This can be done by logging each command before it is passed to the sound engine and storing the command into a log buffer. Periodically, this log buffer is then flushed out to a file.

Your game should provide a boot option so that the logging tool can be active as soon as the game starts. Enabling or disabling the tool should be prohibited while the game is running, as important events may be missed from the log. Your game should also supply a replay mode, where only the sound commands that were logged are executed by the sound engine.

As with the visualizer tool, the user interface for this tool is minimal. When the tool is activated, it can display its interface either onscreen or as a separate GUI application. The interface should allow the sound designer to set a logical breakpoint within the log file. This differs from a code breakpoint, in that it will pause the game and launch any debugging tools required. This is done by marking the last command logged as a breakpoint. When this breakpoint is reached during playback, the game pauses.

Tool design. A SoundLog class is created on the game side, which keeps a short array of the last few commands issued to the sound system. Every so often, this log is flushed out to a file.

A SoundReplay class is also created on the game side when we are playing back a log that was previously generated. This class reads in the log file previously written out and will call the sound system with each command entry.

How to create the playback log. All commands called on the sound engine must be logged so that the sound system can be accurately replayed. This should include all commands being sent to the sound engine, such as sounds being started and stopped and volume changes, as well as all system commands, such as any changes to the listener's position or orientation, any loading or unloading of sound packs, and any reverb areas being activated or deactivated.

The game also requires a replay mode to be added. While in this mode, the log file is read in, and the commands are executed. Commands from the game are ignored while in this mode. Commands coming in from the log file, however, are still played.

Listing 11.7 shows a few simple modifications to the previous example play-sound function in order to support playback logging and replaying from the log file.

The commands being logged require the type of command issued along with the data used by that command being logged. We also need to store how long the game

```
SoundInstance * SoundSystem::playSound( SoundEvent * event,
                                        Params & params,
                                        unsigned int owner_id,
                                                bool  from_log )
{
    if ( SoundReplay::isReplaying() && !from_log )
    {
        return;
    }
    if ( SnapShot::isAllowedCategory( event->m_category ) )
    {
        SoundInstance * inst = SoundEngine::play( event,
                                                  params,
                                                  owner_id );
        SoundLog::logPlaySoundEvent( event,
                                     params,
                                     owner_id,
                                     inst);
        return inst;
    }
    return null;
}
```

Listing 11.7. Sample showing how to add logging to sound calls.

```
enum CMD_TYPE
{
    CMD_SND_PLAY ,
    CMD_SND_STOP ,
     // More CMD enums would be added here.
    CMD_MAX
};

struct SoundCommandEntry
{
    unsigned int m_command; // CMD_TYPE
    float        m_game_time; // When was command executed.
    unsigned int m_size;    // Size of m_data used by command
    void *       m_data;    // Data used by this command.
};
```

Listing 11.8. Sample class for a sound log entry.

was running when the command was issued. Listing 11.8 shows a sample class to
store the command for the log file. It is worth noting that m_data is a pointer to
an unspecified object and m_size is the size of that object to serialize to the file.
The type of object pointed to by m_data is determined by checking the value of
m_command.

Listing 11.9 shows a simple pseudocode sample resembling how we'd log a play
sound event command.

```
// Structure we need to fill in when logging a sound being
// played. We will need to change the size of m_instance_id if
// pointers on the target platform are bigger than the size of
//  an unsigned int.

struct LogDataForPlayingASound
{
    char   m_event_name[ MAX_LENGTH_OF_EVENT_NAMES ];
    Parms m_params ;
    unsigned int   m_owner_id;
    unsigned int   m_instance_id;
};


// Function to log the sound being played.
void SoundLog::logPlaySoundEvent( SoundEvent * event ,
                                  Parms & params ,
                                  unsigned int owner_id ,
                                  SoundInstance * inst )
{
    writeData( CMD_SND_PLAY , sizeof(int) );
    writeData( Game::getTime(), sizeof(float) );

    int data_size = sizeof(LogDataForPlayingASound);
    writeData( data_size, sizeof(int) );
```

```
// Create our log data.
LogDataForPlayingASound new_log_data;

StringCopy( new_log_data.m_event_name, event->m_name );
new_log_data.m_params = params;
new_log_data.m_owner_id = owner_id;
new_log_data.m_instance_id = *(unsigned int*)inst;
writeData( &LogDataForPlayingASound, data_size );
}
```

Listing 11.9. Pseudocode sample of sound command log structure.

As the command log file may end up getting quite large if the replay data are logged for an extended period of game play, it may be worth investigating options to stream this file into memory. This way, we only store the commands for the next few seconds of game play, rather than have the log fill up our, almost certainly restricted, memory pool.

Replaying the sound log. We need a method to play the log file generated by running the game. The easiest method to do this is to run the game in a special sound replay mode. When in this mode, the game will only play sound commands from the log file and not those generated by the game itself. This is easily done by adding a flag to your game, which is set when booting up in replay mode. This flag is used to make sure we only process sound commands retrieved from the log file.

Our SoundReplay class manages loading in the file, potentially streaming it in if the file is too large to fit into memory. The SoundReplay class has to mimic the behavior of the actively playing sounds from the game. Therefore, when creating our log, we note down the address of the SoundInstance pointer used in our sound commands. We must store these addresses so that logged commands that affected a sound instance can be mapped to a new sound instance when we replay them in order to correctly to reproduce the soundscape.

Within our SoundReplay class, we should have a linked list, or an array of LoggedSoundInstances, as described in Listing 11.10. This class allows us to map

```
struct LoggedSoundInstance
{
    unsigned int m_assumed_identity;
    SoundInstance * m_instance;
};
```

Listing 11.10. Sample logged sound instance.

the sound instance identified in the log file with a new SoundInstance returned by the sound engine when running the game in replay mode. This is required, as the memory address of the SoundInstances may have changed between multiple runs of the game. Your implementation of SoundInstance, or your sound engine's equivalent, may provide a neater method of performing this mapping, such as each SoundInstance having a unique identifier.

When a sound command is executed, we check the address of the logged sound instance against the `m_assumed_identifier` within the SoundReplay's list of LoggedSoundInstances in order to find the mapping SoundInstance. We assume an unsigned `int` is the same size as a pointer in this example.

The user should be able to stop the game at any time while the replay is occurring and use other debugging tools, such as the snapshot tool, to examine the soundscape. As well as being able to stop the game while it is running, the user should be able to set a breakpoint within the log file on a particular command. This can be done by setting the top bit of the `m_command` variable of a SoundCommandEntry object. We can set this bit since we should not require the full bit range of the variable, because we will not have too many command types. The overall number of commands this system will have to support varies depending on your application. This top bit can be set either when writing out the command log or by having the sound designer pause the game while it is logging to set breakpoints. This requires a simple user interface element be presented to the designer. When activated, it sets the top bit on the last sound command executed.

Listing 11.11 shows a very simple pseudocode sample of reading and executing a sound command.

```
#define BREAKPOINT_BIT (0x80000000)

void SoundLog::replayNextCommand( void )
{
    unsigned int size_of_data;
    float game_time;
    unsigned int command;
    void * data;

    // Copy the command structure out of our log file
    // and into local variables.
    copyDataAndMoveToNextVariable( &command, sizeof(int) );
    copyDataAndMoveToNextVariable( &size_of_data,sizeof(int) );
    copyDataAndMoveToNextVariable( &game_time, sizeof(float));

    // Now point out local data pointer to the data saved
    // out by this command and move to the next command.
    setCMDDataPtrAndPrepareNextCommand(data,*size_of_data);

    if ( command &  BREAKPOINT_BIT )
    {
        launch_snapshot_tools();
    }

    // Clear the BREAKPOINT_BIT
```

```
command &= 7FFFFFFF;

sleepUntilGameTimeMatchesLoggedTime(game_time);

switch ( command )
{
    case ( CMD_SND_PLAY ):
    {
        // Process play command.
        LogDataForPlayingASound * log =
                    (LogDataForPlayingASound*)data;

        SoundEvent * event = EventDatabase::getEvent(
                                data->m_event_name );

        unsigned int old_inst = log->m_instance_id;

        SoundInstance * new_inst =
                SoundSystem::playSound( event,
                                        log->m_params,
                                        log->m_owner_id,
                                        true );

        createNewInstanceMapping( new_inst, old_inst );
        break;
    }
    case ( CMD_SND_STOP ):
    {
        // Process stop command.
        SoundInstance * inst = findMappedSoundInstance(
                                (LogDataForStop*)data );
        SoundSystem::StopSound( inst, true );
        break;
    }
    ....    // Handle other commands.
}
}
```

Listing 11.11. Pseudocode sample of reading and executing the command.

11.2.4 Streaming Monitor

An increasing problem faced by audio designers is that there are several game systems, aside from audio, which need to stream data from the same storage media. On a device such as a DVD, which has limited streaming bandwidth and long file access times, we can experience delays before an audio sample starts playing. Worse problems occur if a file cannot be serviced frequently enough by the storage device. This leads to choppy audio playback due to the audio buffer not storing a sufficient amount of data to play while the next part of the file is being read.

A solution to this problem is to develop a streaming monitor. The purpose of the streaming monitor is to help organize data so that we can optimally use our storage media. This tool will also help us to debug in-game situations where audio playback may become choppy or where sounds are taking longer to load than expected.

What the tool must provide. The tool should create a log file of all file activity performed by the game while running. This log file should then be examined, and, where applicable, it should flag files which should be positioned close to each other on the storage media used for the game's assets.

Tool design. The streaming monitor requires a FileLog class to be constructed on the game side, which will, in a similar manner to the sound log, store a log of file activity and periodically flush this out to a file. The FileLog class will, in a similar manner as our other tools, make use of static functions and data to store the log of file activity. As well as a FileLog class, we will have a FileSystem class, which is used to wrap up all file I/O functions used by the game. The game developer will use the FileSystem class to open, read, and close files, and this class will, in turn, call the appropriate FileLog function and platform file handling function.

There are two other components to the tool: a runtime visualization of which files are being loaded and a postrun analysis tool. The runtime visualization tool shows file activity as it occurs in the game. Figure 11.3 shows how this tool may look. The postrun analysis tool is a separate application that reads in the file activity log and will generate information on each file's usage, provide hints on how game files should be stored on the game's storage media, and allow the user to step through all the file activity that was performed. An example of this tool is shown in Figure 11.4.

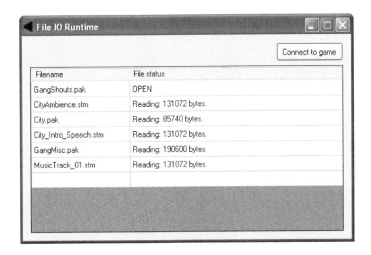

Figure 11.3. Runtime visualization of file activity.

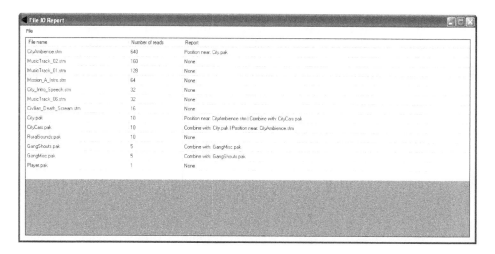

Figure 11.4. Post run report tool.

File logging component. The FileLog class must hook into all the file functions used by the game. When a file I/O function is performed or completed, it is added as a line to the activity log file. You will need to refer to your target platform's documentation on how to hook the file logging into any file I/O completion callbacks. This is so the log being generated is kept accurate. Listing 11.12 shows a sample of the FileLog class being used.

```
// Hook into the platform's open file function.

FileHandle * FileSystem::open( const char * filename )
{
    FileHandle * handle;
    handle = PlatformFileSystemOpen( filename );
    FileLog::log( File open:%s Handle ID: %x ,filename,handle);
}


// Wrap around the platform's read function. Pass in the file
// handle, destination address to read data to, amount of data
// to read in and a callback to call on the read's complection.

void FileSystem::read( FileHandle * handle, void * dst,
                       int amount, FileReadCallback * callback )
{

    // In this example - when calling the platform's read
    // function we also pass in our own callback which is called
    // first when the read has completed.

    handle = PlatformFileSystemRead( handle, dst, amount,
                                     FileReadCompletionCallback,
                                     callback );
```

```
        FileLog::log( File read [start]: Handle ID: %x amount %d ,
                      handle, amount );
   }

   // Log the handle has completed.
   void FileReadCompletionCallback( FileHandle * handle,
                                    FileReadCallback * callback )
   {
        FileLog::log( File read [end]: Handle ID:%s , handle );

        // Now call the game provided callback to let it know the
        // read operation completed.
        callback( handle );
   }
```

Listing 11.12. Sample showing file logging integrated into File IO functions.

The file activity log will need to be written out to a file. Complications arise when trying to write the log file to the same device on which you are trying to test your file's streaming performance. There are several possible solutions to this problem. For instance, you may set up a network connection to another machine that performs the file logging. This machine can be the same one that runs the runtime visualization component as a separate application. With this method, you send the log of file activity data to the connected machine to be written out to a file. Alternatively, you may be able to use a different storage device for writing the log that will not clash with the streamed file I/O you are monitoring.

Runtime visualization component. While the game is running, the runtime visualization part of the tool should be notified of the currently logged line of file activity. The logged string can be parsed to find the type of operation being performed and to update the display accordingly. The component will show the names of all files currently opened and the amount of data being read in from their last read request. The runtime visualization component can either be run in a separate window (possibly as a separate application) or display its data on the game screen if there is enough screen space. If the runtime visualization is executed as a separate application, then the game can send the current line of the activity log to the visualizer and have the component write out the log onto its host PC after it has parsed the results and updated its display.

Post run analysis component. With a file log showing all the file operations that have been performed throughout a game-play session, we have the opportunity to take a closer look at what operations were performed, and this allows us to create some optimizations on how we load our files.

The tool works by parsing the file log and generating a report. Listing 11.13 shows how we parse the file and generate a table of read conflicts (where multiple files are reading at the same time).

```
enum FILE_OPERATION
{
    FILE_OPEN=0,
    FILE_READ,
    FILE_READ_COMPLETE,
    FILE_SEEK,
    FILE_CLOSE
};

// Forward declaration.
struct ReadClash;
class FileEntry
{
public:
    FileEntry() : m_opened( false ), m_reading( false ),
                  m_num_reads( 0 ) {}

    void addEntryToClashList( FileEntry * clash_entry );

    String m_filename;
    bool m_opened;
    bool m_reading;
    int m_num_reads;
    LinkedList< ReadClash * > m_clash_list;
};

// Structure to store any read clashes we find.
struct ReadClash
{
    ReadClash() m_clashed_file_entry( null ),
                m_num_clashes( 0 ) {}

    FileEntry * m_clashed_file_entry;
    int         m_num_clashes;
};

void identifyFileReadClashes( )
{
    LinkedList< FileEntry* > file_list;

    File * log_file = open_file( FileLog.txt );

    // Iterate through our log file.
    while (!feof( log_file ))
    {
        String line;

        read_line_from_file( line, log_file );

        FILE_OPERATION file_op = parse_line( line );

        switch ( file_op )
        {
            case ( FILE_OPEN ):
            {
                FileEntry * entry;
                entry = file_list.find( getFilename( line ) );

                // Check if entry is found else create one for
                // this file!
                if ( entry == null )
                {
                    entry = new FileEntry();
```

```
                                entry->m_filename = getFilename( line );
                                m_file_list.push( entry );
                            }

                            // Mark the file as opened.
                            entry->m_opened = true;
                            break;
                        }
                    case ( FILE_READ ):
                        {
                            // First mark the entry as being read and
                            // increment the number of times this file is
                            // read.

                            FileEntry * entry =
                                file_list.find( getFilename( line ) );
                            entry->m_reading = true;
                            ++entry->m_num_reads;

                            // Now we need to see if there are any other
                            // file entries which are currently reading.
                            // If there are then we need to add this
                            // occurrence of an overlap to our list.

                            Iterator< FileEntry* > ent_it =
                                                    file_list.start();
                            while (;ent_it != file_list.end(); ++ent_it)
                            {
                                if ( (*ent_it) != entry )
                                {
                                    if ( (*ent_it)->m_reading )
                                    {
                                        recordClash( entry, (*ent_it) );
                                    }
                                }
                            }
                            break;
                        }
                    case ( FILE_SEEK ):
                        {
                            // Perform nothing at this time.
                            break;
                        }
                    case ( FILE_READ_COMPLETE ):
                        {
                            // Mark the entry as no longer being read.
                            FileEntry * entry =
                                file_list.find( getFilename( line ) );
                            entry->m_reading = false;
                            break;
                        }
                    case ( FILE_CLOSE ):
                        {
                            FileEntry * entry;
                            entry = file_list.find( getFilename( line ) );
                            entry->m_opened = false;
                            break;
                        }
                }
            }
        }


// Record this clash of reads. This is where both files are
```

```
// reading from the storage media at the same time.

void recordClash( FileEntry* entry, FileEntry * clash_entry )
{
    entry->addEntryToClashList( clash_entry );

    clash_entry->addEntryToClashList( entry );
}


// Add a new entry to this FileEntry's clash list.

void FileEntry::addEntryToClashList( FileEntry * clash_entry )
{
    Iterator<ReadClash*> it = this->m_clash_list.start();
    while(;it != this->m_clash_list.end(); ++it)
    {
        if ( (*it)->m_clashed_file_entry == clash_entry )
        {
            // Increment the number of clashes found
            // and return.
            ++(*it)->m_num_clashes;
            return;
        }
    }

    // No previous entry found so create a new one!
    ReadClash new_clash = new ReadClash();
    new_clash->m_clashed_file_entry = clash_entry;
    new_clash->m_num_clashes =  1;
    this->m_clash_list.push( new_clash );
}
```

Listing 11.13. Building up a table of read clashes.

Once the identifyFileReadClashes function from Listing 11.13 is run, we will have generated the data within our linked list variable file_list containing an entry for each file that was opened when the game was run. Each entry will store the number of times the file was read from as well as a list of all other file entries that were reading whenever this entry was being read.

The information stored in our generated linked list allows us to generate a report for the sound designer. It is from this information that we can check the number of times a file clash occurred compared to the number of times a file was read. If there are files that have a frequent number of clashes, such as a sound pack for city noises and a sound pack for street gang members, then we can combine those two files into a single sound pack. This reduces the amount of seeking performed on the storage media, as the files will be loaded in a single read. We can tell if a file is a sound pack or a streamed sound by either checking the file extension, cross-referencing the file with the sound system, or writing out the file type when the file is opened. If there are files that are mostly accessed at the same time or are streamed files, then we can mark these files out to be placed physically closer to each other on the storage media when we build up the final disk image we intend to create. Files that are repeatedly loaded into and out of memory can be potential candidates to only load once into memory and remain there permanently, although this depends on their file size. You may wish to automate this analysis with a tool that parses the file log to generate a report with recommendations.

11.3   Conclusion

The tools discussed are useful for debugging common problems within a game's audio playback. However, each of your audio systems, such as a speech manager or music controller, can always benefit from having a tool dedicated to tracking that system's state.

With any audio system, it is always worth considering the following:

- How can you clearly the sound designer show how that system is operating?

- How can a tool help track or reproduce a bug within the system? Can you support logging state changes in that system?

- What kind of interface do you present to the sound designer? The easier your tool is to use, the less time will be spent trying to use the tool and the more time spent using it.

It is always best to invest time early in a project to provide sound designers with a set of easy-to-use tools so that they can find and fix problems, as well as demonstrate any problems to you, the programmer.

12

Pragmatic XML Use in Tools

Amir Ebrahimi

12.1 Introduction

In this chapter, you are going to learn how to parse XML in a structured way, serialize/deserialize objects to XML, and see how an XML-based toolchain can assist in the development of an example game, *Minimaxima*. It is assumed that you know what XML is, its format, and its general use on the Internet.

12.2 XML Specification

Serialization is an important topic to any game developer, whether he or she be a tools, engine, or gameplay programmer. As a tools programmer, at some point, you will need to store data for GUI layouts, user preferences, localization, custom game editors, and other intermediate formats used for development purposes. As an engine programmer, you will most likely need to store different model and texture formats, asset metadata, profiling data, and the like. Gameplay programmers are not free from serialization either, with the need to store AI state data, player attributes, and recorded session data. While writing custom binary/text formats can get the job done, using XML properly can save a developer time, allow for flexibility, and ensure portability.

The first XML specification was formalized in 1998, although it began two years earlier among a working group of 11 members [XML 10a]. While coming from SGML, which had been around since the 1980s, XML was born as an answer to two problems, both of which were data related. Firstly, the rise of the Internet begged for a common interchange format that was good for just data and not data and layout (i.e., HTML). Second, programming languages were needing an alternative format to serialize objects in a human-readable form, which is commonly referred to as data binding. Fast-forward ten years to 2008, and you find that most business software had taken to XML quite well with common document formats being saved natively in XML. On the Internet, XML would be used almost everywhere under the buzzword "AJAX" in most client/server web applications. Unfortunately, even now, game development tools haven't quite made full use of XML.

12.2.1 Parsing Approaches

XML can be parsed in a variety of ways:

- as a stream in a forward-reading fashion (e.g., SAX),

- as a tree that can be traversed (e.g., DOM),

- as a transform to convert data to another format (e.g., XSLT, XQuery),

- as an object in memory (e.g., data binding, serialization).

I will summarize these various approaches; however, it is the final approach that we will spend the rest of our time focusing on in this chapter.

Stream parsing. The first approach is quite general and a common one for some developers when they first encounter XML. When reading a stream, each token is parsed sequentially, and state is maintained throughout the parsing process. A common implementation of stream parsing is the simple API for XML, or SAX. While lacking a formal specification, it is still defined as an event-driven API where events are raised for nodes, processing instructions, and comments [SAX 10]. Programming against a SAX API would involve implementing callbacks for each of the events of interest. SAX and stream approaches in general are known for using a minimal amount of memory and being cache friendly. Drawbacks include being a forward-only reader and not having access to the full document, which is needed for some uses, such as XML validation [SAX 10].

Tree traversal. The second approach is most familiar to web programmers, as this is the way you interface with HTML, XHTML, and XML from within the browser. In general, it requires loading the full document into a tree structure in memory that can be navigated. A common implementation is what is referred to as the document object model, or DOM, which was standardized by the W3C in late 1998 [DOM 10]. Programming against a DOM involves walking nodes as siblings, children, or parents and inspecting attributes and contained text. A DOM approach allows for random access and is particularly well suited for XML validation. The drawback to using a DOM approach is the memory usage that is required for really large XML documents.

Transforms. The third approach is more of a utility approach: extracting and transforming XML data. In this approach, an XML document is either queried or converted to another format, which can be XML or entirely different. A common implementation for transforming XML data is extensible stylesheet language transformations, or XSLT. XSLT is a declarative language that itself is represented in the form of an XML document [XSL 10] and can transform data from one schema to another schema. XQuery, on the other hand, is a query language used to extract and transform data, which is commonly compared to SQL, which is a query language for relational databases [XQu 10]. Capabilities of both of these languages overlap; however, the purposes and language verbosity are entirely different.

Data binding. The final approach and the one I find is underused in game tool development is XML data binding. Data binding involves mapping an XML schema to a class definition. Rather than handling the parsing process directly, a programmer provides the class with or without attributes to handle deserializing the XML data. The object can then be modified in memory and serialized back to XML. The benefits of XML data binding include the ability to serialize across programs, languages, and platforms [Dat 10]. Additionally, a programmer doesn't have to maintain parsing code to match the XML schema. Some drawbacks with data binding are that not all data can be serialized properly (e.g., links to other objects), and some data is not preserved (e.g., comments). However, as you'll see later in this chapter, the benefits outweigh the drawbacks for the majority of the use cases in tool development that can be aided by the use of data binding.

12.3 Parsing XML

Before we take a look at data binding, let's look at how we'd parse an XML document via a DOM approach. If you're a seasoned developer, then you have probably written code like this to manually parse an XML document. It's an easy first approach because you hop right in to coding up a mapping between your fields and the incoming XML document.

The task usually comes in the form of either a sample XML document being handed to you by your producer or from the server team or a designer. You're asked to hook it up to the game. It is possible you could go back to the source, which may be a database and query it directly; however, that is not always the case. You may be consuming data from another application or pulling it down from a web service.

Let us take an example of a designer who laid out some character stats in an Excel spreadsheet and exported that to XML for you to use in the game. Listing 12.1 is the document:

```xml
<?xml version="1.0"?>
<Workbook xmlns="urn:schemas-microsoft-com:office:spreadsheet"
 xmlns:o="urn:schemas-microsoft-com:office:office"
 xmlns:x="urn:schemas-microsoft-com:office:excel"
 xmlns:html="http://www.w3.org/TR/REC-html40"
 xmlns:ss="urn:schemas-microsoft-com:office:spreadsheet">
 <DocumentProperties
   xmlns="urn:schemas-microsoft-com:office:office">
  <Author>Amir Ebrahimi</Author>
```

```xml
 <LastAuthor>Amir Ebrahimi</LastAuthor>
 <Created>2010-08-12T19:11:59Z</Created>
 <Version>11.1287</Version>
</DocumentProperties>
<OfficeDocumentSettings
  xmlns="urn:schemas-microsoft-com:office:office">
 <AllowPNG/>
</OfficeDocumentSettings>
<ExcelWorkbook xmlns="urn:schemas-microsoft-com:office:excel">
 <WindowHeight>14980</WindowHeight>
 <WindowWidth>21640</WindowWidth>
 <WindowTopX>180</WindowTopX>
 <WindowTopY>-20</WindowTopY>
 <Date1904/>
 <AcceptLabelsInFormulas/>
 <ProtectStructure>False</ProtectStructure>
 <ProtectWindows>False</ProtectWindows>
</ExcelWorkbook>
<Styles>
 <Style ss:ID="Default" ss:Name="Normal">
  <Alignment ss:Vertical="Bottom"/>
  <Borders/>
  <Font ss:FontName="Verdana"/>
  <Interior/>
  <NumberFormat/>
  <Protection/>
 </Style>
</Styles>
<Worksheet ss:Name="Sheet1">
 <Table
  ss:ExpandedColumnCount="7"
  ss:ExpandedRowCount="4"
  x:FullColumns="1"
  x:FullRows="1">
  <Column ss:Width="94.0"/>
  <Column ss:Width="149.0"/>
  <Row>
   <Cell><Data ss:Type="String">Character</Data></Cell>
   <Cell><Data ss:Type="String">Description</Data></Cell>
   <Cell><Data ss:Type="String">HitPoints</Data></Cell>
   <Cell><Data ss:Type="String">MoveSpeed</Data></Cell>
   <Cell><Data ss:Type="String">AttackPower</Data></Cell>
   <Cell><Data ss:Type="String">Class</Data></Cell>
   <Cell><Data ss:Type="String">Thumbnail</Data></Cell>
  </Row>
  <Row>
   <Cell><Data ss:Type="String">MasterChieftain</Data></Cell>
   <Cell><Data ss:Type="String">One bad mamma jamma</Data></Cell>
   <Cell><Data ss:Type="Number">50.0</Data></Cell>
   <Cell><Data ss:Type="Number">10.0</Data></Cell>
   <Cell><Data ss:Type="Number">30.0</Data></Cell>
   <Cell><Data ss:Type="String">Armored</Data></Cell>
   <Cell><Data ss:Type="String">mstrchf1.png</Data></Cell>
  </Row>
  <Row>
   <Cell><Data ss:Type="String">SolidSerpent</Data></Cell>
   <Cell><Data ss:Type="String">A slick fellow</Data></Cell>
   <Cell><Data ss:Type="Number">63.0</Data></Cell>
   <Cell><Data ss:Type="Number">20.0</Data></Cell>
   <Cell><Data ss:Type="Number">15.0</Data></Cell>
   <Cell><Data ss:Type="String">Standard</Data></Cell>
   <Cell><Data ss:Type="String">solid8.png</Data></Cell>
  </Row>
  <Row>
```

```
    <Cell><Data ss:Type="String">NathanDraco</Data></Cell>
    <Cell><Data ss:Type="String">An adventurous lad</Data></Cell>
    <Cell><Data ss:Type="Number">35.0</Data></Cell>
    <Cell><Data ss:Type="Number">20.0</Data></Cell>
    <Cell><Data ss:Type="Number">18.0</Data></Cell>
    <Cell><Data ss:Type="String">Standard</Data></Cell>
    <Cell><Data ss:Type="String">draco3.png</Data></Cell>
   </Row>
  </Table>
  <WorksheetOptions xmlns="urn:schemas-microsoft-com:office:excel">
   <Print>
    <ValidPrinterInfo/>
    <PaperSizeIndex>0</PaperSizeIndex>
    <HorizontalResolution>-4</HorizontalResolution>
    <VerticalResolution>-4</VerticalResolution>
   </Print>
   <ShowPageLayoutZoom/>
   <PageLayoutZoom>100</PageLayoutZoom>
   <Selected/>
   <Panes>
    <Pane>
     <Number>3</Number>
     <ActiveRow>1</ActiveRow>
     <RangeSelection>R2C1:R4C7</RangeSelection>
    </Pane>
   </Panes>
   <ProtectObjects>False</ProtectObjects>
   <ProtectScenarios>False</ProtectScenarios>
  </WorksheetOptions>
 </Worksheet>
</Workbook>
```

Listing 12.1. An example XML document (CharacterData.xml).

Now, there is a lot of metadata in the XML that is used by Excel, which is not important to us. We need to skip all of these elements as we parse through the document. The real data begins with the first `<Row>` element, which contains the header fields. First, we'll need to create an index for these fields so that we can map the subsequent row data. The C# code for this is is shown in Listing 12.2.

```
{
  static List<CharacterData> characters = new List<CharacterData>();
  static Dictionary<string, int> fields = new Dictionary<string,
    int>();

  static void Main (string[] args)
  {
   var x = new XmlDocument();
   x.Load(args[0]);
   XmlElement root = x.DocumentElement;
   XmlNode node = null;
   if (root.Name == "Workbook")
   {
     // Navigate to the Worksheet child node
     node = root["Worksheet"];

     // Navigate to the Table child node
```

```
node = node["Table"];

// Navigate to the first row, which has the column headers
node = node["Row"];

int index = 0;
foreach (XmlNode child in node.ChildNodes)
{
  if (child.Name == "Cell")
  {
    fields[child["Data"].InnerText] = index;
```

Listing 12.2. C# code to parse the header fields (parsexml.cs).

Next, we need to iterate over each additional row and create objects for each. The following class and enumerations, shown in Listing 12.3, will be used to store our data during parsing.

```
enum CharacterClass
{
  Standard,
  Armored
}

class CharacterData
{
  public string character;
  public string description;
  public float hitPoints;
  public float moveSpeed;
  public float attackPower;
  public CharacterClass characterClass;
  public string thumbnail;

  public override string ToString ()
  {
    StringBuilder sb = new StringBuilder();
    sb.AppendFormat("{0} ({1})\n", character,
      characterClass.ToString());
    sb.Append('\t');
    sb.AppendLine(description);
    sb.AppendFormat("\thp: {0:0}\tms: {1:0}\tap: {2:0}\n", hitPoints,
      moveSpeed, attackPower);
    sb.AppendFormat("\tthumbnail: {0}\n", thumbnail);

    return sb.ToString();
```

Listing 12.3. C# class and enumeration (parsexml.cs).

Now, let us continue in our `Main()` method to parse the remaining rows and create objects for each (see Listing 12.4).

```
      }
    }

    // Grab the first row of data
    node = node.NextSibling;
    while (node != null)
    {
      CharacterData data = new CharacterData();
      data.character = node.ChildNodes[fields["Character"]]
        .InnerText;
      data.description = node.ChildNodes[fields["Description"]]
        .InnerText;
      data.hitPoints = float.Parse(node.ChildNodes[fields
        ["HitPoints"]].InnerText);
      data.moveSpeed = float.Parse(node.ChildNodes[fields
        ["MoveSpeed"]].InnerText);
      data.attackPower = float.Parse(node.ChildNodes[fields
        ["AttackPower"]].InnerText);
      data.characterClass = (CharacterClass)Enum.Parse(typeof
        (CharacterClass), node.ChildNodes[fields["Class"]]
        .InnerText);
      data.thumbnail = node.ChildNodes[fields["Thumbnail"]]
        .InnerText;
      characters.Add(data);

      node = node.NextSibling;
    }
  }

  // Our xml is fully parsed now, so we can do whatever we need
  // with the data

  foreach (CharacterData data in characters)
    Console.WriteLine(data);
  }
}
```

Listing 12.4. C# code to parse the remaining rows (parsexml.cs).

If we're loading many of these objects and runtime performance is an issue, then we can serialize these objects to disk in a binary format to avoid parsing the XML document at runtime. If performance isn't an issue, then we can use the XML documents as-is. It is also possible that for developer builds we can just use the XML directly to allow quick reloading of objects and write out final formats only on release builds.

With the code we have just written, we have now made part of the game data-driven, allowing a designer to tweak values in the game from a spreadsheet. While this was not too difficult, it begs the question: is there an easier way?

12.4   Enter Stage: XML Serialization

12.4.1   An Anecdote

I stumbled across XML serialization in an odd way. As a consultant for a game project, initially I was looking into a performance issue when instantiating existing object hierarchies for a GUI system built on top of Unity. A prototype for a GUI layout was kept around from which new layout instances were launched (e.g., a layout for a specific inventory item). Much of the data were objects in arrays, so I had to perform a deep copy of the actual data. This was expensive for a variety of reasons, one of which was resizing of new arrays. So, I looked at alternative ways of instantiation with serialization methods. I tried both custom binary serializers and decided to also try XML serialization for comparison. In the end, I decided to go with duplication methods that used custom constructors for initializing array sizes and .NET array methods for the actual copy. Even though I discovered XML serialization for the first time while investigating this problem, it still did not occur to me that I should use this for parsing other XML data, much less as a storage format.

The GUI authoring tool that produced the data for the game was a legacy tool that ran under Windows, which natively stored its data in XML. Looking at the source for the authoring tool, the XML for each layout was being written out and parsed in a manual way using a DOM-based approach. Most of the other developers on the team had moved over to using Macs for iPhone development, so either they ran this authoring tool in a virtual machine or kept a separate Windows PC around which they used to export the layouts. Additionally, an exported version of a layout, also in XML, was parsed in Unity to produce GUI objects that were needed for rendering. Unfortunately, this process created an awkward workflow for GUI layouts and caused delay in getting layouts into Unity, which required an export each time from the authoring tool.

The first improvement I made was to allow the XML to be saved directly to the Unity project folder and have that picked up automatically instead of requiring a manual import from within Unity. Unfortunately, this still required an export from the authoring tool. However, the savings of having Unity automatically import this XML with an `AssetPostprocessor` instead of requiring the developer to import each time in Unity were significant. This change smoothed the workflow out a bit; however, I knew that the whole process could be done better.

Code already existed in Unity for parsing an exported version of XML from the layout-authoring tool. However, the source XML document that the authoring tool used could not be read in directly. I adapted this code, which was DOM-based, to parse the source XML document directly instead of the export. Unfortunately, even at this point, I didn't think to switch over to XML serialization for parsing the source format. From this source layout data, I began constructing a layout-authoring tool directly in Unity. My goal became to provide an in-Unity layout editor that was at parity only with the features that were currently being used in the legacy-authoring tool. By keeping parity with a minimal set of features, I could provide a smooth transition to the new tool for the development team.

It was not until I needed to save out data from the new authoring tool that I began to wrestle with formats. Unity, by default, will serialize objects for you with a few API calls. However, Unity stores your objects in a binary format, which doesn't allow for easy merging. The legacy-authoring tool used XML for this reason, since multiple people can work on a single layout and merge changes after. At this point, I remembered that the .NET XML serializer allowed for an easy way to write objects to disk. This allowed me to have the best of both worlds: an XML format for storing the layouts during authoring and a binary version that could be saved elsewhere for runtime. Both of these serialization methods were supported from the same class with custom attributes for each serializer.

12.4.2   .NET XML Serialization

Let's take our XML example from before and have it automatically parsed by the XML serialization class from .NET. First, we need to whip our XML document into shape by converting Listing 12.1 into something digestible by .NET, shown in Listing 12.5.

```xml
<?xml version="1.0" encoding="utf-8"?>
<Characters xmlns:usos="urn:schemas-microsoft-com:office:spreadsheet">
  <CharacterData>
    <Character>MasterChieftain</Character>
    <Description>One bad mamma jamma</Description>
    <HitPoints>50.0</HitPoints>
    <MoveSpeed>10.0</MoveSpeed>
    <AttackPower>30.0</AttackPower>
    <Class>Armored</Class>
    <Thumbnail>mstrchf1.png</Thumbnail>
  </CharacterData>
  <CharacterData>
    <Character>SolidSerpent</Character>
    <Description>A slick fellow</Description>
    <HitPoints>63.0</HitPoints>
    <MoveSpeed>20.0</MoveSpeed>
    <AttackPower>15.0</AttackPower>
    <Class>Standard</Class>
    <Thumbnail>solid8.png</Thumbnail>
  </CharacterData>
  <CharacterData>
    <Character>NathanDraco</Character>
    <Description>An adventurous lad</Description>
    <HitPoints>35.0</HitPoints>
    <MoveSpeed>20.0</MoveSpeed>
    <AttackPower>18.0</AttackPower>
    <Class>Standard</Class>
    <Thumbnail>draco3.png</Thumbnail>
  </CharacterData>
</Characters>
```

Listing 12.5. Simpler XML document (xformed.xml).

We can use XSLT to perform this conversion. You can use a web browser to convert the XML using an XSL document, however, why not just write a simple command line utility (see Listing 12.6)?

```
using System.Xml.Xsl;

class xslt
{
  static void Main (string[] args)
  {
    var x = new XslCompiledTransform ();
    x.Load(args[0]);
    x.Transform(args[1], args[2]);
  }
}
```

Listing 12.6. C# utility to transform XML documents (xslt.cs).

The arguments to this command line utility are the XSL document, the original XML document, and where the converted document should be saved; for example: `xslt.exe transform.xsl CharacterData.xml xformed.xml`.

The XSL document that converts Listing 12.1 to Listing 12.5 is shown in Listing 12.7.

```
<xsl:stylesheet xmlns:usos="urn:schemas-microsoft-com:office
       :spreadsheet"
    version="1.0"
      xmlns:xsl="http://www.w3.org/1999/XSL/Transform"
      xsl:version="1.0">
  <xsl:output indent="yes" />
  <xsl:template match="/">
    <Characters>
    <xsl:for-each select="/usos:Workbook/usos:Worksheet
      /usos:Table/usos:Row">
      <xsl:if test="position()!=1">
        <CharacterData>
        <xsl:for-each select="usos:Cell">
          <xsl:variable name="cellPos" select=
          "position()" />
          <xsl:element name="{../../usos:Row[1]
          /usos:Cell[$cellPos]/usos:Data}">
          <xsl:value-of select="usos:Data" />
          </xsl:element>
        </xsl:for-each>
        </CharacterData>
      </xsl:if>
    </xsl:for-each>
    </Characters>
  </xsl:template>
</xsl:stylesheet>
```

Listing 12.7. XSL transform document (transform.xsl).

Now that we have a simpler XML document, let's mark up our original `CharacterData` class from Listing 12.3 using the XML serializer attributes. The full list of attributes can be found in a document entitled "Controlling XML Serialization Using Attributes" on Microsoft's *MSDN* site. For our purposes, we only need two:

1. `[XmlElement]`: controls the mapping between a field and the element name in the document;

2. `[XmlRoot]`: used to control mapping between a class and the root element name of the document.

Listing 12.8 shows our `CharacterData` class from Listing 12.3 with attributes added.

```
public enum CharacterClass
{
  Standard,
  Armored
}

public class CharacterData
{
  [XmlElement("Character")]
  public string character;
  [XmlElement("Description")]
  public string description;
  [XmlElement("HitPoints")]
  public float hitPoints;
  [XmlElement("MoveSpeed")]
  public float moveSpeed;
  [XmlElement("AttackPower")]
  public float attackPower;
  [XmlElement("Class")]
  public CharacterClass characterClass;
  [XmlElement("Thumbnail")]
  public string thumbnail;

  public override string ToString ()
  {
    StringBuilder sb = new StringBuilder();
    sb.AppendFormat("{0} ({1})\n", character,
      characterClass.ToString());
    sb.Append('\t');
    sb.AppendLine(description);
    sb.AppendFormat("\thp: {0:0}\tms: {1:0}\tap: {2:0}\n",
      hitPoints, moveSpeed, attackPower);
    sb.AppendFormat("\tthumbnail: {0}\n", thumbnail);

    return sb.ToString();
```

Listing 12.8. System.Xml.Serialization attribute mark-up (autoxml.cs).

Finally, let's create the `XmlSerializer` object to deserialize the XML into usable objects (see Listing 12.9).

```
}

[XmlRoot("Characters")]
public class CharacterList
{
  [XmlElement("CharacterData")]
  public CharacterData[] list;

  static public CharacterList FromXml(Stream stream)
  {
    XmlSerializer serializer = new XmlSerializer(typeof
      (CharacterList));
    return serializer.Deserialize(stream) as CharacterList;
  }
}

class autoxml
{
  static CharacterList characters;

  static void Main (string[] args)
  {
    Stream reader = new FileStream(args[0], FileMode.Open);
    characters = CharacterList.FromXml(reader);

    // Our xml is fully parsed now, so we can do whatever we need
    // with the data
    foreach (CharacterData data in characters.list)
      Console.WriteLine(data);
  }
}
```

Listing 12.9. Using XmlSerializer.Deserialize() to parse (autoxml.cs).

Now, wasn't that much easier than a DOM-based approach? We can do better. Why have an extra step for XSLT conversion? Let's just embed it (see Listing 12.10)!

```
class autoxml2
{
  // The embedded XSL document
  static string xslt = @"
  <xsl:stylesheet xmlns:usos=""urn:schemas-microsoft-com:office
      :spreadsheet""
      version=""1.0""
          xmlns:xsl=""http://www.w3.org/1999/XSL/Transform""
          xsl:version=""1.0"">
    <xsl:output indent=""yes"" />
    <xsl:template match=""/"">
      <Characters>
      <xsl:for-each select=""/usos:Workbook/usos:Worksheet/usos:
        Table/usos:Row"">
```

```
                <xsl:if test=""position()!=1"">
                <CharacterData>
                  <xsl:for-each select=""usos:Cell"">
                    <xsl:variable name=""cellPos"" select=""position()"" />
                    <xsl:element name=""{../../usos:Row[1]/usos:
                        Cell[$cellPos]/usos:Data}"">
                    <xsl:value-of select=""usos:Data"" />
                    </xsl:element>
                  </xsl:for-each>
                </CharacterData>
                </xsl:if>
            </xsl:for-each>
            </Characters>
        </xsl:template>
    </xsl:stylesheet>
    ";
    static CharacterList characters;

    static void Main (string[] args)
    {
      // Create a memory stream for holding the transformed XML
      Stream xformedStream = new MemoryStream();

      // Transform the original XML document in memory
      var xform = new XslCompiledTransform();
      xform.Load(XmlReader.Create(new StringReader(xslt)));
      xform.Transform(args[0], null, xformedStream);

      // Reset stream position to beginning, so it can be read
      xformedStream.Position = 0;
      characters = CharacterList.FromXml(xformedStream);

      // Our xml is fully parsed now, so we can do whatever we
      // need with the data
      foreach (CharacterData data in characters.list)
        Console.WriteLine(data);
    }
}
```

Listing 12.10. Embedding the XSLT step (autoxml2.cs).

Now, we can just execute the utility directly on the XML that Excel spits out: autoxml2.exe CharacterData.xml.

There is a tool worth mentioning that is included with .NET: xsd.exe, which can automatically generate C# classes from XML schemas. Additionally, you can generate the initial XML schema definition (XSD) from the XML document itself. When we use xsd.exe on our transformed document from Listing 12.5 we get Listing 12.11.

```
<?xml version="1.0" standalone="yes"?>
<xs:schema id="Characters" xmlns="" xmlns:xs="http://www.w3.org/2001
    /XMLSchema" xmlns:msdata="urn:schemas-microsoft-com:xml-msdata">
  <xs:element name="Characters" msdata:IsDataSet="true"
        msdata:Locale="en-US">
    <xs:complexType>
      <xs:choice minOccurs="0" maxOccurs="unbounded">
```

```
              <xs:element name="CharacterData">
                <xs:complexType>
                  <xs:sequence>
                    <xs:element name="Character" type="xs:string"
                      minOccurs="0" />
                    <xs:element name="Description" type="xs:string"
                      minOccurs="0" />
                    <xs:element name="HitPoints" type="xs:string"
                     minOccurs="0" />
                    <xs:element name="MoveSpeed" type="xs:string"
                      minOccurs="0" />
                    <xs:element name="AttackPower" type="xs:string"
                      minOccurs="0" />
                    <xs:element name="Class" type="xs:string"
                     minOccurs="0" />
                    <xs:element name="Thumbnail" type="xs:string"
                      minOccurs="0" />
                  </xs:sequence>
                </xs:complexType>
              </xs:element>
            </xs:choice>
        </xs:complexType>
      </xs:element>
</xs:schema>
```

Listing 12.11. XSD for xformed.xml (xformed.xsd).

If we were to use this XSD directly to generate the class definition, then all of
the field types would be of type string due to the xs:string type in the XSD.
Let's modify the XSD and provide the correct types (see Listing 12.12).

```
<?xml version="1.0" standalone="yes"?>
<xs:schema id="Characters" xmlns="" xmlns:xs="http://www.w3.org
          /2001/XMLSchema"
  xmlns:msdata="urn:schemas-microsoft-com:xml-msdata">
  <xs:element name="Characters" msdata:IsDataSet="true"
             msdata:Locale="en-US">
    <xs:complexType>
      <xs:choice minOccurs="0" maxOccurs="unbounded">
        <xs:element name="CharacterData">
          <xs:complexType>
            <xs:sequence>
              <xs:element name="Character" type="xs:string"
                    minOccurs="0" />
              <xs:element name="Description" type="xs:string"
                    minOccurs="0" />
              <xs:element name="HitPoints" type="xs:float"
                    minOccurs="1" />
              <xs:element name="MoveSpeed" type="xs:float"
                    minOccurs="1" />
              <xs:element name="AttackPower" type="xs:float"
                    minOccurs="1" />
              <xs:element name="Class" minOccurs="1">
                <xs:simpleType>
                  <xs:restriction base="xs:string">
                     <xs:enumeration value="Standard" />
                     <xs:enumeration value="Armored" />
```

```
                  </xs:restriction>
                </xs:simpleType>
              </xs:element>
              <xs:element name="Thumbnail" type="xs:string"
                  minOccurs="0" />
          </xs:sequence>
        </xs:complexType>
      </xs:element>
    </xs:choice>
  </xs:complexType>
</xs:element>
</xs:schema>
```

Listing 12.12. Modified XSD with correct types (xformedtyped.xsd).

You'll notice that that the `minOccurs` attribute is set to 1 for the `xs:float` fields. It's necessary to set the `minOccurs` attribute so that additional fields aren't generated in the class definition for keeping track of whether the field was specified in the XML document. Also, the possible enumeration values for the `Class` element have to be specified here in order to convert the XML data to an actual enumeration value. With our XSD complete, we can now autogenerate the class using `xsd.exe xformedtyped.xsd /c`, shown in Lisitng 12.13.

```
// ---------------------------------------------------------
// <autogenerated>
//     This code was generated by a tool.
//     Mono Runtime Version: 1.1.4322.2032
//
//     Changes to this file may cause incorrect behavior and
//     will be lost if the code is regenerated.
// </autogenerated>
// ---------------------------------------------------------

//
//This source code was auto-generated by MonoXSD
//
namespace Schemas {

    /// <remarks/>
    [System.Xml.Serialization.XmlRootAttribute(Namespace="",
      IsNullable=false)]
    public class Characters {

        /// <remarks/>
        [System.Xml.Serialization.XmlElementAttribute
          ("CharacterData")]
        public CharactersCharacterData[] CharacterData;
    }

    /// <remarks/>
    public class CharactersCharacterData {

        /// <remarks/>
```

```
        public string Character;

        /// <remarks/>
        public string Description;

        /// <remarks/>
        public System.Single HitPoints;

        /// <remarks/>
        public System.Single MoveSpeed;

        /// <remarks/>
        public System.Single AttackPower;

        /// <remarks/>
        public CharactersCharacterDataClass Class;

        /// <remarks/>
        public string Thumbnail;
    }

    /// <remarks/>
    public enum CharactersCharacterDataClass {

        /// <remarks/>
        Standard,

        /// <remarks/>
        Armored,
    }
}
```

Listing 12.13. Auto-generated class from XSD (xformedtyped.cs).

You might be asking why we'd spend time modifying an XSD when we could just add attributes to a class we've defined from scratch. Writing the class from scratch and adding attributes to map field names certainly provides more flexibility to us, not to mention better-named enumerations and classes. However, generating the class specification from an XSD takes care of one important use case: portability. In the next section we'll make use of this XSD to automatically handle parsing our XML data in another language: C++.

12.4.3 XML Data Binding in Other Languages

Most popular programming languages have XML data binding libraries available. However, it should be mentioned that not all data binding approaches are equal. Some XML data binding formats don't conform to XML schema [XML 10b], formalized by the W3C in 2001, which is the one that .NET uses. For example, the Boost C++ Library has its own XML serialization format. Luckily, there is a good resource for finding libraries for various programming languages. Ronald Bourret has been keeping a list current since 2001 on his personal domain [Bourret 10]. A few are worth mentioning here to get you started:

- C++: XSD library developed by Code Synthesis [CC 10];

- Java: XStream library developed by Joe Walnes [Walnes 08];

- Python: xmlobjects library developed by Mikeal Rogers [Rogers 08];

- Ruby: XMLObject library developed by Jordi Bunster [Bunster 09].

XML data binding in C++. Because C++ is a common language used in conjunction with C#/.NET, let us take a look at how we'd make use of our existing XSD from Listing 12.12 to automatically generate C++ classes. In my evaluation of C++ data binding libraries, the open-source XSD library from Code Synthesis [CC 10] seemed the most robust. In order to not confuse the XSD library from XML schema document (XSD), I'll refer to the library as *XSDlib*. XSDlib comes with example programs, one of which is called "generated." Once you've got the library and it's dependencies installed, simply rename the original library.xml and library.xsd files, copy the XML and XSD from Listings 12.5 and 12.13, and, respectively, rename the new files. On first execution, you'll most likely encounter an error message: `error: no declaration found for element 'Characters'`. This error is covered in the XSDlib documentation and occurs because the validating parser cannot find a schema for the XML document. There are a few ways to fix this issue:

- passing the flag `dont_validate` to the `parse` function in your driver module;

- specifying the `noNamespaceSchemaLocation` in the original XML.

Since the generated example project that we are using generates all of the C++ code, including a sample driver to print out the parsed results, we'll use the second option. We can simply modify our original XSL document from Listing 12.7 to include a `noNameSpaceSchemaLocation` attribute:

```
<xsl:stylesheet xmlns:usos=
        "urn:schemas-microsoft-com:office:spreadsheet"
     version="1.0"
      xmlns:xsl="http://www.w3.org/1999/XSL/Transform"
      xsl:version="1.0">
  <xsl:output indent="yes" />
  <xsl:template match="/">
    <Characters xmlns:xsi=
        "http://www.w3.org/2001/XMLSchema-instance"
 xsi:noNamespaceSchemaLocation="library.xsd">
    <xsl:for-each select=
      "/usos:Workbook/usos:Worksheet/usos:Table/usos:Row">
      <xsl:if test="position()!=1">
        <CharacterData>
        <xsl:for-each select="usos:Cell">
          <xsl:variable name="cellPos" select="position()" />
          <xsl:element name=
```

```
            "{../../usos:Row[1]/usos:Cell[$cellPos]/usos:Data}">
              <xsl:value-of select="usos:Data" />
              </xsl:element>
          </xsl:for-each>
              </CharacterData>
        </xsl:if>
      </xsl:for-each>
      </Characters>
    </xsl:template>
</xsl:stylesheet>
```

Listing 12.14. Updated XSL transform document (library.xsl).

With this new XSL document, we simply regenerate the library.xml document using `xslt.exe library.xsl CharacterData.xml library.xml`. Next, run `library-driver library.xml` from the generated example directory and voila! You'll notice, too, that if you run the newly generated XML through our existing C# autoxml application that it still deserializes properly. We now have serialized object portability between C# and C++!

12.4.4 XML Data Binding Limitations

Most documentation available online for XML data binding will include the limitations to serializing objects via XML. Even in *MSDN*'s introduction to XML serialization there is a section entitled "XML Serialization Considerations." For completeness, I'll include some of the common limitations:

- Private properties and fields cannot be serialized.

- Methods cannot be serialized.

- Serialized classes must have a default constructor.

- Comments and processing instructions are not preserved.

- Circular references are not supported.

- Generic Dictionary and List fields are not supported.

For some of these limitations, such as generics support, there are generally good workarounds that can be had with a simple search query at your favorite search engine. Usually, when you encounter one of these limitations, you can rework your classes to accommodate.

12.5   Minimaxima: A Case Study

12.5.1   Background

When I began writing this chapter, I set a goal to provide a real case of XML data binding in a game pipeline. There are quite a few applications that either use XML natively or export to XML. We've already seen how Excel supports exporting to XML. I looked at other products that might be useful in a game pipeline, such as iMovie or Final Cut Pro. I also looked at data in abundance on the web, such as Google's Keyhole Markup Language (KML) which is used for expressing geographic data. In the end, I decided on a common application known to many: Apple's iTunes. The iTunes Library metadata is stored in an XML format. Unfortunately, this format isn't readily usable by .NET serialization. Listing 12.15 shows a snippet of what it looks like.

```
<?xml version="1.0" encoding="UTF-8"?>
<!DOCTYPE plist PUBLIC "-//Apple Computer//DTD PLIST 1.0//EN"
 "http://www.apple.com/DTDs/PropertyList-1.0.dtd">
<plist version="1.0">
<dict>
    <key>Major Version</key><integer>1</integer>
    <key>Minor Version</key><integer>1</integer>
    <key>Application Version</key><string>10.0.1</string>
    <key>Features</key><integer>5</integer>
    <key>Show Content Ratings</key><true/>
    <key>Music Folder</key>
        <string>file://localhost/Users/amir/Music
            /iTunes/iTunes%20Media/</string>
    <key>Library Persistent ID</key><string>42DAF318AC521979</string>
    <key>Tracks</key>
    <dict>
        <key>79</key>
        <dict>
            <key>Track ID</key><integer>79</integer>
            <key>Name</key><string>Air Swell Intro</string>
            <key>Artist</key><string>Chiddy Bang</string>
            <key>Album Artist</key><string>Chiddy Bang</string>
            <key>Composer</key><string>Xaphoon Jones</string>
            <key>Album</key><string>Air Swell</string>
            <key>Genre</key><string>Hip Hop</string>
```

Listing 12.15. iTunes Library XML document (iTunesLibrary.xml).

As you can see, the dict, key, and string elements are not ready to be consumed by .NET XML serialization directly. However, this can be remedied with a handy XSL document [Staken 03] (see Listing 12.16).

```
<xsl:stylesheet version="1.0"
        xmlns:xsl="http://www.w3.org/1999/XSL/Transform"
        xsl:version="1.0">
```

```
    <xsl:output indent="yes" />
    <xsl:template match="/">
        <songlist>
            <xsl:apply-templates select="plist/dict/dict/dict"/>
        </songlist>
    </xsl:template>

    <xsl:template match="dict">
        <song>
            <xsl:apply-templates select="key"/>
        </song>
    </xsl:template>

    <xsl:template match="key">
        <xsl:element name="{translate(text(), ' ', '_')}">
            <xsl:value-of select="following-sibling::node()[1]"/>
        </xsl:element>
    </xsl:template>
</xsl:stylesheet>
```

Listing 12.16. iTunes XSLT document (iTunesTransform.xsl).

You will get something more digestible using `xslt.exe`, `iTunesTransform.xsl`, `iTunesLibrary.xml`, and `iTunesXformed.xml` (see Listing 12.17).

```
    <?xml version="1.0" encoding="utf-8"?>
<songlist>
  <song>
    <Track_ID>79</Track_ID>
    <Name>Air Swell Intro</Name>
    <Artist>Chiddy Bang</Artist>
    <Album_Artist>Chiddy Bang</Album_Artist>
    <Composer>Xaphoon Jones</Composer>
    <Album>Air Swell</Album>
    <Genre>Hip Hop</Genre>
    <Kind>MPEG audio file</Kind>
    <Size>1681866</Size>
    <Total_Time>34977</Total_Time>
    <Disc_Number>1</Disc_Number>
    <Disc_Count>1</Disc_Count>
    <Track_Number>1</Track_Number>
    <Track_Count>6</Track_Count>
    <Year>2010</Year>
    <BPM>110</BPM>
    <Date_Modified>2010-04-06T20:08:06Z</Date_Modified>
    <Date_Added>2010-08-01T23:50:26Z</Date_Added>
    <Bit_Rate>320</Bit_Rate>
    <Sample_Rate>44100</Sample_Rate>
    <Part_Of_Gapless_Album>
    </Part_Of_Gapless_Album>
```

Listing 12.17. Transformed iTunes Library XML document (iTunesXformed.xml).

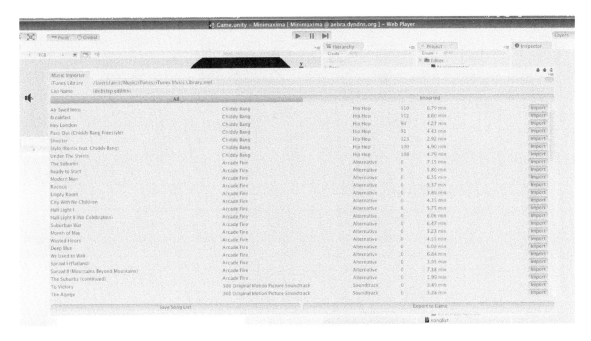

Figure 12.1. Screenshot of the custom *Minimaxima* Editor.

12.5.2   An XML-Based Toolchain

After prototyping a few different audio-based game mechanics, I finally landed on a pong-ish, arcade-style boss fight that was driven by the audio of a song (see Color Plate VIII for a screenshot of *Minimaxima*. I decided to name it *Minimaxima* since I would be scrubbing the waveform data, extracting FFT frequency data, and performing beat detection. Depending on the type of song that was used, it was necessary to tweak gameplay values (e.g., watching a different frequency subband for beats). In the end, I wrote a custom editor that could read the iTunes Library metadata and allow for importing of specific songs into the game and tweaking gameplay values. With XML data binding, I was able to use the same classes for serializing the song list to be used in the game, keeping custom gameplay values, and for writing out a binary runtime version of the data. For the sake of brevity, I'll spare you the 1000+ lines of code and leave it to you to take a look at the project files shown in Figure 12.1.

12.6   Conclusion

XML can be used in a flexible way for game development tools. With XSLT, you can transform XML data from one format into an easier-to-parse format (e.g., something that .NET can use). When schema definitions are available, XSD can produce class templates in C# and other languages. Combined with XML data binding, you can skip having to write quite a bit of code required to parse individual XML data and use first-class objects directly. While there are limitations to XML data binding, which have been mentioned, in practice there are far more appropriate uses despite the limitations.

I'd like to thank Thomas Grové for his help in designing *Minimaxima* with me, Tyler Bryant for his play-testing feedback on *Minimaxima* and Jeffrey Aydelotte for peer review.

Bibliography

[Bourret 10] Ronald Bourret. "XML Data Binding Resources." Available online (http://www.rpbourret.com/xml/XMLDataBinding.htm), 2010 [cited October 2, 2010].

[Bunster 09] Jordi Bunster. "XMLObject." Available online (http://xml-object.rubyforge.org/), 2009 [cited October 2, 2010].

[CC 10] Code Synthesis Tools CC. "XSD: XML Data Binding for C++." Available online (http://codesynthesis.com/products/xsd/), 2010 [cited October 2, 2010].

[Dat 10] "Wikipedia: XML Data Binding." Available online (http://en.wikipedia.org/wiki/XML), 2010 [cited August 12, 2010].

[DOM 10] "Wikipedia: Document Object Model." Available online (http://en.wikipedia.org/wiki/Document_Object_Model), 2010 [cited August 11, 2010].

[Rogers 08] Mikeal Rogers. "xmlobjects." Available online (http://code.google.com/p/xmlobjects/), 2008 [cited October 2, 2010].

[SAX 10] "Wikipedia: Simple API for XML." Available online (http://en.wikipedia.org/wiki/Simple_API_for_XML), 2010 [cited August 11, 2010].

[Staken 03] Kimbro Staken. "Cleaning up iTunes plist XML." Available online (http://www.xmldatabases.org/WK/blog/1086?t=item), 2003 [cited October 3, 2010].

[Walnes 08] Joe Walnes. "XStream." Available online (http://xstream.codehaus.org/), 2008 [cited October 2, 2010].

[XML 10a] "Wikipedia: XML." Available online (http://en.wikipedia.org/wiki/XML_data_binding), 2010 [cited August 11, 2010].

[XML 10b] "Wikipedia: XML Schema (W3C)." Available online (http://en.wikipedia.org/wiki/XML_Schema_(W3C)), 2010 [cited October 2, 2010].

[XQu 10] "Wikipedia: XQuery." Available online (http://en.wikipedia.org/wiki/ XQuery), 2010 [cited August 11, 2010].

[XSL 10] "Wikipedia: XSLT." Available online (http://en.wikipedia.org/wiki/ XSLT), 2010 [cited August 11, 2010].

13

Low Coupling Command System

Gustavo A. Carrazoni

13.1   Introduction

Applications developed for the daily work of artists and game designers have a rich user interface and usability that is designed to increase the performance of the development team. In this chapter, we propose a versatile and flexible command system to manage the user input that is suitable for monolithic applications and open and extensible systems.

13.2   The Most Basic Command

An example generally used to justify the necessity of a command system is the user interface as it consists of several elements, such as buttons and menus, with logic that does not really need to know the details of the operations it executes; it just needs to know which operation to execute.

Thus, the operation details are bundled into objects called *commands* (each command is a class that performs a specific operation), and our user interface is

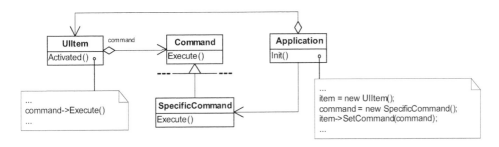

Figure 13.1. Command pattern.

given the ability to work with these commands. The result is basically the command pattern [Gamma et al. 95] which can be modeled as shown in Figure 13.1.

According to this model, the `Application` class is responsible for creating the elements and commands of the user interface, and for linking each item of the interface with its corresponding command. In the model proposed here, we go a step further in the separation of user interface and application logic by eliminating the necessity of an entity that links every element of the interface with its corresponding command.

13.3 Low Coupling

For a low-coupling system, we will eliminate the necessity of the command consumer to know the specific types of commands in order to be able to create them. Each command will be identified by its name, and with the help of a factory, we will create an instance of the command from anywhere in the system. Coming back to the example of the user interface, a button can create and run an associated command and only needs to know its name to do so. This can be modeled as in Figure 13.2.

In this diagram, we appreciate that there is no link to the specific type of commands. The command consumer (in this case `UIItem`) only knows the `Command` interface and the `factory` used to create the instances. Moreover, the `Application`

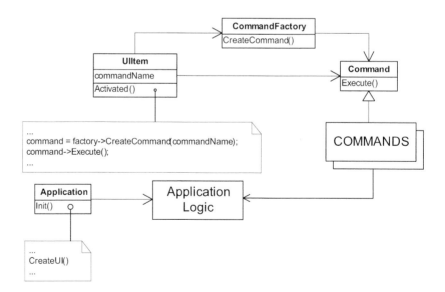

Figure 13.2. Low-coupling command system.

class does not need to know specific user interface components, because these are able to create command instances on their own. The `Application Logic` box represents the data that commands act on and the algorithms used to modify that data.

13.3.1 Command Factory

The key element of the model proposed here is the `CommandFactory` that must be able to create a command instance based on the command's name. It is much more convenient for developers to not have to touch the factory's code every time a new command is added. The extent to which this is possible depends very much on the programming language used for implementation.

With the .NET framework and other modern languages, we can create an instance based on a class name, so if we match the command name with the name of the class that contains the command, the implementation of the factory is easy.

In the case of C++, we have to decide whether to implement a dictionary that translates a command name into a specific factory function or to give commands the ability to autoregister in the static initialization of the application.

From the point of view of design the command factory is a singleton, and therefore, there can only be one instance in the system.

13.3.2 Commands with Parameters

Let's look at a command that changes the color of a selected object in our model editor. This command needs to know both the object on which it acts and the new color to apply. In order to achieve this, we could establish a mechanism for the command to know the elements that are necessary for it to perform the operation correctly. However, this might imply that the command logic accesses the user interface, which is not desirable and should be avoided if possible. Thus, we will improve the commands with a generic parameter-passing mechanism instead. This mechanism agrees with the low-coupling philosophy we have been working with so far.

We will identify the parameters by their name and add the `SetParam` method to the class `Command` (see Figure 13.3).

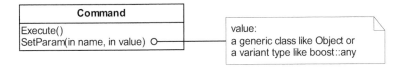

Figure 13.3. Command extended with a parameter setting mechanism.

The user interface code that executes this command is the following:

```
Command setColorCmd;
setColorCmd = factory.CreateCommand("SetColor");
setColorCmd.SetParam("OBJ_ID",object->GetId());
setColorCmd.SetParam("COLOR",COLOR_RED);
setColorCmd.Execute();
```

For the implementation, we can take advantage of the facilities of .NET languages like C# that are able to assign values to object properties knowing only their names. This way, we will not have to implement the `SetParam` method specifically for every single command in our system.

13.3.3 Practical Applications

Advantages for the development of the user interface. Development and maintenance of the user interface becomes more flexible as it does not depend on the application logic. Many user interface development kits offer the possibility to extend the interface components with user properties that can be accessed in the form editor. If we use one of these properties to save the name of the command, we can configure an operation that is performed by a button, for example, without having to touch a line of code.

It is also a lot easier to create different views of the same application; thus, the user interfaces for artists and designers can be different.

Use in extensible systems. It is increasingly common to develop open systems that can be extended with plugins or other mechanisms. Using a low-coupling command system in this scenario has two beneficial effects:

1. Independent development between the host applications and the plugins is easier because dependencies in source code are reduced, especially since the need to know specific command types has been removed.

2. Any component of the system, either the host application or a plugin, can invoke commands of any other component by knowing the name of the command to be run. Host-plugin interaction is the typical case of interaction in this kind of architecture, but with this command system there is no restriction for a plugin to run an operation in another (see Figure 13.4).

To make this possible, the command factory must be able to create commands available in any component of the system. Again, the use of modern frameworks like .NET makes our work easy because we can create instances of classes resident in external modules with the class name and the assembly name that contains it. In other cases, it may be necessary that each plugin implement and expose its own

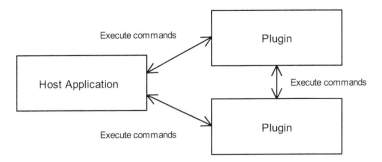

Figure 13.4. Commands can be invoked between system components without restriction.

command factory: access to these factories must be centralized in a global factory based in the host application.

Plugins should be developed with the possibility to execute commands from other components or to load other components. Consider the case in which our game editor has a model editor and a material editor implemented each as separate plugins. The model editor may desire to use the functionality of the material editor to change the material of a particular model. In such a case, however, the model editor may need to explicitly open the material editor before issuing any commands. The follow code shows how this is done:

```
Command openMatEditor;
openMatEditor =
  factory.CreateCommand("OpenMaterialEditor");

//if material editor is not installed the factory
//will fail to create the command returning null
if (openMatEditor != null)
{
  openMatEditor.SetParam("MATERIAL",myMaterial);
  openMatEditor.Execute();
}
```

Macro recording and batch execution. Since the commands use a common interface and are created by means of their name, it is easy to generate command execution scripts. This can be useful during the build process of the game or to make batch changes to the content of the game. To save a script we can use, for example, an XML file like Listing 13.1.

With the same philosophy, we can record the history of the commands that are running on the editor. It is sufficient that every command stores its name and the information of its parameters at the moment of its execution. Keeping this kind of

```
<?xml version="1.0" encoding="UTF-8"?>
<MyGameCommandBatch >
    <command name="loadmap">
        <param name="`infile" value="level1.map" />
    </command >
    <command name="ps3build">
        <param name="outfile" value="level1.ps3map" />
    </command >
    <command name="x360build">
        <param name="outfile" value="level1.x360map" />
    </command >
    <command name="closecurrentmap"/>
<MyGameCommandBatch />
```

Listing 13.1. Example batch file.

history is useful for repetitive tasks or for debugging purposes because it allows us to know the operations the user has made and be able to reproduce them.

13.4   Improvements to the Command System

13.4.1   Undo/Redo

Undo/redo is a feature available in most modern applications and is also desirable for our development tools. To obtain this feature, on the one hand, each command must be able to undo its operation, and on the other hand, we need to store the commands (a list, for example) that have been executed (see Figure 13.5).

Within that list there must be a reference to the last executed command. Thus, if the user wants to undo a command, the previous command in the list will be

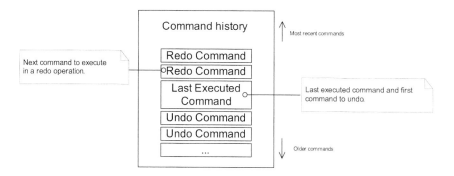

Figure 13.5. Undo/Redo command history.

established as the last executed command. In a redo operation, the `Execute` method will be applied to the next command and set it as the last one executed.

What happens when a single user action results in the execution of several commands? In this case it is mandatory to enclose all commands in a macro command and put only the latter in the undo/redo stack. It should be noted that to undo a macro command, you must execute undo operations in the contained commands in reverse order.

13.4.2 Macro Commands

In the specific case discussed in this section, we define a macro as a command that consists of several other commands. This might be a command to change the material of an object, which can be a composition of the two commands that set the object's color and texture. Another frequent example are commands that perform operations on several items at the same time, for example, moving multiple selected objects around on the map. The composite design pattern [Gamma et al. 95] is useful for implementing these commands (see Figure 13.6).

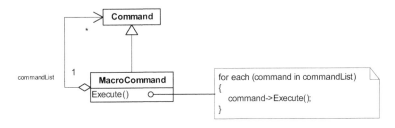

Figure 13.6. Macro command model.

13.4.3 Preview

The preview mechanism is used to demonstrate the effect of a command without actually executing it. A common example is the movement of an object in a 3D scene by dragging it with the mouse. The command is not executed until the user stops moving the mouse, but it is helpful to simulate the movement to show the user the result of this motion as accurately as possible.

For the preview function, it is not a good idea to generate a command in response to every event generated by the user (in the example of moving an object around, there may be hundreds of mouse motion events in a single movement). This would disable the undo/redo system due to the creation of a large sequence of commands that represent small incremental changes.

To implement this mechanism, we add a `Preview` method to the command interface and delegate its implementation to each command that requires a preview. This method will be invoked every time we want to update the feedback for the user (e.g., every mouse motion event) and should only change the visual status of the edited item. When the user finishes editing, the `Execute` method is activated. See the example code below:

```
OnMouseButtonDown:
MoveCmd = factory.CreateCommand("moveObject");
MoveCmd.SetParam("OBJ_ID",selectionID);

OnMouseMove:
MoveCmd.SetParam("POSITION",mousePos3D);
MoveCmd.Preview();

OnMouseButtonUp:
MoveCmd.Execute();
```

13.4.4 Notifications

Usually, the execution of commands generates notifications to alert interested systems that there has been a modification. A common example is that the changes caused by a command have to be reflected in the user interface.

Let's consider the case that in which we have a list of items on the user interface and a command to delete one of these elements. Every time an item is deleted, a notification is sent to the user interface so that it updates its status.

If we delete several items at once, for example with a macro command that contains various individual delete commands, the interface will receive a change notification for each removal. The result is usually a slowdown of the application due to the continuous update of the user interface.

A way to avoid this undesired effect is to have the system that sends the notifications retain them until all commands from a certain single action have completed their execution. Then, all corresponding notifications can be generated together in a batch, and the system that receives them can process all notifications at the same time and act accordingly and efficiently.

To facilitate the process of building notification batches, commands must inform the notification manager when they start and finish their execution. In the `Execute` method, this can be achieved as shown in Listing 13.2

Of course the notification manager must be aware that commands may be arranged in groups to decide when to send a batch of notifications.

```
notificationManager.BeginChangeBatch();
...
/*
Command execution code. In case of a macro will execute several
commands more. Every command can dispatch some notifications.
*/
...
notificationManager.EndChangeBatch();
```

Listing 13.2. Command execution code.

13.4.5 External Utilities

We can create a command to execute command line utilities if our tools or pipelines use this kind of application. The parameters provided to this command are both the name of the tool to be run and the arguments it needs for its functioning. Running these kinds of tools from anywhere in our system is easy:

```
Command clToolCmd;
clToolCmd = factory.CreateCommand("CommandLineTool");
clToolCmd.SetParam("TOOLNAME","fxc");
clToolCmd.SetParam("ARGS","/T fx_4_0 /Fo aex.fxo aex.fx");
clToolCmd.Execute();
```

Bibliography

[Gamma et al. 95] Eric Gamma, Richard Helm, Ralph Johnson and John Vlissides. *Design Patterns: Elements of Reusable Object-Oriented Software.* Reading, MA: Addison-Wesley, 1995.

14

Object-Oriented Data

Alan Kimball

14.1 Introduction

As engines become more data driven, responsibilities are shifting. Entire games can be created without writing any scripts or code. This shift in capabilities has given much more flexibility to content creators. With this flexibility, we have been able to create more interesting, vibrant worlds. While this expanding of capabilities has been a great boon to game development,in the transition, the self-descriptive abilities of programming has been lost. In many ways, content-creation packages are at the same level of maturity as pure procedural programming languages. When representing game information in data files instead of inside a structured language, it is more difficult to make reusable, generic data structures. But, by borrowing concepts from object-oriented programming, data systems can regain some of the safety that was lost. Much like the transition from C to C++ enabled many programmers to create larger, more componentized systems, the transition from traditional data models to object-oriented data can lead to the same advances. Many concepts from object-oriented data have already been embraced on the web with Cascading Style Sheets (CSS), but it is not necessary to completely implement their functionality to take advantage of some of the core concepts.

14.2 Data Inheritance

When designing a system in an object-oriented programming language, inheritance is integral to the design. A programmer is able to abstract shared functionality into base classes, minimizing duplicated information. This allows for individual subclasses with the responsibility to change which functionality is required for the specific implementation.

This concept transfers very well to data design. When creating an object-oriented class, care is taken to reuse methods and functionality whenever possible. When creating object-oriented data, one reuses individual field values. Instead of having virtual functions, object-oriented data has virtual fields. When deriving one piece of data from another, you start with an identical copy of that data. Then, modifications made to the child object are overlays on top of the existing data. If a field has not been "overloaded," then it keeps the same value as a parent.

This overloading concept is vital for reusability. In many cases, different pieces of data are only slightly different, but they must be tweaked and modified. By inheriting most information from parent data, tweaking shared concepts is easy. Any change made to the parent data automatically cascades to all derived data. This can be thought of as design-time instancing. At runtime, instancing an asset can be used to optimize the runtime, and using data inheritance can save the time of content creators by allowing them to reuse their work.

14.2.1 Example

Traditionally, when creating data for a role-playing game, a designer may have created the following four types of goblins:

```
<object name="Goblin"
   HitPoints="50"
   Model="goblin.model"
   Color="Green"
   Allegiance="Enemy"
   Weapon="Axe"
   Weakness="Red"/>
<object name="Blue Goblin"
   HitPoints="50"
   Model="goblin.model"
   Color="Blue"
   Allegiance="Enemy"
   Weapon="Axe"
   Weakness="Red"/>
<object name="Red Goblin"
   HitPoints="50"
   Model="goblin.model"
   Color="Red"
   Allegiance="Enemy"
   Weapon="Axe"
   Weakness="Blue"/>
<object name="Red Goblin King"
   HitPoints="100"
   Model="goblinking.model"
   Color="Red"
   Allegiance="Enemy"
   Weapon="Axe"
   Weakness="Blue"/>
```

Each entity, or game object, may have been copied and pasted or created from scratch, but after the data have been created, each entity is completely unique. The first issue here is when looking at the data, it is hard to tell ex-

actly what the differences are. As the data becomes more complicated, the number
of fields begins to grow, and it becomes increasingly difficult to manage all of the
information.

Second, if the model for goblins needs to be updated, a designer has to update
each individual asset. This busy work can be time consuming and bug prone if
every instance is not found and swiftly remedied.

Conversely, with object-oriented data, repeated information is removed. By
adding a concept of parent data, more semantic information is added. Here, via inheriting from the base goblin data, it is made explicit that the red and blue goblins
are types of goblins:

```
<object name="Goblin"
    HitPoints="50"
    Model="goblin.model"
    Alligance="Enemy"
    Weapon="Axe"/>

<object name="Blue Goblin"
    Base="Goblin"
    Color="Blue"
    Weakness="Red"/>
<object name="Red Goblin"
    Base="Goblin"
    Color="Red"
    Weakness="Blue"/>
<object name="Red Goblin King"
    Base="Red Goblin"
    Hitpoints="100"
    Model="goblinking.model"/>
```

This data is more concise, and more importantly readable. The extra noise of
resetting individual weapon characteristics is gone. If all of the goblins had too
many hit points, a designer would be able to update the hit points in the base data
to update all different types of goblins.

14.2.2   Implementation

Much like class inheritance, data inheritance can occur completely at build time.
The existence of inheritance is only a tool for adding more semantic information
for the user. During the build, the inheritance hierarchy can be removed. For each
piece of data that has a base object defined, a tool can walk the fields of that object.
If a field is set in the base data but not set in the child data, this build tool can
copy the value to the child data. After this conversion tool has been run over all
of the data files, the end result will have all of the inheritance hierarchy removed
from the files, leaving no need to modify the runtime (see the following code):

```
// Iterate through all of the input objects
foreach(node : InputObjects)
{
    // Find the "base" node for this piece of data
        baseNode = GetObjectWithName(node["@Base"]);
    if (baseNode != null)
    {
        // Iterate through the attributes of the base
        foreach (field : baseNode.Fields)
        {
            // If this field is in the parent but
            // not the child, copy the value
            if (node[field.Name] == null)
            {
                    node[field.Name] = field.Value;
            }
        }
    }
}
```

14.2.3   Complications

The act of data inheritance is quite simple, but much like poorly designed code, inheritance can lead to problems, as can poorly designed data inheritance. Just because two pieces of data share the same fields, it does not mean that there should be an inheritance relationship between the two. Inheritance is an implicit contract that two are related: one is a specialized version of the other.

Additionally, from an implementation point of view, data inheritance adds a significant amount of work to the build system. Dependencies must be strictly obeyed with inheritance. Much like a header file that defines a class, all inherited data that depend on a piece of base data will need to be reconditioned (compiled) when that base data changes. Children will have to be recursively reconditioned. Without careful thought about the inheritance of data, this can lead to significant build time issues. A small tweak to an object may have larger repercussions if it is the base of a tall inheritance tree.

14.2.4   Additions

Inheritance is only the first possible step toward more expressive object layout. Building off of the parallels of object-oriented programming, other concepts can follow just as cleanly. Multiple inheritance is sometimes used to combine different inheritance trees together, and the same can be used for combining different trees of data into one composite piece of data. Instead of setting an individual base data, multiple base data can be conglomerated together. Much like object inheritance, multiple data inheritance comes with its own set of problems. For example, if two base objects define the same field, the child classes will need to properly handle these conflicts. Resolving these and other issues is merely a matter of coming up with a simple rule of thumb. Depending on the expectations of the users, it may be an error case, or the runtime can choose the first value.

Sometimes when implementing a derived class, it is still important to refer to the base implementation of a method. The same can be done for data inheritance; instead of strictly overriding a value, a designer could add or subtract a constant from the base value. By transforming the base value, incremental changes can be made while keeping the advantages of data inheritance.

14.3 Constants

Another tool available in almost every programming language, which is so fundamental that we take it for granted, is named *constants*. By using constants, programmers are able to talk about concepts, not specific unlabeled values. When information is moved into data, we often lose this ability. Individual pieces of data are often named, but it is often impossible to name individual pieces of data inside an object.

14.3.1 Example

Continuing from the example above, a designer may be looking at the number of hit points which different entities have:

```
<object name="Goblin" HitPoints="50"    />
<object name="Goblin Knight" HitPoints="100"    />
<object name="Goblin King" HitPoints="150"    />
<object name="Kobold" HitPoints="50"    />
<object name="Kobold King" HitPoints="150"    />
<object name="Peasant" HitPoints="100"    />
<object name="Knight" HitPoints="150"    />
<object name="King" HitPoints="50"    />
<object name="Dragon" HitPoints="1000"    />
<object name="Lich" HitPoints="1000"    />
```

There is not a large amount of variety in these data, but they are still quite heterogeneous. In general, these objects are significantly different, so changing the inheritance hierarchy would be quite detrimental to understanding the data. But, at the same time, these values were all set for a reason. For the purpose of balancing, it is very important to keep track of these values, and it is very intentional that the same values repeat. If these data were all written in code, named constants would be used to limit the amount of repeated data. Below, the data have been converted to use named constants:

```
<var name="WeakHitpoints" UnitType="HitPoints" value= 50 />
<var name="MediumHitpoints" UnitType="HitPoints" value= 100 />
<var name="StrongHitpoints" UnitType="HitPoints" value= 150 />
<var name="MegaHitpoints" UnitType="HitPoints" value= 1000 />

<object name="Goblin" HitPoints="WeakHitpoints"  />
<object name="Goblin Knight" HitPoints="MediumHitpoints"  />
<object name="Goblin King" HitPoints="StrongHitpoints"  />
<object name="Kobold" HitPoints="WeakHitpoints"  />
<object name="Kobold King" HitPoints="StrongHitpoints"  />
<object name="Peasant" HitPoints="HumanHitpoints"  />
<object name="Knight" HitPoints="StrongHitpoints"  />
<object name="King" HitPoints="WeakHitpoints"  />
<object name="Dragon" HitPoints="MegaHitpoints"  />
<object name="Lich" HitPoints="MegaHitpoints"  />
```

Much like data inheritance, by using semantic information instead of hard-coded values, it is much easier to understand the meaning of the data instead of seeing only the values. Now, if it is determined that the entities are too easy or hard, only a small number of constants need to be tweaked. These constants trickle down into each associated class.

But it is important to keep in mind that just because two values are the same, they do not have to use the same constant. Above, the `Peasant` and the `Goblin Knight` may have the same number of hit points, but by using two different values we will not accidentally change one value when we are tweaking another.

14.3.2   Implementation

In the raw data, data constants can be treated like any other object in an object database. Existing tools do not need to handle these constants in any special way—they are just small objects. Then, during the build, a tool can process all of the objects. Whenever an object refers to a constant, the value of that constant can be copied into that object directly. This copy step would be completely tool only.

Additionally, while embedding the constant values into the actual objects where they are used, additional semantic verification can be done. Constants do not have to be of type `integer`; instead these values can be marked by what the data represent. Constants can have their actual units attached to them. Instead of marking a field as an `integer` or `float`, a field would be marked as distance or temperature. These units can prevent designers from using a constant that may currently have the value they expect, but conceptually may have a different meaning. In the future, data can be refactored without inadvertently modifying unrelated information.

```
// Iterate through all of the input objects
foreach(node : InputObjects)
{
    foreach(field : node.Fields)
    {
        // Try to find a variable reference by name
        var = FindVariableByName(field.Value);
        if (var != null)
        {
            // Ensure that the variable is the same
            // type as the field.  This type may be
            // application specific.
            Assert(var.Type == field.Type);
            // Unflatten the variable
            field.Value = var.Value;
        }
    }
}
```

14.4 Conclusion

By using basic concepts from object-oriented programming, it is possible to make custom data more powerful and safer for designers. By relying on a build-time data transformation, much like a code compiler, there is no performance cost to these features, and they can be added to an existing tool chain without significant risk or overhead added to the tool chain as a whole.

15

Improving Remote Perforce Usage

Mike O'Connor

15.1   Introduction

Love it or hate it, most of us find ourselves using Perforce in our daily routines, from syncing to the latest changes at the beginning of the day to digging through the revision history of a file to track down when and where a bug was introduced. For the majority of us that's as much as we need to think about it.

But what if that Perforce server, which you interact with frequently throughout the day, wasn't tucked away in a server room just down the hall? What if it was on the other side of the country, or even another continent? How would that affect you?

15.2   Remote Reality

I found out just how much working with a remote version control server would affect me when I joined a startup specializing in technical consulting. As a consultant, I would spend all my time working on another team's Perforce server, and the majority of that work would be done remotely.

It was several days before I got my first true taste of remote performance when I attempted to sync to the latest changes. I knew it would be a slow operation, but I had no idea just how slow. On most previous projects, an incremental sync generally took no longer than a few minutes. With the remote server, I needed to start the sync at night so that it would be finished by the morning!

While the nightly sync was generally an effective workaround, it had one critical flaw: any interruption in internet service during the sync would completely destroy productivity for the next day. Unfortunately, we were experiencing disconnects often enough that we could feel the loss of productivity. We had a real problem on our hands, and we needed to do something about it.

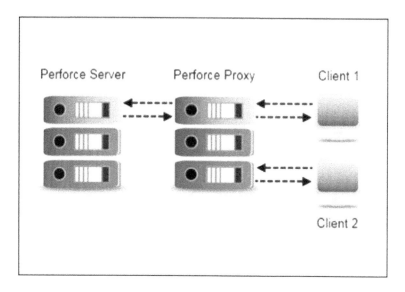

Figure 15.1. An illustration of a proxy server setup.

15.3   Productive by Proxy

Our first solution was to set up a Perforce Proxy server, also known as P4P. For those unfamiliar with P4P, it's a special server provided by Perforce that functions as a local cache of a remote server. When a user requests a file at a particular revision, the proxy will first check the cache to see if it has that revision already. If it does, it will just return the local copy, but if it doesn't, it will route the request to the remote server and cache the file once it has been retrieved (see Figure 15.1).

Under normal circumstances, a proxy server would have solved our problems. However, we had no central office; everyone worked from home. This meant that the proxy server shared by the company had to be located remotely. Furthermore, while our server had more bandwidth, it still needed to be seeded from the remote server. Instead of removing the bottleneck, the proxy had just shifted its location in our pipeline.

It became clear that the proxy server would not save us, so we continued to search for another solution.

15.4   Here Comes a New Challenger

Since we failed to solve the speed issue, we focused on stability instead. The idea was to create a program that would start a sync to a specified changelist and then wait to detect a disconnect. If the sync was interrupted, the program would restart the sync. We called this tool SyncBot, and it would eventually evolve to become our final solution to working remotely.

The first incarnation of SyncBot was a simple C# command line application that I put together in a couple days. That might have been the end of it, except for something peculiar I noticed in the output logs. Whenever a sync restarted, I noticed that many files that Perforce had seemingly finished were being synced again. To be sure that it wasn't something I had caused, I verified that the same behavior was present in the Perforce client. Further investigation revealed that Perforce does this to prevent overwriting an existing file until the new file has been fully synced.

This was important because many of the files that we were syncing were huge, well over a hundred megabytes. Because the sync process was so slow, needlessly syncing hundreds of megabytes of data a second time seemed wasteful. I was determined to fix that.

15.5   A Parallel Approach

My plan to fix the redundancy was to sync every file individually, which would guarantee that the server would recognize it as finished. I accomplished this by modifying SyncBot to first run a sync preview command, then iterate through the list of files returned, syncing them one at a time.

As I was making that change, though, I couldn't help but think about how the data would be easy to divide up among several threads. Several past colleagues had claimed that syncing different folders in separate instances of P4Win increased bandwidth utilization, so I decided that it was worth investigating.

It ended up being a fairly simple task. I had already done the work of generating the list of files using a sync preview command, so I just needed a way to distribute those files among several worker threads. The solution I settled on was to treat the list as a queue and let the worker threads grab files from the queue until it was empty.

To be honest, I didn't expect to see much benefit from adding multithreading. I assumed that we were already getting as much bandwidth from the server as possible. However, after using this new version for several nights, it seemed like my syncs were completing much faster than before.

I wanted to be sure that I wasn't just imagining things, so I compared the network utilization of SyncBot and P4Win in the Task Manager. It wasn't my imagination: SyncBot was getting more bandwidth from the server! Excited by this new development, I timed several syncs while varying the number of threads used. Figure 15.2 shows these results.

The secret to SyncBot's increased bandwidth is in the multiple connections that it establishes with the Perforce server. Many networks cap bandwidth on a per-connection basis, but SyncBot conveniently circumvents this limitation.

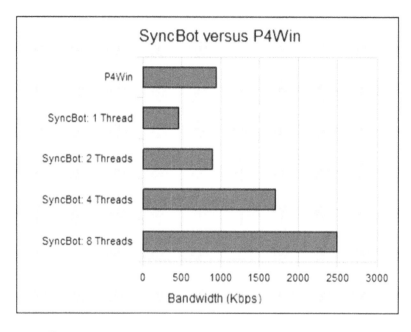

Figure 15.2. Bandwidth utilization of SyncBot and P4Win.

15.6 Putting It All Together

Once I shared the good news with my coworkers, we decided to see what would happen if we combined SyncBot with the proxy server, which had a larger upload bandwidth than the remote server. First we ran SyncBot on the proxy server to cache a given changelist. Once that finished, we ran SyncBot on our computers, syncing to that same changelist from the proxy server.

We hoped that this combination would lead to even faster syncs, and we were not disappointed. We were able to fully utilize the download bandwidth of our internet connections, which were in excess of 15 megabits per second!

Using SyncBot, caching the proxy server with a specified changelist now only took a few hours instead of the entire night. And once it was cached, we could complete a sync in roughly an hour. Toward the end of the project, we realized that we could even sync in the middle of the day, something that was previously impossible.

The combination of the proxy server and SyncBot was the key to increasing our productivity. Freed from the distractions of the remote server, we were able to focus on the tasks at hand.

15.7 Conclusion

While working remotely is likely to hinder your productivity, there are ways that you can minimize the impact. This article has presented two tools, the Perforce Proxy and SyncBot, which can be used separately or together to improve productivity when working remotely.

Part III

Third-Party Tools

So far, this book has described some ways to approach your asset pipeline and what tools you might have decided to build to improve your workflow and productivity.

In this part, we discuss how to use some tools that are made by third-party vendors. We start off with an article on "Vector Displacement in the Sculpting Workflow"(Chapter 16), which generates images that are simply gorgeous. Speaking of gorgeous images, Lambe and Roufas have contributed a chapter on a texture synthesizing tool called Genetica which has some very compelling results (Chapter 18).

Pretty images aren't everything though (I think my 3D Graphics Guy card just revoked for that statement). We have a chapter on using TBB to increase your frame rate (Chapter 17), on YAML to configure your severs (Chapter 20), Parallel Nsight to find your graphics bottlenecks (Chapter 21), and FBX to make importing your 3D files trivial (Chapter 22).

You doubtlessly know about many of these tools. Hopefully, these articles will open up new insights into using them in your projects that will gain you performance and improve your workflow.

16

Vector Displacement in the Sculpting Workflow

Craig Barr

16.1 Introduction

Vector displacement mapping in Mudbox provides artists with a very powerful toolkit for the extraction and storing of complex, multidirectional displacement. Intricate forms with appendages, undercuts, folds, and bulges, such as a human ear can be stored and reused throughout the sculpting and detailing process. These details are stored in a 32-bit floating-point image format that can be used as brush stamps or stencils in Mudbox to paint complex detail onto meshes in a single stroke. Artists can build up a library of commonly used forms and reuse them on any model. Artists can access a library of specific features that follow the exact look and style of a project and apply this data to the creation of characters, props, or environments. A vector displacement map (VDM) library is a more efficient data set than a collection of high-resolution models or scene files, thus allowing for a more portable and accessible pipeline solution.

There are many tools available to the digital artist today that allow for the creation of highly detailed and sculpted models. Vector displacement mapping provides artists with the ability to customize tools for specific sculpting effects. Sculpting workflows can also benefit from the storage of VDMs in libraries that are quickly and easily accessed. The use of vector displacement mapping to help preserve, or maintain, a specific look, design, or style can aid in any sculpting-based pipeline.

Vector displacement mapping allows artists to take advantage of these techniques and, therefore, aids in the sculpting workflow. This chapter briefly examines an effective and efficient means of storing, transferring, and sculpting with high-resolution geometric data stored in a two-dimensional image format.

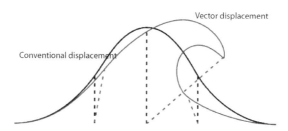

Figure 16.1. Conventional displacement (black) in comparison with vector displacement (gray).

16.2   Overview: Vector Displacement

Unlike conventional displacement maps, a VDM stores distance data as well as *directional* data (see Figure 16.1). Based on the pixel-color value of the map image, a VDM stores the height, or distance, a vertex will be displaced and the direction of the vertex displacement [Autodesk 10]. This allows for complex geometric structures, such as overhangs and undercuts, to be stored in a 2D image format.

16.2.1   Mudbox and Vector Displacement

Vector displacement mapping in *Mudbox* provides a very powerful toolkit that allows displacement data to be stored as a 32-bit (per channel) floating-point color image and captures all of the detail from a mesh without any loss in quality from the original sculpted detail. The maps accurately record complex sculpted features that undercut, overhang, or occlude other detail on a model. Provided that the UV-coordinates are laid out efficiently, 32-bit displacement maps can record 4,294,967,295 unique height data as floating-point values. *Mudbox* stores the XYZ-coordinate data in the RGB values of the image, where X=red, Y=blue, and Z=green. The maps are extracted in 32-bit (per channel) floating-point TIFF or OpenEXR format, or as a Ptex file (with the Autodesk Mudbox 2011 Subscription Advantage Pack).

Map creation and extraction in Mudbox. Allowing for the storage of geometric data in an image format, VDMs are easily and quickly created in Mudbox. Sculpted details are extracted to a map by recording the directional and distance data (as a color value) between user-specified subdivision levels from a source and target mesh (i.e., between the top-level subdivision resolution and the base mesh). Similar to the process of extracting conventional displacement, VDMs can be extracted in resolutions of up to 8K. The subdivision map extraction process (recording the distance between subdivision levels on the same model) in Mudbox provides virtually artifact-free results of specific details or of an entire model.

16.2.2 Sculpting with Vector Displacement

There are four basic means by which vector displacement can prove useful in the sculpting workflow: via direct surface imprinting with stencils and stamps, as a tool or brush-tip modifier to produce different sculpting effects, as a means of transferring details between meshes, and to recreate detail in supported renderers.

Stamps and custom tools. Vector displacements can be utilized in the form of stencils or, at a more finite level, as stamps. Mudbox allows access to VDMs as stamps to enhance existing or custom sculpting tools. Stamps can be applied to allow specific details to repeat across a surface or as a means of shaping, or customizing, a brush tip. This is extremely valuable for achieving specific design elements such as trims, stitching, buttons or hard-surface aspects (corners, bevels, onlays, etc.) where precision is desired (see Figure 16.2).

Stencils. VDMs accessed as stencils are typically used for, but not limited to, larger details and more complex structures. Stencils are useful for sculpting interesting features and irregular textured effects that would otherwise be difficult

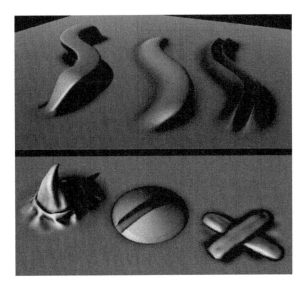

Figure 16.2. Vector displacement stamps used as custom tools (top) and repeatable details (bottom). (See Color Plate IX.)

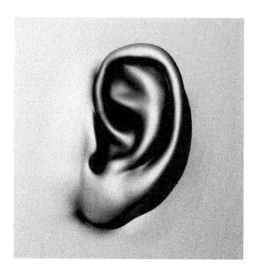

Figure 16.3. Vector displacement applied as a stencil to achieve complex details such as this ear map. (See Color Plate XI.)

to achieve. Vector displacement stencils provide an efficient manner for applying complex and time-consuming details (see Figure 16.3).

Transferring details. An entire mesh can be represented via a VDM. This provides a means by which details can be transferred between meshes. A character head, leg, or hand, for example, could be detailed separately and then extracted as a VDM and applied to another mesh sharing the same UV layout. This allows for pieces or components of a mesh (i.e., a character's hand) to be detailed separately and at much higher resolutions than the entire mesh (i.e., the full character) would allow.

Rendering. In supported renderers, such as Pixar's RenderMan, vector displacement can be used to recreate complex details at render time while working with the lower-resolution model within a viewport.

16.3   Creating Vector Displacement Maps: A Workflow Example in Mudbox

16.3.1   Sculpting Details

The creation of VDMs in Mudbox is a fast and straightforward process. Sculpted details can be created and stored in a VDM format at any time during an existing sculpting session, or created on their own in a separate Mudbox session. A fast and efficient way to create, extract, and store sculpted details in a vector displacement

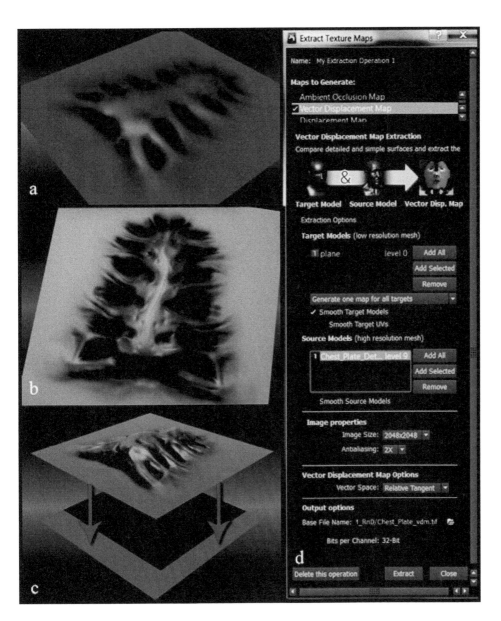

Figure 16.4. The basic sculpting process for sculpting details and extracting a vector displacement map in Mudbox. (a) early sculpt; (b) final detail sculpt; (c) illustration of detail as the source and a base plane as the target; (d) map extraction menu in Mudbox 2011. (See Color Plate X.)

format is to work with simple planes. This geometry can be created within Mudbox or imported from another digital content creation package (i.e., Maya, 3ds Max, or Softimage). Taking advantage of the tools and layer system within Mudbox, the details can then be sculpted at a variety of subdivision levels. The images in Figure 16.4 illustrate the process by which detail is sculpted on a plane that has been subdivided many times.

Extracting vector displacement maps. Once the high-resolution details have been sculpted, the map extraction process within Mudbox could not be easier. The process involves accessing the extraction options menu (Maps> Extract Texture Maps>New Operation) and selecting Vector Displacement Map from the Map Generation list (see Figure 16.4(d)). In the menu box, we simply define the low-resolution mesh as the target (where you want the details to transfer to) and the high-resolution mesh as the source (where you want the details to transfer from). The target and source geometry must share identical topology where, either the target is a lower subdivision level from the same model or another model that shares the exact same topology. For creating VDMs that are storing details to be accessed in a sculpting session, it is a good idea to use a separate version of the base mesh, in this case, the simple plane. This insures a flat, untouched base plane for the target mesh. This can be accomplished by either creating another plane within Mudbox or by importing a new version (see Figure 16.4(c)).

To define the properties of the image to output, we simply select an Image Size (resolution up to 8K), Antialiasing (if required), the Vector Space (specifies the coordinate space for calculating the output map) and, a Base File Name (the name and location of our output image). The Base File Name is output as 32 bits per channel by default and the file type is (currently) limited to .tif, .exr, and .ptx (Autodesk Mudbox 2011 Subscription Advantage Pack). The final output filename is tagged with a `_vdm` suffix (i.e., `Chest_Plate_vdm.tif`) (see Figure 16.4(d)).

Applying VDMs. As with regular textures, displacements or reference images, accessing VDMs in Mudbox is just as easy. The built-in Image Browser is a 32-bit image viewer and can be used to preview a library of VDMs. As with 32-bit HDR images, the exposure can be adjusted for viewing the VDM using the "+" and "−" hotkeys (see Figure 16.6). From the Image Browser, VDMs can be viewed and selected as a stamp or stencil to work with directly in the 3D viewport by selecting the Set Stamp or Set Stencil commands. Stamps and stencils can also be added to the existing libraries in the tabbed trays at the bottom right of the 3D viewport by accessing the menu (the arrow icon) and selecting "Add...". This allows for several VDM stamps and stencils to be stored in their appropriate trays for quick and repeated access throughout a sculpting session.

To apply VDMs, the mesh will need to be subdivided to a suitable resolution to utilize the details stored within the VDM image. VDMs can be used with any of the primary sculpt tools within Mudbox; however, the main sculpt brush will produce the most accurate reproduction of stored VDM details. In the Properties box for the sculpt brush, it is a good idea to work with the strength at 100% to produce details accurate to the VDM.

To apply a VDM as a stamp, there are two principles to consider: repeated and/or randomized patterns (rivets or teeth, for example) or as a tool-tip modifier (like a chisel tip shape). For repeated or randomized patterns that do not overlap, the Stamp Spacing will need to be adjusted to accommodate the desired placement of details. The Randomize properties can also be adjusted to apply random ro-

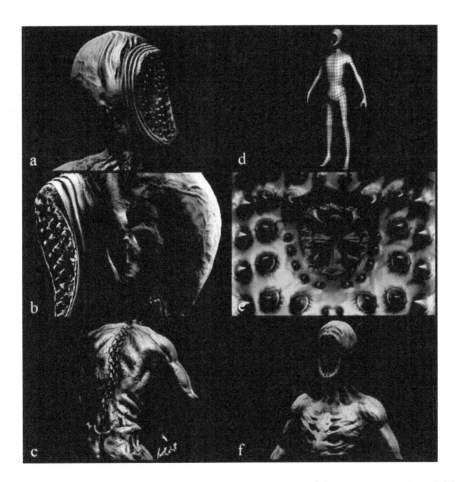

Figure 16.5. (a) VDM stamps applied for repeating teeth; (b) VDM stamps for gill-like structures; (c) VDM stamps used to repeat and overlap along spine; (d) the base mesh; (e) VDM stencil applied for throat-iris detail; (f) VDM stencil placed for chest detail. (See Color Plate XII.)

tational, scaling, positional and strength effects to the VDM stamp. It is also a good idea to adjust the Falloff used for the stamp placement. The falloff tray in the bottom right-hand corner of the viewport contains some useful presets to apply varying degrees of edge falloff (and custom presets can be created and stored here as well). For the most part, VDM stamps are best suited for little to no falloff to apply the VDM detail to full effect. The effect of the VDM stamp can be seen when simply dragging the brush across the subdivided mesh (see Figures 16.2 and 16.5 (a)–(c)).

Although similar to the application of stamps, VDM stencils are applied with slightly different properties adjusted on the sculpt brush. Stamp spacing should remain very low or at the default setting (0–6.25). A soft falloff is usually a good idea when applying organic details to allow for blending between existing sculpted features. Properties applicable to the Use Stamp Image settings are generally avoided for the placement of stencils (although they can certainly be used to blend with stamps for varying effects). The Buildup property affects the overall rate that the deformation (or applied VDM detail) will reach the strength value (the higher the number value, the faster the rate of buildup). Stencils appear as a semitransparent guide in the viewport, allowing for easy positioning, scaling, and rotating of the VDM image. The sculpt brush is simply used to rub across the stencil to transfer the VDM details to the surface of the subdivided mesh (see Figures 16.5(e)–(f)).

Of course, all of these settings are merely guides and suggestions and will need to be adjusted to the artist's liking. For more detailed information on settings and techniques for sculpting with stamps and stencils, refer to the Mudbox Documentation [Autodesk 10]. Several tutorials are also available at http://www.The-Area.com and the "Mudbox Blog" (also on The-Area website).

16.4   Vector Displacement and the Art Pipeline: Further Applications and Considerations

The integration of new tools and technology into an existing pipeline can often be costly, time consuming, and can involve intricate debugging processes [Carter 04]. Complicating the matter is the need to provide training to existing artists or the acquisition of application-specific talent. Both scenarios add to the overall financial and time budgets allocated for a specific project. The use of vector displacement in a sculpting workflow, however, requires a very low learning curve, little-to-no research and development time, and can enhance pipeline and workflow efficiency as a substantial time saver for sculpting intricate and complex details.

16.4.1   Enhancing Sculpting Pipeline Efficiency

Establishing consistency and efficiency in any pipeline is of paramount importance. The challenges encountered in the art pipeline within the game development process are of no exception. Approval processes between artists and creative and artistic directors can take up valuable time and resources in the production workflow. Providing artists with a library of data that fits the overall creative style and artistic look of the game allows for a much more streamlined approach to the creative process. VDMS can be stored on servers much like other texture directories and will have a much lighter data footprint compared to the storage of high-resolution geometry.

Libraries. Vector displacement mapping provides several benefits to existing and new game-art pipelines. Vector displacement libraries can easily be created, stored, and accessed on a network in the same manner as other texture, reference, and image directories. This means that VDMS can be implemented into existing pipelines with little to no programming support and can follow the same rules as existing directory structures [Davies 00]. If a 32-bit HDR image viewer is available, artists can view these directories in the same manner as a regular image-based directory. This allows artists to start sculpting components, attributes, or specific details before an overall concept is approved. The benefit here is that artists can focus on specific components or details that contribute to the overall style or look of the game. Furthermore, access to a specific library of pre-approved details and components creates a more efficient approval process with Creative and Artistic Directors (less back-and-forth during asset creation).

Maintaining look and style. Teams of artists are often tasked with the goal of maintaining the overall look integrity of game assets. The visual quality of a game usually garners a specific style that all characters, environments, and props must adhere to. In large-scale projects, preserving specific elements of design in the modeling and detailing process presents its own challenges in the areas of overall unity and balance [Bernard 10]. Access to VDMS of pre-built, pre-approved detail can aid in the preservation and communication of the design and style while also providing a means of control for the overall visual and look development. Allowing artists to access look-specific details also allows them to focus on larger tasks. This also provides an additional means of control over reinventing the wheel, where Artist A spends time unknowingly building what Artist B and Artist C have already previously built [Carter 04].

Reusing work that has already been completed is a huge benefit of the digital workflow, as it is important to automate routine tasks whenever possible [Williams 09]. Pre-approved components in the form of VDMs also provide artists with a starting point, template, or reference for a character, environment, or prop (or components of all). Mudbox also allows artists to access VDMs to aid in the sculpting process before final UVs are applied to the mesh. The sculpting of details can take place while the base mesh is undergoing the UV layout process in another department. The UVs can be imported to a mesh within Mudbox at any time in the sculpting process.

Figure 16.6. A sculpt of an organic structure (left) at 1.6 million polygons and a file size of 200 MB (.obj format) compared to the same structure stored as a (.tif) vector displacement map (right) at 1024 × 1024 resolution and a file size of 17 MB. (VDM exposure adjusted in Mudbox Image Browser). (See Color Plate XIII.)

Smaller data footprint. Geometric details stored in the form of 32-bit (per channel) floating-point images are a much smaller and efficient dataset than a directory of high-resolution models. Large datasets can result in bloated directories and impact the pipeline negatively. This is especially true with high-resolution geometry (see Figure 16.6, where VDMs can be stored in a variety of image resolutions: smaller resolutions for stamps and stencils, and, when necessary, larger resolutions for complete objects (characters, props, environments, etc.). Furthermore, VDMs can be applied in a manner that allows for quicker scaling and placement as well as control over blending into the existing surface of the mesh.

UV-less workflows: Ptex. The future of workflows that do not rely as heavily on UVs provides enormous potential for the use of vector displacement in a sculpting workflow. Developed for production use at Disney Animation Studios, Ptex is a new texture-mapping method that requires no explicit parameterization [Burley and Lacewell, 08]. Ptex is free of tedious UV setup and allows for the easy transfer of details between arbitrary meshes. Mesh topology and textures are free to change throughout a pipeline without the fear of details becoming invalidated. Ptex allows sculpted details to be stored and re-applied to a mesh even after substantial topological changes [Burley and Lacewell, 08].

Hardware-accelerated tessellation. Hardware companies are continually pushing the limits of graphics processing power and, as a result, the next-generation GPU will handle much higher geometry resolutions. Hardware-accelerated tessellation will allow for the rendering of dense subdivision surfaces in real time. This allows for greater levels of detail within a game engine or any real-time rendering environment. Tools, such as Mudbox, allow for the creation of highly detailed meshes and VDMs to store geometry data in a 2D image format. The use of VDM images opens up the possibility of providing a compact and more efficient approach (see Section 16.4.1 in this article) to rendering highly detailed surfaces in a hardware accelerated, real-time environment.

16.5 Conclusion

Vector displacement mapping provides an effective and efficient means for the storage and transfer of complex geometric details. Tools and brushes within Mudbox can be customized with vector displacement to provide specific effects on a mesh. Furthermore, vector displacement libraries also allow intricate and complex details to be quickly accessed and used in a sculpting workflow. The use of vector displacement mapping to help preserve, or maintain, a specific look, design, or style can aid in any sculpting-based pipeline.

Bibliography

[Autodesk 10] Autodesk. "Autodesk Mudbox 2011 Help Documentation." Available at http://download.autodesk.com/us/mudbox/help2011_5/index.html ?url=./files/WS73099cc142f487552b5ac6c412649166e6e-66e7.htm, topicNumber=d0e22071, 2010.

[Bernard 10] Teresa Bernard. "Principles of Good Design: Unity, Art Lesson #9." Available at http://www.bluemoonwebdesign.com/art-lessons-9.asp, 2010.

[Burley and Lacewell, 08] Brent Burley and Dylan Lacewell. "Ptex: Per-Face Texture Mapping for Production Rendering." In *Eurographics Symposium on Rendering 2008*, The Eurographics Association and Blackwell Publishing Ltd., 2008.

[Carter 04] Ben Carter. *The Game Asset Pipeline*. Charles River Media, 2004.

[Chiang 08] Doug Chiang. *Mechanika*. Portland, OR: Impact Books, 2008.

[Davies 00] Dianna Davies. "Common Methodologies for Lead Artists." Available at www.gamasutra.com, 2000.

[Williams 09] Freddie E. Williams, II. *The DC Comics Guide to Digitally Drawing Comics*. New York: Watson-Guptill Publications, 2009.

17

Optimizing a Task-Based
Game Engine

Yannis Minadakis

17.1 Introduction

Before 2005, the CPU-side of game code was single threaded. Optimizing for the CPU meant improving algorithms and data layout and removing unnecessary code. Sampling profilers and call graphs were the tools of choice to find bottlenecks. Parallelism was reserved for the GPU. The graphics APIs restricted developers to expressing their code in a form that could be parallelized by the hardware. The developer focused on how much load was placed on either the CPU or GPU and tried to load-balance to achieve the highest frame throughput.

With the arrival of the Xbox 360 and PlayStation3, developers were given up to three CPU cores to work with. The PC platform was also quickly moving to multiple CPU cores. Writing straightforward code that utilized the whole machine was manageable. There were multiple systems in a game engine. The systems were executed sequentially and could be run on separate threads as long as their inputs and outputs were pipelined. I call this the thread-per-system paradigm. For example, thread0 would submit frame(N), while thread1 animated frame($N + 1$) and thread2 processed user input for frame($N + 2$). Frame latency increased, but the game also ran faster and with richer content so the trade-off was reasonable. Once the systems were broken out, the traditional CPU optimization opportunities remained. Using mature profiling tools, the CPU's potential was there to be had just as it was in the single-core days.

Fast-forward to 2010. Intel is shipping six core CPUs with twelve hardware threads.[1] CPUs with eight hardware threads and on-chip integrated graphics are now the mainstream CPU for both desktop and laptop. In a few years, these parts

---

[1] A physical CPU core has at least one hardware thread. A hardware thread appears as a CPU to the operating system and is also called a logical CPU. All hardware threads on one physical core share the physical core's processing power.

will be the majority of the PC install base. With eight threads, there simply are not enough systems to move into threads. Either we leave a lot of CPU performance on the table, or we move to a task-based architecture.

This chapter will demonstrate how to move from a thread-per-system approach to a fully scalable task-based system. We will see how to decompose different game engine systems into tasks. We will learn how to efficiently schedule work across the machine and how to use new performance tools to visualize tasks as they run on the CPU. Using a simple example animating a skinned model we will implement a task-based animation and rendering system and we will use the Intel Graphics Performance Analyzer (GPA) to review our work.

17.2   From Threads to Tasks

Programming threads directly made a lot of sense when an entire system was separable. The inputs and outputs were straightforward and could be synchronized to the main thread via a semaphore. Adding queues allowed for pipelining of multiple frames to increase throughput. The scheduling of all this work was simple, and each game created a custom implementation.

Figure 17.1 shows a pipelined, threaded architecture on the CPU. The dark grey state boxes represent a frame moving from user input through scene submission to the GPU. Time moves from left to right. The main thread created one worker thread for each system, in this case the animation and physics systems. The main thread processed user input for frame $N + 1$ and would push work into the input queue of the animation and physics systems. The work is pipelined so that the main thread can submit rendering calls from frame N while the worker threads

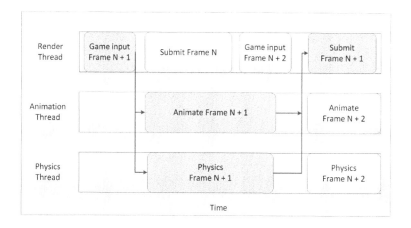

Figure 17.1. Example thread-per-system game engine.

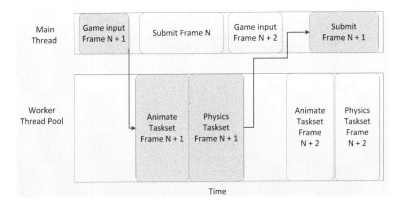

Figure 17.2. Example Task-based game engine.

process data from the $N + 1$ frame. When the worker threads complete, the main thread will submit frame $N + 1$.

To take parallelism to the next step, we need to break up the systems across threads. The first step is to decompose the work of each system into data-independent logical tasks. A task is a unit of work for a system that can execute asynchronously. To complete the work of the system, the task function is executed multiple times. The set of task executions needed to complete the work of a system is called a taskset. A task can access thread-specific data, but cannot synchronize data between itself and other task instantiations in its taskset. At runtime, a taskset can execute on any available thread, maximizing the use of all the CPU cores on a machine without having to create code for the particular number of available threads. Figure 17.2 shows how the game in Figure 17.1 can be converted to a task-based approach. The worker thread pool can scale from one thread to one thread per CPU core.

17.2.1 Task-Based Animation

Animation is probably the best system to start with. Let us consider a very simple example. We have a scene with a variable number of animated models. The models are stationary and loop through an animation. The animation system takes the animation data as input and produces the bone matrices as output. Pseudocode for the animation loop in the main thread is given below (example code is available on the website):

```
Foreach Model in ModelList
        ComputeBoneMatrices(Model, Time, OutputBones);
```

```
TaskDecl AnimateModel(TaskId, NumberOfTasksInSet)
{
    ComputeBoneMatricies(
        ModelList[ TaskId ],
        Time,
        OutputBones[ TaskId ] );

}

TaskSetHandle = CreateTaskSet(
    AnimateModel,
    NumberOfModels,
    NoDependecies);

// Other processing on the main thread.

WaitForTaskSet( TaskSetHandle );

// Consume data produced by taskset.
```

Listing 17.1. Pseudocode for creating a taskset.

We can extract parallelism with threads by separating the loop into another thread. We can write code to use all the threads on the machine that would detect the number of threads and try to distribute the work. Each game would have to implement its own thread scheduling as well as any interoperation between the different systems. All middleware used by the game would have to be compatible with the game's custom scheduling for maximal efficiency. Scheduling code is difficult to debug since deadlock or timing bugs can be harder than average to find. Game developers want to spend time making great games, not working on infrastructure code.

With a task-based implementation, the scheduling of tasks is delegated to the tasking system. The programmer only needs to specify the task function. The AnimateModel function in Listing 17.1 is a task. The game animates the models in the frame by creating a taskset. When the animation data are needed, the main thread can wait for the taskset to complete.

The tasking system abstracts the scheduling of tasks and the number of hardware threads on the machine. The programmer can divide up the work into tasks based on the workload and create tasksets. Task sets from multiple game systems are scheduled cooperatively by the tasking system. The tasking system maintains a list of all tasksets in the game and executes only tasksets that are ready to run. There is no execution overhead from tasksets that are not ready to run. Task sets are ready to run when all of their dependent tasksets have completed. Consider the case where taskset B requires the output of taskset A. The main thread can specify to the tasking system that taskset B depends on the completion of taskset A

```
TaskSetAHandle = CreateTaskSet(
    TaskSetAFunction ,
    NumberOfTasksInA ,
    NoDependecies);

TaskSetBHandle = CreateTaskSet(
    TaskSetBFunction ,
    NumberOfTasksInB ,
    TaskSetAHandle);

/* Other processing on the main thread.  The tasking system will
execute taskset A then taskset B.  WaitForTaskset will not return
until taskset B is complete. */

WaitForTaskSet( TaskSetBHandle );

// Consume data produced by taskset B that.
```

Listing 17.2. Specifying dependencies.

(see Listing 17.2). The main thread can then continue executing while the tasking system instantiates taskset B when the dependencies for B are met.

When waiting means working. `WaitForTaskSet` does not actually wait in the OS sense. Blocking a thread that participates in the tasking system would be inefficient. Rather, `WaitForTaskSet` notifies the tasking system that the main thread cannot proceed until the specified taskset completes its work. As part of `WaitForTaskSet`, the main thread will start processing tasks itself until the taskset it is waiting on completes. That way, the main thread is drafted into being a worker thread when no other useful work can occur on the main thread.

Generally, tasking systems will create $N - 1$ OS threads, where N is the number of hardware threads on the machine. Creating N threads would compete for execution time with the main thread whenever work was executing in the tasking system. Also tasks should never block, meaning they should not call any function that might put the OS thread to sleep. The tasking system only creates one OS thread per CPU core. If one of those threads block, there is no other OS thread available within the tasking system to continue processing tasks. As a result, performance will be lower, as one CPU core will be unused until the blocking condition is resolved.

17.2.2 Code with Data Dependencies

Task parallelism works by exploiting the property of data independence between tasks. If a system does not have that property, tasking is more challenging. For example, an AI system with a collision detection algorithm for models moving on a plane might need to resolve movement conflicts between models. Execution order of tasks in a taskset is not constrained. Models may collide since the taskset can only rely on the initial positions. A nave tasking implementation would cause inconsistencies.

Dependencies between individual tasks require a new approach. The task must be broken into pieces that are guaranteed to be independent of each other. In the case of the AI example, the plane can be divided into sections. Models moving toward the interior of the section can be resolved in parallel by processing the sections as a taskset. After the taskset completes, the set of models that move across sections can be resolved serially in a single task. Even though there is more work in the task-based approach, overall running time improves since significant portions of the AI algorithm run in parallel using otherwise idle cycles.

The key observation from the AI example is that a task-based algorithm that has more overhead runs significantly faster overall than a more optimal single-threaded approach. Work performed while the machine would otherwise be idle is essentially free. The game's performance is gated by the completion of the frame on the main thread. Therefore, a more complex task-based approach can increase frame throughput even if it takes more cycles to compute.

17.3   Profiling a Task-Based Game Engine

Using a task-based approach simplifies the problem of scheduling work on machines with large and varying number of cores. The complexity of enforcing dependencies between tasksets and scheduling optimally is delegated to the tasking system. However, tasking does create a new class of issues. While these new issues may seem simple to find, in a full game with many systems it is challenging. I have seen both these examples occur during the development of AAA games.

17.3.1   Data Dependencies

Assume you have two tasksets; an animation taskset and a rendering taskset. The rendering taskset depends on the output of the animation taskset, but the rendering taskset does not specify a dependency to the output of the animation set. The tasking system may schedule both tasksets to run concurrently leading to incorrect rendering. A small cut-and-paste error can lead to unpredictable timing issues manifested as corrupt memory or access violation exceptions.

Sampling-based CPU tools fall flat when trying to diagnose data-dependency errors. A sampling profiler may happen to catch both the render taskset function and the animation taskset running concurrently. Most sampling profilers aggregate samples over small time slices. The render taskset should run right after the animation taskset, so even correct data dependencies between tasksets will appear to be violated. Also, many other types of bugs can cause memory corruption. You could spend hours diagnosing the memory corruption before concluding it to be a data-dependency issue.

17.3.2   Insufficient Performance

Consider a serial algorithm that runs in 8 ms. It can be broken into tasksets but will require a serial portion which requires an extra 2 ms to compute. On a quad-core CPU the expectation that the algorithm will run in about 4 ms $(8/4 + 2)$. When the tasksets are added to the game, the frame time improves only to 6 ms. Where are the extra cycles going?

Sampling profilers report the total number of samples taken in a function for a given time range relative to the total samples for the entire process. Comparing the original serial implementation to the taskset implementation shows more samples in those functions. However, there is no indication if the extra samples used are cycles that would otherwise be idle or cycles that could have been used by another taskset. Also, functions in the game can be called from multiple tasksets. Sampling profilers only know about functions so cannot attribute samples to the taskset that called the function. Call stacks on the samples can help attribute even tasksets. The sampling profiler would have to be aware of the tasking system to aggregate the call-stack data. As of the writing of this chapter no sampling profiler has the flexibility to give robust performance data for tasking systems.

Perhaps the biggest deficiency of the most current tools is that they are function based. In creating a task-based system, work is purposefully split into tasks meaningful to the game. That higher-level information makes optimizing the game much easier. What we need is a tool designed with tasking in mind. One such tool is the Intel Graphics Performance Analyzer (GPA).

17.3.3   The `TaskingGameEngine` Sample

To demonstrate how to use Intel Graphics Performance Analyzer (GPA) to find issues in task-based code, I have written a simple sample called `TaskingGameEngine` (TGE). The source code, detailed setup instructions, as well as directions to download and run the latest version of GPA are available on the book's website. TGE animates and renders a set of models. While TGE is very simple, the issues are very real. All of the issues I will discover and analyze using GPA in this chapter are issues I have seen in AAA game titles using GPA. I encourage you to install GPA and look for the issues yourself.

The tasking system implemented for TGE (in TaskMgrTBB.cpp/h) is based on Intel Thread Building Blocks (TBB). TBB is open source and provides the complex scheduling logic needed to run the tasking system efficiently. TaskMgr is a simple wrapper API to create and wait on tasksets. GPA, however, will work with any task system, including custom in-game systems.

TGE has two major systems: animation and rendering. The example is based on the DirectX SDK's DXUT framework. It is designed to illustrate the tasking system-related issues I have observed while working with game developers.

Depending on the CPU and GPU the example runs on, it may be either CPU or GPU bound. If the example is GPU bound, any improvements in CPU throughput will not be visible in the frame rate. That does not mean that the optimizations are not worth it. When more powerful GPUs become available, the already shipped game will scale, and there are more opportunities to add features to future titles based on the same engine. For the rest of the chapter, we will optimize the example for CPU performance.

17.3.4   Decorating Tasks and Other Important Work

Sampling profilers use function names to give context to reported execution time. For example, a sampling profiler might show that you spent 80% of the total execution time on a particular function. This approach works well when a function encompasses the interesting work and when the set of interesting functions are small. With a task-based game engine, there are many different tasksets executing potentially from different frames at once. During optimization, we want to improve the execution time of tasksets to increase framerate. However, we can also refactor tasksets so the throughput of tasksets increases, even if that increases overall execution. Remember the goal of optimizing a task-based game engine is to increase the framerate. Using idle CPU cores to do more work is a win if that work reduces the total time it takes to compute a frame.

GPA provides a simple, generic, hierarchical API for adding context to a section of code. The macros `BeginTask/EndTask` are used to decorate code with a name that is meaningful to the game. Although the macros contain the word "Task," there is no requirement that the work decorated be a task. Any code can be decorated.

In the example the highest-level decoration in the hierarchy are the DXUT callback functions `MoveFrame()` and `OnD3D11FrameRender()`. The TaskMgr will automatically decorate tasks created using the name specified during the call to `TaskMgr::Createtask` set. With decorated code, GPA provides unique insights into what is happening in the code.

For a step-by-step guide to running the example and gathering the data used in the rest of the chapter, please refer to the example code on the website.

17.3.5   Comparing Single-Threaded versus
Task-Based Animation

Running the example with all animation on the main thread and with tasking enabled, then disabled, produces the following results. The model count is set to maximum, and the sample is set to be CPU bound. The data was gathered on an

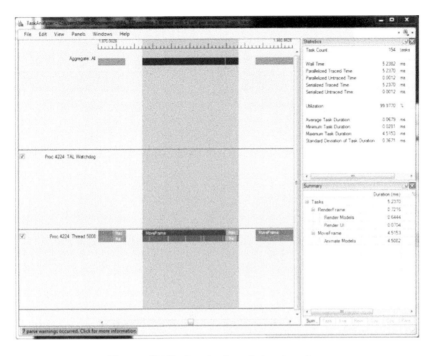

Figure 17.3. Single-threaded animation.

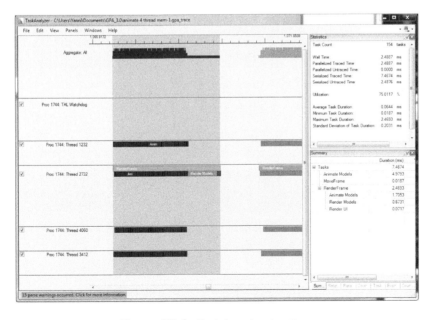

Figure 17.4. Task-based animation.

Intel Gulftown limited to four cores. What I call a frame is the time DXUT gives
TGE in `OnFrameMove()` and `OnD3D11RenderFrame()`, which is highlighted in Figures
17.3 and 17.4. The time where no GPA tasks appear is time spent in DXUT. This
time is not counted as frame time. DXUT is not a performance render engine and
is used here for simplicity. A real application would have a more optimal render
path for performance. GPA supports zooming into the timeline to better view the
data. Figures 17.3 and 17.4 are zoomed to show relevant events, so the horizontal
scale varies for each figure. Time is measured using the statistics and summary
windows on the left. The data in those windows is limited to the highlighted region
in GPA.

The first cut of the data looks promising (Figures 17.3 and 17.4). The animation
tasks are scheduling well. GPA tells us the wall time for the frame went from 5.23 ms
to 2.48 ms. Note that GPA times should be treated as approximate. The overhead
of logging data can affect absolute task execution time. Blank space on the thread
timeline indicates time not in a decorated task. This includes both driver time and
DXUT overhead. The total time spent in Animate Models increased from 4.5 ms

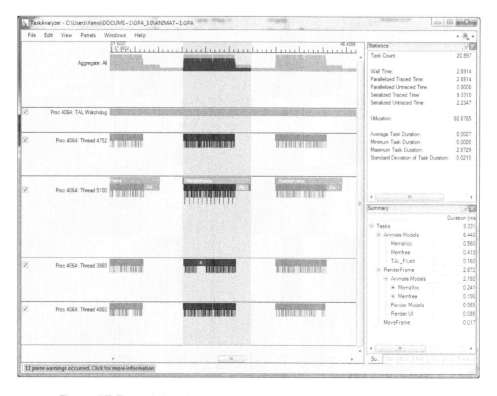

Figure 17.5. Task-based animation with memory allocations decorated.

to 6.68 ms. Benchmarking the tasking system separately showed about 1.5 ms spent scheduling or about .3 ms of wall time (1.5 ms /4 cores). The animation tasks appear to be running slower than expected. The excess execution time is inside the animation tasks themselves. To analyze where that time is going, we can decorate other parts of the system as we did with tasks. The most important code to decorate is code that contains synchronization points such as memory allocation.

With memory operations decorated (Figure 17.5), we can now see where the problem is. The model allocates memory during the animation phase. Memory allocation is single threaded, thereby synchronizing all the various threads. There are multiple ways to address memory allocation in tasks. The best case is to remove the allocation. If that is not possible, perhaps the memory can be pre-allocated. If it is memory only used in a single frame, a temporary heap could be used. The temporary heap could allocate a fixed-size buffer and satisfy local frame allocations and reset at the end of the frame. Also, using the context id provided by the tasking system allows temporary per-hardware thread heaps, making them even more efficient to allocate from.

The key take-away is to remove any OS synchronization points from inside task functions. For this example, I will remove the allocation since it is not needed in

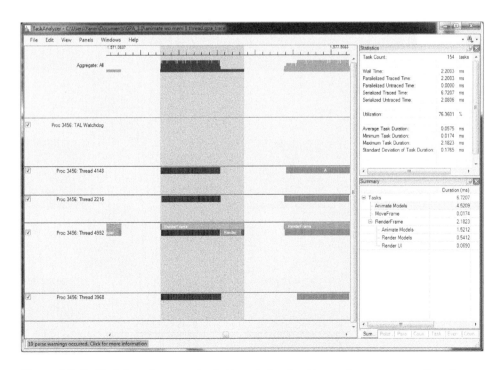

Figure 17.6. Task-based versus single-threaded animation and no memory allocation.

this location. The animation task execution time drops to 5.92 ms, and the wall time drops from 2.89 ms to 2.2 ms or about a 20% improvement in frame time (see Figure 17.6). Running TGE without GPA shows 3.53 ms per frame with the allocations versus 3.38 ms without, or a 4.2% improvement in frame time. The difference is attributable to the logging overhead of GPA. Using GPA helps focus on opportunities to improve performance, but it is difficult to predict the absolute improvement.

17.3.6   Animation and Rendering Task Set Scheduling

The next step is rendering. The thread-based implementation usuallys involve waiting on the animation system before generating D3D11 command lists[2]. In the task-based approach, waiting for the animation taskset to complete before creating the render taskset will result in idle worker time waiting for the main thread to create the render taskset. Creating the render taskset right after the animation tasksets, specifying the animation taskset as a dependency, will achieve the fastest possible scheduling for both tasksets. The animation taskset starts immediately upon creation, and the rendering taskset starts as soon as the animation taskset completes without intervention from the main thread.

```
// During OnFrameMove function
gTaskMgr.CreateTaskSet(
        AnimateModels ,
        &gAnimationInfo ,
        guModels ,
        NULL ,
        0,
        "Animate Models" ,
        &hAnimationSet );

// During D3D11OnFrameRender function

gTaskMgr.CreateTaskSet(
        RenderModels ,
        &gRenderInfo ,
        guTasksPerSet ,
        &ghAnimationSet ,
        1,
        "Render Models" ,
        &hRenderSet );
```

---

[2]The D3D11 API is available on Windows Vista and above for D3D9 hardware. D3D11 allows command lists to be created on multiple threads and requires their submission on the main thread. For games that ship on Windows XP, a slightly more complex solution is possible. DX9 does not have command lists and allows only single-threaded rendering. The game can implement a simple token scheme and using a taskset to generate the tokens for each of the draw calls in your frame. With such token lists, the main thread can submit the D3D9 frame similarly to how it does this on D3D11, and the game should get similar performance benefits relative to single-threaded D3D11 drivers.

```
gTaskMgr.WaitForTaskSet(hRenderSet);

// Submit Command lists generated in hRenderSet to pd3dDevice
ID3D11CommandList** pList = gRenderInfo.pCommands;

for( UINT uIdx = 0; NULL != pList[ uIdx ] && uIdx < MAX_TASKS; ++uIdx )
{
    pContext->ExecuteCommandList(
        pList->pCommands[ uIdx ],
        FALSE );

    gRenderInfo.pCommands[ uIdx ]->Release();
    gRenderInfo.pCommands[ uIdx ] = NULL;
}
```

Listing 17.3. Code from TGE for animating and rendering a frame.

Listing 17.3 shows the TGE code for creating the animation and render tasksets specifying the proper dependency between them. The D3D11 `OnFrameRender` waits on `hRenderSet` and submits the set of command lists generated by the taskset.

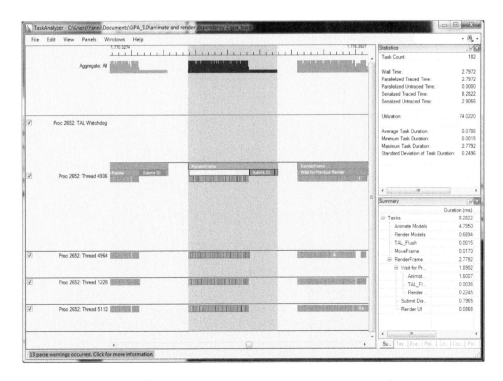

Figure 17.7. Render taskset depends on animation taskset.

Reviewing the GPA trace in Figure 17.7, the frame shows the animation and render tasksets executing in sequence. Wall time for the frame increased to 2.8 ms. That is unexpected. The GPA trace shows that both animation and rendering take about 1.8 ms which is an improvement. The submit task is forcing a serialization point, however. The drivers used to gather these data do not support multithreaded command lists. Internally, the D3D11 API creates tokens which are then played back in the `ExecuteCommandList` function. The multithreaded emulation slightly increases the frame cost, yet all is not lost. Even for drivers where multithreaded submission is not enabled, we can use the drain-out time (defined below) with pipelining.

17.3.7   Pipelining Systems across Frames and Latency

The tasksets are now free of synchronization points and their dependencies are properly specified. There are surely many more algorithmic and implementation optimizations possible for this example. From a tasking perspective, however, the scheduling is as efficient as possible for this frame. The tasking system schedules the various game systems' work as soon as the dependencies allow, and the system's tasks run concurrently. To get to the next level of tasking utilization, multiple frames need to be in flight at once.

Pipelining in a thread-per-system game. With the thread-per-system model, the number of frames in flight to achieve the maximum possible throughput is equal to the number of dependent systems in a frame[3]. Let us assume a game has three systems A, B, C and that the frame is CPU bound. System B depends on the output of A and system C depends on the output of B. If the game systems are run on one thread, total frame time is the sum of the running time of A, B, and C and the Latency $=1$:

$$\text{Time(Frame)} = \text{Time(A)} + \text{Time(B)} + \text{Time(C)}.$$

If each system is on a thread, then to achieve maximum throughput, the latency will be three frames and

$$\text{ExecTime(Frame)} = \max(\text{ExecTime(A)}, \text{ExecTime(B)}, \text{ExecTime(C)}).$$

Also, the memory footprint expands since the inputs and outputs of the systems need to be queued. For simplicity, we can describe the memory usage as a function of the latency because each pipelined frame needs independent memory to operate on.

---

[3]Complex threading systems that more closely resemble tasking can result in lower frame latency at the cost of code complexity. There are a continuum of solutions between the ridged thread-per-system model and the tasking model.

To achieve maximum throughput for this game three frames of latency are needed:

$$\text{TotalMemory} = \text{Latency} \times \text{MemorySize(Frame)}$$

Pipelining in a Task-Based Game A task-based system with the same constraints can achieve full throughput with significantly less latency. Each system runs its tasks on all cores. Running the systems in sequence means the entire taskset of A must complete before B can run. Since the tasking system schedules B as soon as A completes, the longest B has to wait to run after A completes is the length of one task, where $\text{WaitTimeToStart(B)} = \text{TaskTime(A)}$:

$$\text{SetTime(A)} = \text{TaskTime(A)} \times \text{TaskCount/NumberOfCPUs},$$

This loss of execution time is referred to as drain-out time. Figure 17.8 shows three tasksets executing in the tasking system. The white space is drain-out. The calculation of execute time for this scenario, which has a latency of 1 is

$$\begin{aligned} \text{ExecTime(Frame)} = \text{SetTime(A)} + \text{WaitTimeToStart(B, A)} + \text{SetTime(B)} \\ + \text{WaitTimeToStart(C, B)} + \text{SetTime(C)}. \end{aligned}$$

As the number of CPU cores increase, the thread-per-system cannot scale past the number of systems while the task-based system can run concurrently on all

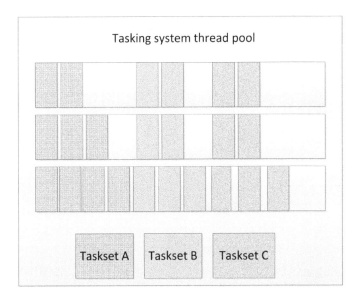

Figure 17.8. Three tasksets executing in the tasking system (task-based game).

available cores. $\mathrm{SetTime}(x) + \mathrm{WaitTimeToStart}(x)$ will always be small relative to $\mathrm{Time}(x)$. However, comparing the pipelined case becomes more complex. If the latency is three frames, then the task scheduler will be able to fill all idle time with tasks from the frames in flight. The running time of the task-based game is the same as the thread-per-system game if the number of hardware threads is equal to the number of systems. As the number of hardware threads increase, the task-based game $\mathrm{Time(Frame)}$ continues to drop, while the thread-per-system $\mathrm{Time(Frame)}$ remains constant. This property holds as long as the number of hardware threads is less than the number of tasks in the tasksets. This is a good result, but we can do better.

Let us assume that

$$\mathrm{SetTime(A)} + \mathrm{SetTime(B)} + \mathrm{SetTime(C)} > \mathrm{WaitTimeToStart(B, A)} \\ + \mathrm{WaitTimeToStart(B, C)}.$$

This is true if the tasksets have a significant amount of work to complete. If two frames are always in flight on the CPU, then the drain-out time for frame N can be filled with tasks from frame $N + 1$ as follows, with a Latency $= 2$:

$$\mathrm{ExecTime(Frame)} = \mathrm{SetTime(A)} + \mathrm{SetTime(B)} + \mathrm{SetTime(C)}.$$

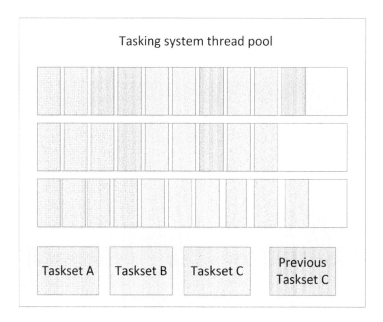

Figure 17.9. Three tasksets executing in the tasking system with one frame pipelined.

Figure 17.9 illustrates how pipelining one frame can use drain-out time from another frame. The empty CPU time created by taskset B, depending on the result of taskset A, and taskset C, depending on taskset B, are utilized by the taskset C executing from the previous frame. Note that, since the latency is two frames, the memory footprint is smaller than the thread-per-system case while achieving maximum throughput. The result of moving CPU pipelining to a task-based approach is a more responsive game with a lower memory footprint.

Bringing pipelining to the tasking game engine. The rendering taskset in the example is not really the entire process of rendering. D3D11 allows for creating command lists on separate threads, but submission of those command lists can only occur on the main thread. The main thread waits for the render taskset to complete command list creation and submits the command lists. The first step to pipeline frame submission is to double-buffer the command list array. The animation and rendering tasksets can work on the frame $n + 1$, while the main thread submits frame n. Each system selects which buffer to use based on whether the frame is odd or even, ensuring that each taskset works on the data for the correct frame without heavy OS synchronization. Finally, the submit code skips the first frame rendered since there are no command lists to submit.

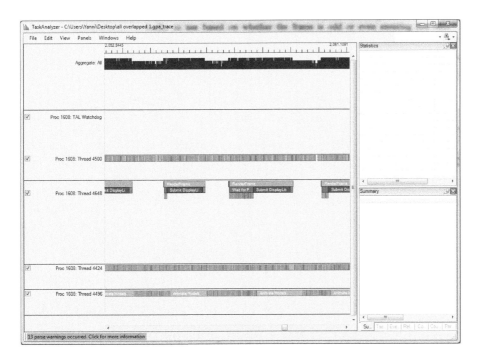

Figure 17.10. TGE with pipelined frame submit.

It is difficult to say how much a single frame now takes in GPA (see Figure 17.10). Work from the previous frame is part of the current frame. We do see all worker threads busy executing tasks. The gaps between frames are gone for the worker threads. DXUT is single-threaded, running on only the main thread. Running TGE without GPA now runs at 3.05 ms raher than 3.38 ms, the best execution time TGE had before pipelining. This confirms the intuition that DXUT was not using the cycles on the three worker threads and that overlapping two frames on the GPU allows these cycles to be used for frame rendering.

17.4   Task, Task, Task

Moving a real game engine to tasking is complex. There are many data-dependent systems that need to be rethought, but the long-term benefits of scalability are huge. CPU core counts will continue to increase, and so will the mix of products in the marketplace. Currently, shipping PCs already start from two hardware threads and go all the way to twelve. Trying to figure out the best scheduling of threads is tedious and best left to someone with lots of time on their hands. With tasking, you can focus on the capabilities of the PC, not the core count. With systems broken into tasks along logical lines, scaling up or down becomes a tractable problem. Finally, with generic scheduling implemented in the task system, you are free to focus on what makes your game rock!

18

Efficient Texture Creation
with Genetica

Ichiro Lambe and Atlas Roufas

18.1 Introduction

AaaaaAAaaaAAAaaAAAAaAAAAA!!!—A Reckless Disregard for Gravity (also referred to as *Aaaaa!*), is an award-winning action title by Dejobaan Games that brings the thrill of BASE jumping to the PC. Players attempt to leap off tall structures, navigate levels in challenging ways, perform tricks, avoid obstacles that are liable to break bones or at least smear mascara, and then safely land with the aid of a parachute. One of the game's levels is shown in Figure 18.1.

Figure 18.1. Aaaaa! offers a vibrant, stylized vision of the future. (See Color Plate XIV.)

A challenge of creating *Aaaaa!* was to keep the game visually fresh as the player progresses through 81 levels. This involved the creation of hundreds of bitmap assets to be used as model textures, glowing effects, and item icons. At the same time, preserving the game's unique look required visual continuity to be maintained between all assets created.

Genetica, a seamless texture and effects editor by Spiral Graphics, was the tool selected by Dejobaan Games to aid development. It was chosen for two reasons. First, its approach to texture generation allowed the creation of exceptionally intricate textures in a fraction of the time required by other tools. Second, Genetica's node-based approach allowed non-artists (level designers) to also iterate on the designs, creating additional thematically consistent assets wherever needed.

The purpose of this chapter is to introduce readers to Genetica. The first section will acquaint readers with Genetica's underlying philosophy, interface, and workflow. The second section will discuss principles that game artists can follow to get the most out of Genetica, while drawing on specific instances of Genetica's use in the creation of *Aaaaa!*

18.2   Genetica's Workflow and Philosophy

While there are countless bitmap editors for game artists to choose from, nearly all are variations on the traditional photo-editor model where bitmaps are opened and directly manipulated through various destructive operations. This section surveys key aspects of Genetica that make it unique among bitmap editors.

18.2.1   Node-Based Workflow

In Genetica, textures and visual effects are constructed by arranging nodes into networks. Each node represents a graphics operation, such as creating a pattern or modifying the output of a previous node.

Figure 18.2 shows a simple example that consists of opening a photograph in Genetica and then adjusting its contrast. When the photograph is opened, it appears as an Imported Image node in the middle of the workspace. To adjust the image, a Change BCI (Brightness Contrast Intensity) node is dragged from the library panel at the right of the interface and dropped below the imported image. Finally, the Change BCI node's 'contrast' property is modified to obtain the desired result.

Each operation involved in an asset's construction is fully nondestructive. In the previous example, either the Imported Image or the Change BCI node could be modified at any time. Regardless of the number of nodes found in a document, all changes automatically propagate through to the final result.

One of the first things new users will notice is that node networks in Genetica don't resemble the networks found in most other node-based applications. Instead of allowing nodes and interconnections to be placed freely throughout the

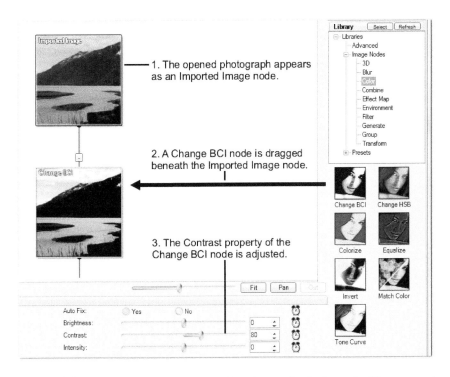

Figure 18.2. Assets are constructed by dragging nodes in from the library panel.

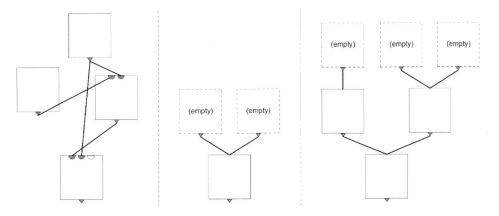

Figure 18.3. Traditional node-based apps allow nodes and connections to be placed anywhere (left). Genetica allows nodes to be placed only in specific slots (center). As existing slots are filled, Genetica creates new ones (right).

workspace, Genetica attempts to enhance network orderliness by only allowing nodes to be placed into specific input slots, as shown by Figure 18.3. As users fill empty slots with additional nodes, new slots appear where needed.

This distinctive characteristic causes all networks in Genetica to exhibit certain design commonalities, even for assets created by different artists. First, nodes are always arranged in such a way that information flows downwards through the network, with nodes towards the top of the workspace signifying the initial components involved in an asset's production and lower nodes representing additional refinements of previous steps. Second, each asset ends in a single root node at the bottom of the workspace that represents the final output of the network. Because of this structure of many branches coalescing into a single root, node networks in Genetica are referred to as *node trees* or even just *trees*.

18.2.2   Groups

Node trees can be packaged into single nodes called groups. Consider a glow or bloom effect, which can be created in any image editor by combining a picture with a blurry version of itself. The right half of Figure 18.4 shows how such an effect would be structured in Genetica. The Change BCI node influences the strength of the effect, the Gaussian Blur node creates a blurry version of the image, and the Combine node blends the blurry version with the original sharp image. As previously indicated in Figure 18.2, such a setup would be constructed by dragging the mentioned nodes from the library panel into the workspace.

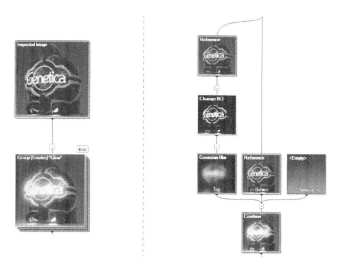

Figure 18.4. A glow effect packed into a single group node (left). The contents of that group (right).

The left half of Figure 18.4 shows the glow effect packaged into a single group node. After a group is created, it can be positioned as simply as any other node, regardless of whether the group contains just a few nodes or hundreds.

Once a Group has been created, it can be given any input image, and the Group will automatically apply the same set of actions to the new input. Groups can therefore be thought of as the visual equivalent of scripting in more traditional image editors, and as such, represent a way for users to expand upon Genetica's core functionality.

18.2.3 High-Level Tools

A trait shared by most node-based applications is for all the nodes at the users' disposal to represent fairly simple operations that must be painstakingly assembled to produce complex results. One of Genetica's most distinguishing characteristics is that its nodes don't only represent low-level operations, but also include high-level tools, such as those depicted in Figure 18.5.

Shown in Figure 18.5 are the Canvas node, which represents an entire vector drawing tool, the Synthesis node, which contains a texture synthesis tool capable of creating seamless textures from photographs, and the Make Environment node, which can be used to create cube maps. These nodes will appear in examples throughout the following section.

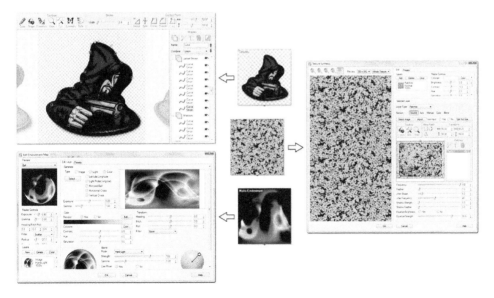

Figure 18.5. Some nodes, such as Canvas, Synthesis, and Make Environment, reveal entire mini-applications when double-clicked. (See Color Plate XV.)

18.3   Principles for Efficient Asset Creation

Genetica easily doubled the speed with which seamless textures and other bitmap assets were created for *Aaaaa!* As with any art tool, there are countless ways to achieve any one result, many of which differ dramatically in production efficiency. This section covers key design principles that allowed Dejobaan Games to realize their considerable productivity gains, as well as some additional tips of relevance to game projects in general.

18.3.1   Group Nodes into Logical Units

A node tree should tell a story. By making use of Genetica's ability to group nodes into logical units, the overall process involved in constructing an asset can be made apparent from the first glance. Consider the two variations shown in Figure 18.6.

If an artist were asked to look at the left half of the figure for a few moments and describe what they saw, their answer would likely be along the lines of "various shapes are combined to form a hazard-striped wall with a biohazard sticker on it." While technically accurate, that's about as informative as asking someone to describe a housing construction site and learning that "various materials are combined to form a house."

Repeat the experiment with the other half of the figure and the response will more likely sound like this: "A hazard-striped wall and a biohazard sticker are created. The sticker is placed onto the wall." The three essential elements of the construction process have been made apparent by organizing the nodes into three groups. The node tree now tells a story that can be understood at once.

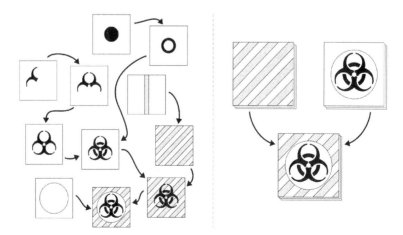

Figure 18.6. "Noodle-soup networks" lack organization (left). Disciplined node trees tell a story from the first glance (right).

Figure 18.7. Sensible node groupings expedite the creation of asset variations. The top-left quadrant shows the original asset. The other quadrants show the result of replacing individual node groups.

One might argue that the left half of Figure 18.6 could be organized into a few vertical lines in order to better organize the process. Though this would organize the nodes somewhat, it would still be less understandable than the right half of Figure 18.6. Our method is analagous to the reasoning behind using functions in a program: it is a way of organizing a process to better communicate and segment the work being done.

As shown in Figure 18.7, a well-organized node tree also expedites further artistic exploration by suggesting quick, yet high-impact, customizations. For example, the node-group representing the hazard-striped wall could be replaced with a different surface, such as a brick wall. The biohazard group could be replaced with a wanted poster. And the group that combines the two images could be made to add tears to the top one, allowing the bottom image to show through in spots.

But this is only the beginning. As discussed in the following section, node groups boost workflow down the road by encouraging component reuse.

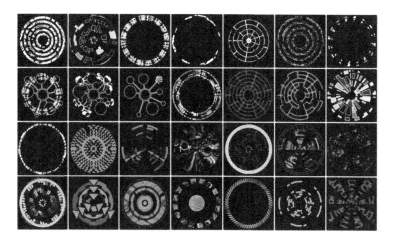

Figure 18.8. A sampling of dozens of light ring variations created for *Aaaaa!* (See Color Plate XVI.)

18.3.2 Reuse Components

Node groups can be thought of as the subroutines of a programming language, and as such, can be constructed to perform arbitrarily complex tasks. Similar to how subroutines can be called from multiple places, groups can be reused for the creation of multiple assets, or even as part of a batch processing operation.

Spending time during the early stages of a project to properly group nodes into discrete functions allows significant time savings later due to the reusability that is gained. For *Aaaaa!*, preparing and reusing groups enabled the rapid creation of several large sets of related assets, such as the light rings shown in Figure 18.8.

Figure 18.9 provides a closer look at one of these rings. At the top of the tree are nodes responsible for generating the base pattern, followed by a group that colors the pattern and brightens its edges, and ending with a group that adds a glowing halo to the image. These latter effects were created once and then reused for the majority of the light rings, providing immediate visual continuity between the variations. Different versions of the base pattern were constructed with similar rapidity by mixing and matching several pattern-generating components. In this manner, hundreds of bitmaps were created with relative ease. For a more detailed look at one of these groups, refer to Section 18.2.2, which explains the construction of the glow group.

Although the stylized world of *Aaaaa!* required predominantly abstract texturing work, node groups can also be created to perform organic tasks such as the surface weathering shown in Figure 18.10. Other tasks may include artistic filtering, bump- and specular-map generation, placing graffiti on walls, adding burn marks to paper, making a design appear as if printed on cloth, and so on.

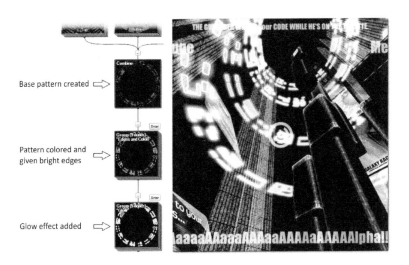

Figure 18.9. A light ring created in Genetica (left), and shown in-game (right). The node groups forming this texture were reused for the creation of multiple assets. (See Color Plate XVII.)

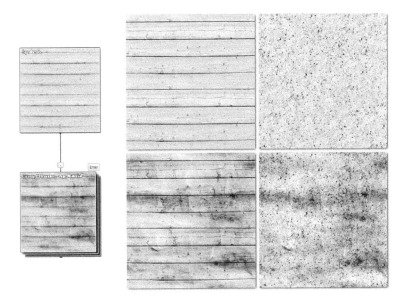

Figure 18.10. Node groups can be reused to perform just about any job. In this case, a group has been created (left) that will batter and smudge any input image (center and right). (See Color Plate XVIII.)

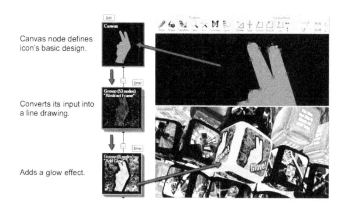

Canvas node defines
icon's basic design.

Converts its input into
a line drawing.

Adds a glow effect.

Figure 18.11. The "Flip-It Glove" icon created in Genetica (upper right and left). The icon appearing in *Aaaaa!*'s extensive menu of unlockable content (lower right). (See Color Plate XIX.)

18.3.3 Avoid Fixed Designs

It could be said that the object of BASE jumping is to make it through each jump while retaining as many teeth as possible. *Aaaaa!* takes this a step further by rewarding players with additional teeth as they complete new levels, beat previous times, and perform stunts such as spray-painting government buildings. Teeth then serve as the game's currency and can be spent to unlock over a hundred additional pieces of content such as new levels and items. With each piece of content needing an icon to represent it, this presented another opportunity for using Genetica to expedite the creation process.

One example of unlockable content in *Aaaaa!* is the "Flip-It Glove," which allows players to give detractors the finger as they hurtle by. Pictured in Figures 18.11 and 18.12, the glove's icon is comprised of an intricate pattern of glowing lines, some of which follow the shape of the hand. Such a pattern could be created in a fixed manner by individually drawing each line. However, by avoiding fixed designs and instead relying on procedural means to create patterns, it becomes much easier to make artistic adjustments and to reuse the original work in the production of derivatives.

As shown in Figure 18.11, the hand shape for the "Flip-It Glove" icon is defined as a vector drawing within a Canvas node, which as mentioned earlier is the seamless drawing tool included in Genetica. This makes the icon exceedingly easy to modify, with the output of the Canvas node being passed to a pair of node groups below it that will process their input into a glowing, futuristic line drawing.

This setup streamlines the creation of icon variations. Figure 18.12 shows how simply modifying the vector shape in the Canvas node causes Genetica to automatically recreate the entire icon, with the output of the Canvas node being passed to

Figure 18.12. The icon as it appeared in *Aaaaa!* (left). Modifying the shape drawn in the Canvas node (center) will automatically propagate down to the final result (right). (See Color Plate XX.)

the nodes below it. Notice that when the hand's pinky is extended, the surrounding line pattern automatically adjusts to the new shape.

This practice of avoiding fixed designs is an extension of the component reusability concept discussed previously. Whereas fixed designs will often benefit only the asset for which they were initially created, procedural creations can be readily re-purposed. Figure 18.13 shows a few of dozens of different icons that were created for *Aaaaa!* by reusing and adjusting the same components utilized to create the "Flip-It Glove" icon.

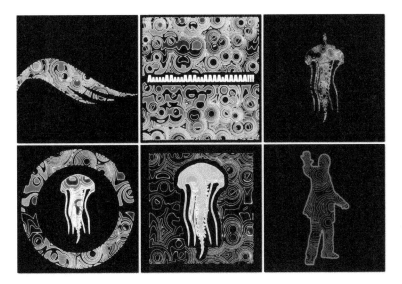

Figure 18.13. Avoiding fixed designs allowed numerous icon variations to be created for *Aaaaa!* with exceptional speed. (See Color Plate XXII.)

Figure 18.14. A barebones example of how the component library for a fantasy game might be organized.

18.3.4 Build Component Libraries

Up until now, we've demonstrated how the creation of reusable components can lead to a significant production speedup. To take full advantage of this, components should be added to a well-organized library as they are created throughout the asset production phase. Figure 18.14 shows a simplified view of what such a library might look like for a game with a traditional fantasy setting. The primary branches of the library are Generators, which produce designs and textures, and Filters, which add further detailing to their inputs.

The categories of Figure 18.14 simply represent folders created by the user with their operating system's file manager. Things get more interesting when Genetica is directed to load the root folder of the asset library, after which Genetica will automatically traverse the library and integrate all the categories and assets it finds into its interface, where they will appear alongside all the standard nodes and components that come included with the application.

The integrated library then serves as a toolbox of all the reusable components of relevance to the project. As the library increases in size, building new assets increasingly becomes a matter of drag-and-dropping previously created components. For example, a stone generator can be dropped into a filter that will turn it into a stone wall. This in turn can be dropped into a filter that will add bloodstains to the surface. The result of this rapid assembly is a unique stone wall material that appears to have gone through a recent battle.

Figure 18.15. Cube, normal, and opacity maps created in Genetica (left) form convincing compact discs in a game engine when applied to a standard reflection shader. (See Color Plate XXI.)

18.3.5   Use Cube Maps with Baked Effects

Genetica includes an environment map editor that is able to generate cube maps with a variety of lighting effects baked into them. When used with standard reflection and refraction shaders, this results in a range of exotic surfaces, many of which would otherwise require specialized shader code. By using cube maps with baked effects, unique surfaces are much quicker to create, can be customized by artists without modifying code, and will run on older hardware as well as mobile platforms that may offer fixed-function reflection shaders but may not have programmable GPUs.

Figure 18.15 shows one example of this. With three standard assets produced in Genetica and an ordinary reflection shader, realistic compact disc surfaces were created in a game engine with light patterns that shift in a convincing way as the viewing angle is changed.

Genetica can filter cube maps with a variety of effects including diffusion, light scattering, and anisotropic effects. As shown in Figure 18.16, different versions of an environment can be assigned to different objects within a scene, creating the impression of various surface types lit by the same environment. The steps used to create this example appear in Figure 18.17.

The skin shader shown in Figure 18.18 is again little more than a reflected cube map. If needed, the cube map could be rotated by the shader to ensure the brightest part of the cube map always faces the primary light source. The cube map was designed in Genetica to create the impression of subsurface scattering, but the resulting shader renders without the overhead associated with many other techniques.

Figure 18.16. Genetica is able to bake a variety of lighting effects into cube maps. The left cube map is unfiltered, while the right one has been modified to create the impression of polished bronze. (See Color Plate XXIII.)

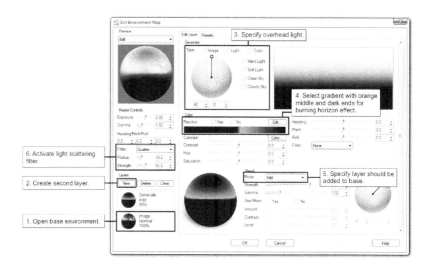

Figure 18.17.   The polished bronze effect can be baked into a cube map using the Edit Environment Map dialog, found by clicking the Render Environment Map button in Genetica's main button bar. (See Color Plate XXIV.)

Figure 18.18. Genetica-created cube maps find uses in unexpected areas, such as this super-efficient skin shader.

The steps used to create the skin cube map are almost identical to the ones that were shown in Figure 18.17. The main differences were that in Step 4 a gradient with more fleshy tones was selected, in Step 5 normal blending was selected, and in Step 6 a diffuse filter was chosen instead of scatter.

18.3.6   First Photographs, Then Procedurals

The extensive array of nodes offered by Genetica allows just about any material to be created procedurally, but there are still trade-offs to consider. Procedural textures require more attention to create but offer ultimate control over every aspect of the result. On the other hand, Genetica also includes a texture synthesis tool, shown in Figure 18.19, that can create seamless textures from photographic sources. Synthesized textures can be created much more quickly than procedural ones while readily delivering photorealistic results, but they depend on the availability of photographs that resemble the desired surface.

Genetica's node-based system allows texture synthesis to be freely mixed with procedural techniques to any extent, which means that each asset can fall anywhere on a spectrum from the purely procedural to the purely photo-based. A good approach for finding the ideal balance along this spectrum is to initially create all new assets using texture synthesis, and then to begin adding procedural elements to the extent that the desired look was not already achieved. This method allows artists to take maximum advantage of the speed and realism benefits offered by texture synthesis, while using procedural techniques to whatever extent they're needed.

Figure 18.20 shows an example resulting from this method. First, a seamless texture was created for a ship hull by synthesizing it from a photograph. A more aged appearance was desired, so the result was run through a procedural node that was configured to apply a number of weathering effects to its inputs.

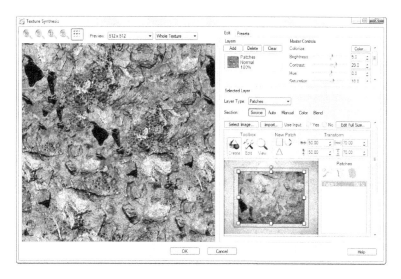

Figure 18.19. As an alternative to procedural generation, Genetica includes a texture synthesis tool that creates seamless textures from photographs.

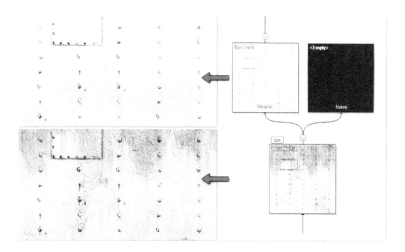

Figure 18.20. In this example a seamless texture for a ship hull was created from a photograph (top). A more aged surface was desired, so it was weathered procedurally (bottom). (See Color Plate XXV.)

18.4 Conclusion

This chapter introduced readers to Genetica and explored how it was used by De-jobaan Games to realize significant productivity gains in bitmap asset production, as well as a few additional techniques of relevance to game projects in general. Like any flexible art tool, while there are many ways to approach the creation of each asset, they are far from equal in terms of production efficiency. We touched on key techniques such as node-grouping and component reuse, which allow Genetica's full potential to be realized.

19

Reducing Video Game Creation Effort with Eberos GML2D

Frank E. Hernandez and Francisco R. Ortega

19.1   Introduction

In this section, we discuss some concepts we found to be common for all 2D games during the development of the Eberos Game Modeling Language 2D. It is important to note that this is by no means the only or best language approach to modeling 2D games, but rather it is the approach we developed to reduce our game development effort. This approach is also by no means complete; we present it in this article with the hope of demonstrating the savings in development that similar approaches can give your project.

While exploring, we have identified the following requirements for the game modeling language:

- *Simplicity.* Part of the reason for the increase in effort of developing games is the overhead for translating the game requirements into source code (see Figure 19.1(a)). Eberos GML2D aims at reducing this cost by providing an intermediate step between game specification and game code (see Figure 19.1(b)).

- *Platform-Independent.* Since the game logic is independent of the underlying platform, so too must the language be that expresses it.

- *Library/Game Engine-Independent.* Similarly, the modeling language must not be linked to any specific development library or game engine.

- *Expressiveness.* It must be able to model a large majority of game development projects.

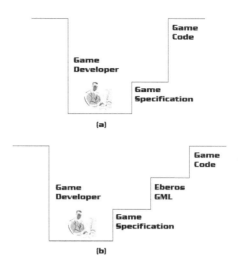

Figure 19.1. Gap between game specification and development. (a) Current gap, where developers must rely on a combination of intuition and experience when bridging the gap between the stages. (b) Eberos GML aims at reducing the gap by providing developers with an intermediate stepping stone between stages.

In order to develop Eberos GML2D, we began by abstracting some concepts common to 2D games. We accomplished this by identifying some of the major components common to all 2D game such as sprites, animation, sound effects, etc. Once we identified these components we continued to identify subcomponents, for example, the frame delay, which is a subcomponent of all animations. During this process, we also identified the logic and source code segments that were common among our previous 2D games. This latter information was then used in the development of the semantics of our language as well as the translators from Eberos GML2D model to source-code implementation.

Before we move on to explain the constructs of Eberos GML2D, let's first look at the specification for a simple game of *Pong* for the PC. First, we'll show how it would look in plain English and then how it would look with Eberos GML2D.

Specification for *Pong*: Plain English

This game of *Pong* has two players. Each player controls a paddle at each side of the screen. Player1 controls the paddle at the left of the screen, while Player2 controls the paddle at the right side of the screen. Player1's controls are the A key for moving the paddle up and the Z key for moving the paddle down. Player2's controls are the up arrow key for moving up and the down arrow key for moving the paddle down. The ball in the game will start at the center and will begin each round with a random direction. When the ball crosses the left or right limit of the screen, the opposing player will gain a point and the ball will reset at the center. The game will be a windowed game with dimensions of 800 pixels wide by 600 pixels high.

Specification for *Pong*: Eberos GML2D

The game has two `UserDefinedEntities`: Player and PongBall. The Player entity has one `Sprite2D` with the bar graphics. It has a global state which listens to the MOVE_UP and MOVE_DOWN `GameMessages`. The Player entity has a `BoudingRectangle` for collision detection. Finally, it has two `CompositeActuators`; MoveUp and MoveDown, which handle the translation of the entity up or down. The PongBall entity has one `Sprite2D` with the ball graphic. It has a `BoundingRectangle` for detecting the collision with the player's paddle and the screen limits. The PongBall entity has three `CompositeActuators`; MoveBall, ResetBall, RandomizeDirection. The PongBall entity also has two `States`: BALL_RESET and BALL_ACTIVE for supporting the logic of the PongBall entity. Since the game is a windowed game, the GameRoot entity is 800 pixels wide by 600 high. The GameRoot also has three `EntityReferences`: Player1, Player2, and PongBall. The player references are then controlled by two `InputHandlers`: Player1Input and Player2Input. The Player1Input responds to the A and Z keys, and notifies the Player1 reference of MOVE_UP and MOVE_DOWN `GameMessages`. Similarly, Player2Input responds to the up arrow and down arrow keys, and notifies Player2 reference of MOVE_UP and MOVE_DOWN `GameMessages`.

19.1.1 Source Code

Once the game has been defined, the Eberos GML2D model created can be automatically translated into source code, and the initial game version is created (see Figure 19.2). The game might still require some programming to complete, but you

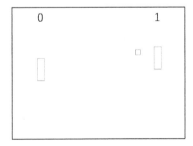

Figure 19.2. Simple Game of Pong.

have just saved yourself the repetitive work of creating the states, implementing the input handling logic and collision detection. We discuss these benefits in the last section of this article.

19.1.2 Entities

Entities in Eberos GML2D are akin to actors in a game. The same way that actors are the meat of all games, entities are the meat of Eberos GML2D. Entities are used to model the actors in a game. There are two kinds of entities in Eberos GML2D: user-defined entities and specific entities. While specific entities are entities that abstract a specific concept such as a game message, user-defined entities allow the language user to create new kinds of entities not specified in the language by combining other Eberos GML2D constructs.

GameRoot. The GameRoot represents the entry into the game; this is similar to the main function in a C++ program. In Eberos GML2D, the game model is viewed as a graph, where at least one of the entity edges must be connected to the GameRoot. The GameRoot is also used to specify an initial setup of the game. Currently, the GameRoot entity specifies the screen resolution and whether the game is windowed or full screen.

GameMessageTracker. The GameMessageTracker entity controls all the possible GameMessages that exist in the model. This entity ensures that any message by any of the other entities is a valid message. Game messages in Eberos GML2D are represented by the GameMessage entity. Just like in any game, messages in our language represent a single, specific piece of data.

GameMusicManager. Similar to the GameMessageTracker, the GameMusicManager entity specifies the music and sound effects available in the game model. The GameMusicManager also controls which sounds and music can be played by the PredefinedActurators. This entity is populated by SFXTrack and BGMTrack entities, which specify information specific to the audio file. The Track ID is a unique identifier that allows for each specific track to be used by the PredefinedActuators, while the Track URL is used to specify the location of the music and sound effects in the system. The Track URL is used when translating the Eberos GML2D model into source code to transfer the file to the project's folder. This is done as a means for reducing the errors of specifying the project's path to each sound file.

UserDefinedEntity. UserDefinedEntities are meant as the catch-all of entities, and can be used to model any of the specific entities (see Figure 19.3). Entities are the center of Eberos GML2D; everything is treated as an entity in the game model. Since entities/actors can range from menus to dialog choices to players and much more, entities must support a range of properties common to all of these actors. UserDefinedEntities can be composed of zero or more entities, which allows for

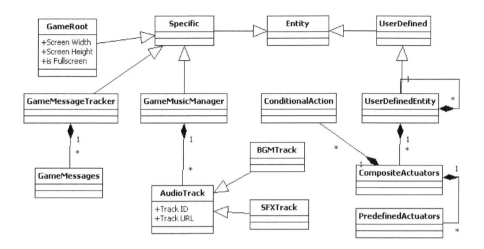

Figure 19.3. Basic class diagram with an overview of the entity relationships.

the modeling of nested entities, such as would be the case of a menu composed of menu choices.

Entities are also composed of `CompositeActuators`, which represent actions that the entity can perform in the game. `CompositeActuators` are composed of `PredifinedActuators`, which are a small subset we have found to be common to all 2D games.

In the following list, we catalog the `PredefinedActuators` found during the development of Eberos GML2D.

- `Translate`. Displace an entity by a given amount.

- `Place At`. Place an entity at the given location.

- `Notify Self`. Allow the entity to send itself a message.

- `Play/Stop Sound`. Play/stop a sound effect.

- `Play/Stop Music`. Play/stop a music track.

- `Invert Axis`. Invert a given coordinate axis.

- `Play/Stop Animation`. Play/stop a given animation.

`Actuators` can also have `ConditionalActions`, which represent actions that only occur if a specified condition is met. These are composed of two parts: conditions and actuators. The condition evaluates to true/false, and the actuators are a set of `Predefined/CompositeActuators` to be executed when this condition becomes valid.

The follwoing is a list of conditions found during the development of Eberos GML2D.

- **Check Collision.** Is set as true if a collision has happened between the entities.

- **Check Position.** Check if the entity position is at or around the specified position.

Finally, entities can also have zero or one `State/GlobalState` representing the initial state of the entity's state machine (see Section 19.1.3), zero or one `Sprite2D` (see Section 19.1.4), zero or one `BoundingObject` for collision detection (see Section 19.1.5), and zero or one `InputHandler` for modeling input (see Section 19.1.6) .

19.1.3 Logic

The game logic is probably one of the most important and most time-consuming aspects of any game project. While there are many approaches to implementing the behavior of actors in a game, finite state machines (FSM) seem to be one of the more versatile approaches available. In Eberos GML2D, we have two constructs, `State` and `GlobalState`. These constructs were modeled based on the state architecture presented by Mat Buckland in [Buckland 05]. Similar to his approach, `States` and `GlobalStates` have one owner entity (see Figure 19.4).

`State/GlobalState`. A `State/GlobalState` directly attached to an entity in the model means that such a state is the initial state for that FSM. Each state is composed of `Actuator_Calls`, which represents actions that entities can take in the game. These `Actuator_Calls` can be placed inside the `OnEnter`, `OnExit`, `OnUpdate`

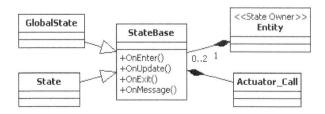

Figure 19.4. Basic class diagram for entity to state relationship.

and `OnMessage` sections of the states. As the names implies, an `Actuator_Call` placed inside the `OnEnter` section execute when the state is entered. Any `Actuator_Call` placed inside the `OnUpdate` section is called on every update, and any `Actuator_Call` placed inside the `OnExit` section is called when the state is being exited. The `OnMessage` section of the states is a bit different from the other sections. Any `Actuator_Call` placed inside this section must have a `GameMessage` specified along with it, and is only called when that `GameMessage` is received by the state.

An FSM is built in Eberos GML2D by linking states together with `TransitionEvent` links. Currently, a `TransitionEvent` link represents an edge from one `State` to another `State`, or one `GlobalState` to another `GlobalState` and specifies the message that triggers the transition from such state to another. Finally, a FSM modeled in Eberos GML2D is only valid if every state in the Eberos GML2D game model is reachable.

19.1.4 Sprite and Animations

In Eberos GML2D, a `Sprite2D` represents the resource image file for a sprite or sprite sheet (see Figure 19.5). This construct holds the information specific to that file, such as the resource URL, the image width and height (in pixels), and where in the screen it will be drawn by default. The screen detination is used in particular in the case of modeling a heads-up display (HUD) or a menu. In the case when the sprite is actually a spritesheet containing multiple animations, this can be modeled using one of the two animation constructs, `AnimationStrip2D` or `CompositeAnimation2D`.

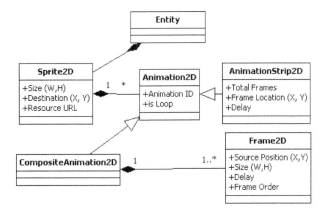

Figure 19.5. Basic class diagram for entity-to-sprite relationship.

Animation2D. Animation2D is an abstract representation of all animations, so every animation construct in the language is derived from this. Every animation contains an animation ID for addressability purposes inside the language and information as to whether or not the animation loops.

AnimationStrip2D. We have found that in most cases of a spritesheet, the animations tend to be on a given line from left to right. Eberos GML2D models these with the AnimationStrip2D construct, which represents a single strip of frames on the spritesheet. The strip is composed of uniformly sized frames. This is a somewhat rigid construct that allows rapid specification of simple animations. Each instance of this construct contains information about a single animation such as the total number of frames, the size of the uniform frames, the position in the sprite image where the first frame appears, and the delay (in milliseconds) of each frame.

CompositeAnimation2D. There are also times when an animation inside the spritesheet might be made up of frames of different sizes, or frames that are not necesarily adjacent to one another; to model this kind of animation, we have the CompositeAnimation2D construct. A CompositeAnimation2D is another kind of Animation2D, and is used to represent animations at a deeper level of detail. Each CompositeAnimation2D is composed of one or more Frame2D.

Frame2D. A Frame2D represents a single frame of the animation. This construct gives a lower level of control over the modeling of the animations by allowing their spcification of an animation on a frame-by-frame basis. Each Frame2D contains information about its X and Y position on the source spritesheet, its width and height, its delay (in milliseconds), and its position in relation to other frames in the animation.

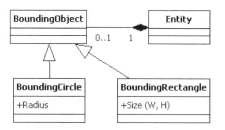

Figure 19.6. Basic class diagram for entity and collisions relationship.

19.1.5 Collisions Detection

Currently, the language only models bounding object collision detection with bounding rectangles and bounding circles. An entity in the game model becomes a candidate for collision detection when a `BoundingObject` is defined for it (see Figure 19.6). This means that now the entity can be a target for actuators that deal with collisions, as is the case for the `ConditionalActuator CheckCollision`. For Eberos GML2D, we only model two kinds of `BoundingObjects`: `BoundingRectangle` and `BoundingCircle`. The `BoundingRectangle` contains information about its width and height in pixels. Similarly, the `BoundingCircle` contains information about the size of its radius in pixels.

19.1.6 Input Handling

In Eberos GML2D, every entity reference is capable of having an `InputHandler` construct attached to it. When an entity has an `InputHandler`, it means that such an entity is controlled by an input device in some way. At the time this article was written, `InputHandler` only models keyboard input.

Keyboard input is modeled by adding a `KeyboardKey` to the `InputHandler` construct (see Figure 19.7). In Eberos GML2D, a `KeyboardKey` contains three pieces of information: the key to detect, the state of the key we are interested in, and the `GameMessage` to dispatch when the key and key state are matched. Currently, there are four possible states that can be modeled: `DOWN`, `RELEASED`, `WAS_PRESSED`, and `IS_HOLDING`. Once the input is matched, that is, the key specified is in the desired state, the entity attached to the `InputHandler` is notified of the `GameMessage` specified for that key. This `GameMessage` is then used as a link between the entity logic and the input.

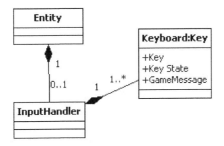

Figure 19.7. Basic class diagram for entity to input relationship.

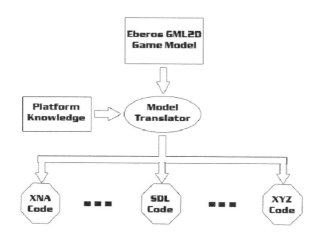

Figure 19.8. Model translation: Once the game model is created, it can be translated into source code for different underlying platforms.

19.2   Reducing Effort

Up to this point, we have presented the concepts we abstracted during the development of Eberos GML2D, which we found common in the 2D game domain. By doing this, we have taken would-be repetitive work and encapsulated it into simple language constructs. In implementation terms, we have taken what would have been repetitive code and reduced it to a simple operation. Also, by developing a language, we are now constrained by the language semantics and have reduced the number of errors that can be made during the development of these repetitive tasks. However, before we can profit from our language, we must first develop the means to translate it into implementation artifacts, such as source code or any other artifact specific to the desired technology (see Figure 19.8).

The final step before we can enjoy our saving of effort is to develop a translator for the language. This last step, however, does require some platform knowledge by the translators. That is, the translator must know what is the equivalent of the language on the target platform or engine. In our specific case, we have implemented translators for Microsoft's XNA and SDL, so our language constructs translate to either a set of classes or a set of function calls specific to the libraries.

In the case of our implementation, this abstraction meant reduction in the amount of code that was needed for items like state machine, animations, and game logic (see Figure 19.9), and an overall reduction of as much as 86.4% in the entire game code. Before Eberos GML2D, programming a state machine meant we would copy and paste most of the architecture code for each state class and

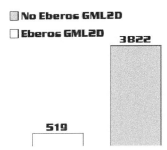

Figure 19.9. Number of lines of code a developer needs to write the same game to completion, both with the aid of Eberos GML2D and without. Results from experimental game *SpaceKatz*.

then modify it to add the code specific to the logic we wanted to implement. For state machines containing 20+ states, this was time consuming and error prone as mistakes would inevitably be made when linking the right states together. Currently, this process is developed graphically using Eberos GML2D, and the code is automatically generated, thus reducing the chances of programmer errors. Also, with the additions of the `CompositeActuators`, a large set of the code specific to each state has been reduced. Similarly, the code for input handling, animations, and collision handling has been partly automated.

19.3 Conclusion

In this article we describe the constructs, which we found during the development of the Eberos Game Modeling Language 2D to be common among all 2D games. We also describe some of the requirements to keep in mind while creating a game modeling language, and the possible effort amount such a language could reduce. This effort reduction, comes from abstracting common concepts into language constructs, which can then be used to express the game in this new intermediate language. Once the game is represented in this language, it can then be translated in order to generate artifacts to be used during the development of the game. In our specific case, we translated from Eberos GML2D models right into code. However, this model can in turn be translated into another language, which can model other components of the game not expressed by Eberos GML2D, thus reducing the effort even further than with Eberos GML2D alone. The Eberos GML2D presented here is not a complete language; there are still many concepts common to 2D games that it does not encapsulate. At its current stage, however, it has shown some promising results, and we hope that it will entice the reader to further explore the benefits that domain-specific languages can bring to the game development process.

Bibliography

[Buckland 05] Mat Buckland. *Programming Game AI by Example*, First edition. Plano, TX: Wordware Pub, 2005.

20

YAML for C++ :
Applied Data-Driven Design

Sebastien Noury and Samuel Boivin

20.1   Introduction

Data-driven design (DDD) is a way of organizing software so that the logic code is completely independent from the data structures on which it acts [Wilson 02]. This kind of design greatly reduces integration time in game projects where developers frequently iterate over the engine's code while artists and other content providers integrate their assets and finely tune the gameplay. When the code/data separation is not clear, incorporating these changes can be a daunting and time-consuming task for developers, especially when using a statically typed language like C++.

Many solutions exist to implement DDD principles, relying on various data formats, but most fail to address all of the following requirements at the same time:

- human legibility of the data;

- ease of integration into the code;

- support for structured data containers.

While data description languages are plentiful, ranging from the simple comma-separated values (CSV) format to the full-fledged XML format, very few of them address the aforementioned requirements needed for adoption on both sides of the equation: developers and content providers.

In this chapter, we first introduce YAML, a human-readable, structured data serialization language. Then, we present the yaml-cpp library for parsing YAML and provide a thin wrapper to seamlessly integrate it into C++ projects. Finally, we solve three real-world scenarios with our DDD solution to demonstrate its strengths and ease of use.

20.2 YAML Ain't Markup Language

Human readability is one of YAML's design goals. It is achieved by minimal use of structural characters. YAML's syntax is as minimally intrusive as possible, and it reads like natural note-taking: hierarchical structure is achieved through indentation, key-value pairs are associated with colons and lists are created using simple dashes.

We will briefly describe the most common elements of its syntax. Further detail can be found in the YAML 1.2 specification [Ben-Kiki et al. 09], freely available online. YAML's base type, known as scalar, can represent any primitive data type: strings, numbers, booleans, etc. These can be structured using two kinds of YAML containers: sequences and mappings, which can later be translated into C++ STL vectors and maps (Listing 20.1).

```
# mapping of scalars
pi: 3.1415
language: YAML

# sequence of scalars
- tutorial
- play
- options

# mapping of sequence of mappings of scalars
resolutions:
  - width: 1024
    height: 768
  - width: 800
    height: 600
```

Listing 20.1. Sample YAML syntax introducing hierarchical data structures.

These containers can be combined at will to describe the most complex data structures, as we will see in the last section of this article. YAML mappings and sequences can also be written in a more compact way, called flow style, to make them fit on a single line; for example, to represent colors, vectors, or matrices (Listing 20.2).

```
# mapping of sequence of scalars
gravity: [ 0, -9.81, 0 ]

# mapping of mapping of scalars
yellow: { r: 1.0, g: 1.0, b: 0.0, a: 1.0 }
```

Listing 20.2. Flow-style notation of YAML sequences and mappings.

YAML's natural flow is visually striking: unlike most markup languages, its syntax is not cluttered by cryptic tags, quotation marks, and redundancy. It can also be noted that YAML is a superset of the JavaScript Object Notation (JSON) [Crockford 06] since version 1.2, which means that a YAML parser can understand any JSON file. This language is widely used as a configuration and data interchange format on the Internet for its compactness and readability.

Two of our requirements for the adoption of DDD principles are achieved by YAML's simple but powerful syntax:

- Human legibility of the data,

- Support for structured data containers.

We can now focus on the last and most important requirement for developers: ease of integration into C++ code.

20.3 Seamless C++ Integration

Our goal is the seamless integration of YAML-defined data into C++ code with minimal wheel reinventing. We provide a thin wrapper for the yaml-cpp library [YCL 10], intended to exploit most of the features of this open-source project while having a single entry point for our game engine code.

```cpp
#include <yaml.h>

class Config
{
  public:
    typedef YAML::Node Node;
    Config(std::istream &input) throw();
    const Node &operator[](const std::string &key) const throw;

  protected:
    Node _doc;
};
```

Listing 20.3. Our minimal YAML configuration wrapper interface for C++.

The `Config` wrapper interface (Listing 20.3) is minimalist and achieves only two tasks: reading a single YAML document through its constructor, and accessing YAML elements through their YAML key path. The yaml-cpp library exploits modern C++ features like lexical casting and templated cast operators [Meyers 96], automagically translating YAML scalars, mappings, and sequences into C++ base types, STL maps, and vectors, whenever possible.

```
int main(int argc, char **argv)
{
  std::ifstream f("engine.yaml"); Config cfg(f);
  unsigned int width = cfg["screen/width"];
  unsigned int height = cfg["screen/height"];
  std::map<std::string, double> consts = cfg["constants"];
}
```

Listing 20.4. Excerpt from Engine.cpp, game engine implementation file.

The only extension we have added to yaml-cpp's implementation is the ability to access nested objects without necessarily chaining calls to the square-bracket operator ([]) by using the slash character (/) as a delimiter; see, for example, Listing 20.4.

Instead of describing every feature of our generic solution, we will demonstrate its strengths and practicality through three real-world scenarios, thus validating the third requirement for DDD adoption: ease of integration into C++ code.

20.4 Applying DDD to Real-World Scenarios

20.4.1 General Engine Configuration

Our wrapper can be used for simple configuration, to read key/value pairs from a YAML file (Listing 20.5). When values are nested, hierarchical key paths can be used to directly access them. Scalar values can be deserialized into basic C++ types like int, double, or std::string, while mapping and sequence structures can be automatically deserialized into the appropriate STL containers without having to explicitly specify their type (Listing 20.4).

```
screen:            # each key/value under "screen" will
  width: 1920      #   be read independently
  height: 1080
constants:         # the whole "constants" mapping will
  e: 2.7183        #   be read in one row in a std::map
  pi: 3.1415
```

Listing 20.5. Excerpt from engine.yaml, configuration file read by Engine.cpp.

20.4.2 Data-Driven Class Deserialization

More complex classes can be deserialized from YAML node objects by extending them with the C++ right stream operator (>>). This way, we can read an arbitrary number of engine classes in any container at runtime and use standard STL iterators to loop through them inside the logic code, maintaining zero dependency with the game data (Listing 20.6).

```cpp
struct float3 { float x, y, z;};

struct Player
{
  std::string name;
  unsigned int life;
  float3 position;
};

void operator>>(const Node &n, float3 &f3)
{
  assert(n.GetTag() == "!float3"); // optional type-check
  n[0] >> f3.x; n[1] >> f3.y; n[2] >> f3.z;
}

void operator>>(const Node &n, Player &p)
{
  assert(n.GetTag() == "!Player"); // optional type-check
  n["name"] >> p.name;
  n["life"] >> p.life;
  n["position"] >> p.position;
}

int main(int argc, char **argv)
{
  std::ifstream f(argv[1]); Config cfg(f);
  std::vector<Player> players = cfg["players"];
  return 0;
}
```

Listing 20.6. Sample C++ code for the deserialization of Player and float3 objects.

Stronger type checking can be enabled with YAML's tagging feature. Each scalar can be assigned an arbitrary number of tags, preceded by an exclamation

```yaml
players:
  - !Player
    name: Player 1
    life: 100
    position: !float3 [1.0, 0.0, 0.0]
  - !Player
    name: Player 2
    life: 80
    position: !float3 [0.0, 1.0, 0.0]
```

Listing 20.7. Sample YAML description of Player and float3 objects.

point, to associate meta-information with the data. We can use this feature to enhance our deserialization by making sure that the data responds to the correct interface we intend to map it to (Listing 20.7).

20.4.3   A DirectX Effects-like File Format for OpenGL

Finally, we introduce the last element of YAML's syntax: aliases. Aliases are analogous to C pointers, the & character creates a named anchor and the * character points to this anchor. This process is entirely transparent for the configuration parser: the aliased nodes look like they have been duplicated.

This kind of behavior is useful for cases where data structures can be reused multiple times in order to avoid redundancy and reduce errors. We illustrate this scenario with a very simple metashader file format, similar to DirectX's Effects files, where multiple shaders can be combined into sequential passes to form techniques (Listing 20.8).

Of course, other creative uses of YAML's scalars, containers, tags, and aliases can be thought of to answer the many problems encountered in game development. We leave these as an exercise for the reader.

```
phong_vs: &phongvs
  varying vec3 N, v;
  void main()
  {
    v = vec3(gl_ModelViewMatrix * gl_Vertex);
    N = normalize(gl_NormalMatrix * gl_Normal);
    gl_Position = gl_ModelViewProjectionMatrix * gl_Vertex;
  }

phong_fs: &phongfs
  varying vec3 N, v;
  void main()
  {
    vec3 L = normalize(gl_LightSource[0].position.xyz - v);
    vec4 Idiff = gl_FrontLightProduct[0].diffuse *
                                  max(dot(N, L), 0.0);
    gl_FragColor = clamp(Idiff, 0.0, 1.0);
  }

techniques
  - name: PhongShading
    passes:
    - name: PhongPass0
      vertex_shader: *phongvs
      fragment_shader: *phongfs
```

Listing 20.8. DirectX effects-like definition of a simple Phong lighting shader.

20.5 Conclusion

We have presented a simple and efficient data-driven design solution for C++ projects based on the YAML data description language. This solution successfully meets adoption requirements both on the developers' and the artists' side by making it easy to integrate structured and human-readable data into C++ code at runtime.

The yaml-cpp library, on which our solution is based, can also serialize C++ classes into YAML through its emitter. This is very useful to save game states and objects or to exchange structured objects over a network. Moreover, as YAML is a widely adopted standard, many other languages, like Python or Ruby, have YAML bindings and can be used to quickly develop new tools. A full list of these bindings and supported languages can be found on YAML's website, http://yaml.org/.

Bibliography

[Ben-Kiki et al. 09] Oren Ben-Kiki, Clark Evans, and Brian Ingerson. "YAML Ain't Markup Language (YAML™) Version 1.2." Available at http://yaml.org/spec/1.2/spec.html, 2009.

[Crockford 06] Douglas Crockford. "RFC 4627: The Application/JSON Media Type for JavaScript Object Notation (JSON)." Available at http://www.ietf.org/rfc/rfc4627, 2006.

[Meyers 96] Scott Meyers. *More Effective C++*. Reading, MA: Addison-Wesley Professional, 1996.

[Wilson 02] Kyle Wilson. "Data-Driven Design." Available at http://www.gamearchitect.net/Articles/DataDrivenDesign.html, 2002.

[YCL 10] "yaml-cpp—A YAML Parser and Emitter for C++." Available at http://code.google.com/p/yaml-cpp/, 2010.

21

GPU Debugging and Profiling with NVIDIA Parallel Nsight

Kumar Iyer and Jeffrey Kiel

21.1 Introduction

Over the last few years, the programmability of GPU hardware has exploded in capability and popularity. Games routinely have hundreds of shaders per rendered frame. In addition, a new generation of games expands the use of the GPU even further by using DirectCompute, CUDA C/C++, and other GPGPU technologies to simulate physics, particles, image space effects, animation, and more.

NVIDIA Parallel Nsight is a development tool integrated into Microsoft Visual Studio that can help you debug and profile the rendering and GPGPU code in your game. Any application using Direct3D 10 or 11, running on a Tesla class chip or beyond, can utilize the powerful Parallel Nsight features inside the Visual Studio 2008 and 2010 IDEs. The graphics API inspection capability, simple frame profiling, and some of the tracing capabilities are available when running on graphics hardware from other vendors, including AMD and Intel.

In this chapter, we'll show you how to use Parallel Nsight to

- capture a Direct3D frame live and scrub through draw calls in real time to see how the rendered frame gets built;

- debug the source of your Direct3D HLSL shaders, including pixel, vertex, compute, hull, and domain shaders using the standard Microsoft Visual Studio source debugging tools and workflows;

- find out if you are CPU or GPU bound;

- find the most expensive draw calls in your frame, both on the CPU and GPU;

- profile expensive draw calls, using metrics for each draw call like CPU time, GPU time, hardware unit bottleneck, utilization, shaded pixel, pixel count, and primitive count;

- trace activities across both your CPU and GPU.

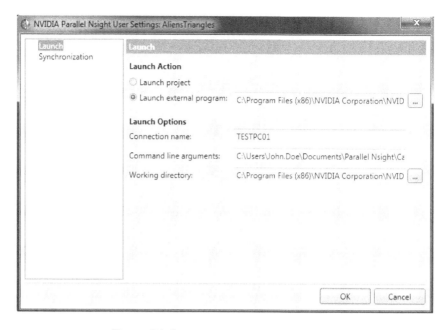

Figure 21.1. Parallel Nsight user settings.

21.2   Debugging a Full Direct3D Frame with the Graphics Inspector

21.2.1   Setting Up Your Application

There are two configurations you can use to run your application with Parallel Nsight. If you are just going to use the API inspection features, called the Graphics Inspector, you can run on the local system and still be able to inspect the state of the Direct3D runtime at each point in the frame, as well as profile a frame using the Frame Profiler. If you would like to debug a shader, you will need to set up to run on a remote machine because the GPU that is running the application will also be running the Visual Studio GUI, which means you cannot interact with it after a breakpoint has been hit.

When you right-click on the project, you can select Parallel Nsight Settings from the menu, allowing you to configure how Parallel Nsight will run (see Figure 21.1). For running locally, simply leave the Connection name as "localhost", and change it to the proper machine name for remote debugging. Also, you can tell Parallel Nsight just to run the normal output from the project or to give it an external program to run, as well as specifying the command line options and working directory. Finally, Parallel Nsight can sync files from the host to the target, which can be especially useful with small projects. The second screen allows you to specify what directories and file extensions to synchronize. Obviously, this is not efficient when running with exceptionally large data files, so you can disable syncing and simply use a network share to access the files from both the host and target.

21.2.2   Capturing a Direct3D Frame

The typical workflow for debugging applications is to run them over and over until you see a problem and then try to reproduce that problem by replicating the steps that lead to the bug. Once you have a reproducible case, you then go through the typical debugging cycle of instrumentation and inspection, code modification and recompilation, and retry the scenario. This is a reasonable workflow, but can be tedious because of the long turnaround time from bug detection to testing the fix.

Parallel Nsight improves this workflow by allowing the developer to capture entire frames of rendering calls while the application in question is still running. So, instead of having to exit the application and try to reproduce an issue, the developer can capture the bug while the application is still running and inspect the call stream and the state of the Direct3D runtime for the cause.

When the frame is captured, Parallel Nsight intercepts all of the timing functions in the system so that the application will not change any state (world updates, physics, animation, etc.). All of these systems will need to handle a very small or even zero time delta properly to prevent application errors, and possible divide by zero crashes. The easiest thing to do is to check the time delta at the top of the routine and exit out early if the delta is 0 or so small that the system cannot handle it.

If postmortem analysis is preferred, say, when trying to illustrate an issue with a coworker, these saved frames can be serialized to disk and reloaded. This saved frame can also be used as representative benchmark frames, for reporting bugs to IHVs, and more.

Finally, the developer can exit the captured frame and return to the application, which was dormant during that analysis session. The application will come back to life right where the developer left off and from there he or she can continue playing the game, looking for other issues to debug or analyze for performance.

21.2.3   Understanding Your Frame's Structure

Modern engines typically use a number of different passes on their frame database to construct the final image. Shadow pass, Z prepass, albedo pass, even full-fledged deferred rendering are all examples of multipass techniques. Then, once the scene is rendered, many applications do any number of full-screen effects for HDR rendering, glow effects, depth of field, etc., in order to achieve an amazing cinematic quality in the final rendering. On top of all of this, there is a huge process distance between an artist constructing some assets, running that through a content pipeline to prepare

Figure 21.2. Scrubbing in the HUD. (See Color Plate XXVI.)

it for rendering, loading it into the engine, and finally rendering it on the screen. All of this complexity makes it difficult to understand certain levels of details, such as why a certain pixel is the color that it is.

Parallel Nsight allows you to scroll, or scrub, through each draw call in your frame and watch the scene as it is constructed through the various passes. We typically call it scrubbing because it is similar to interacting with a video clip where you scrub frame by frame to see a scene unfold. This scrubbing can be done both through the HUD, right on top of the application (see Figure 21.2), and also on the host from within Visual Studio.

It is often useful to see the entire frame at a glance. This is why Parallel Nsight starts on the Frames Page when entering the Graphics Inspector. This screen provides an overview of the captured frame(s), including Actions (clears, draw calls, dispatch calls, etc.), and Direct3D performance markers. There is a marker for the current scrub location that you can select and move with the left mouse button. Note that as you scrub on the host, the target will update the current location and vice versa.

As you scrub through the scene, you can look for different errors in the scene like rendering calls that have no impact on the final image, maybe because the rendering

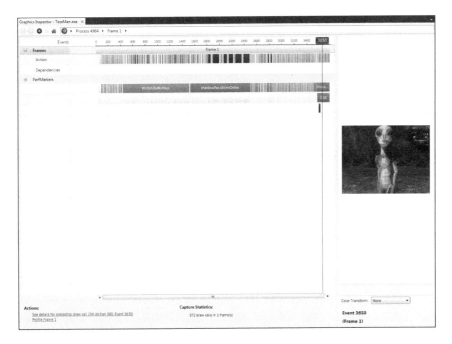

Figure 21.3. The Frames Page.

is off-screen or so small that the object is not noticeable. Another example is rendering that happens before a clear, or even examples of bad portal culling where you render objects within a room or space, only to draw a wall or other large structure on top of them. You can also see hard-to-find errors like the drawing of opaque objects back to front, which hurts your performance because you won't take advantage of fast z-culling hardware. Another surprising bug can be double rendering of portions of the scene, which is nearly impossible to see without this type of scene decomposition.

Underneath the Actions line on the Frames Page (see Figure 21.3) is the Dependencies line. This line shows producers and consumers of the currently selected draw call. For instance, say you do a shadow pass to determine the distance of an object from a light source. This is the "production" of a given resource. When you render that object later in the frame, you "consume" that resource when you read the depth back and compare it to the current distance to the light, showing if the fragment is lit or in shadow. When you click on the second rendering call, you will see a line or a link back to the shadow pass call(s) that produced the light's depth map.

This can be useful for performance tuning because you can look for draw calls that consume a resource immediately after it is written to. This will usually require the GPU to flush all of the current work in order to make sure that all updates have completed before kicking off the new draw calls. It is also helpful in debugging because you can check to make sure that the correct resources are used at all stages in rendering the scene.

Finally, something that you can do to help absorb and differentiate all of the actions and various passes in the Frames Page is to use Direct3D performance markers. You can use these to annotate the frame and each pass within the frame so you can understand what each draw call in the pass does. The screenshot in Figure 21.3 shows how the performance markers are visualized under the Dependencies line. The API used for this functionality is `D3DPERF_BeginEvent` and `D3DPERF_EndEvent`.

21.2.4   Debugging Textures and Render Targets

Once you find a draw call of interest, you naturally will want to inspect all of the Direct3D setup as well as the resources used for that draw call. You can double-click a draw call on the Frames Page, or click the link in the lower-left corner to begin drilling down through all of that information.

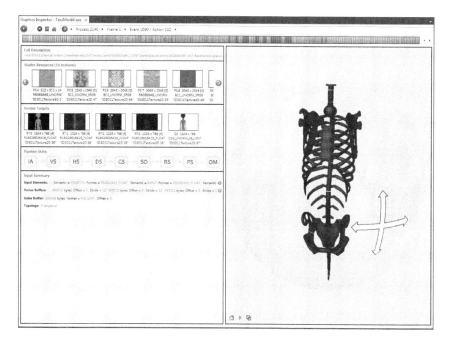

Figure 21.4. The Draw Call Page. (See Color Plate XXVII.)

When you enter the Draw Call Page (see Figure 21.4), you will see on the right-hand side a display of the pretransform geometry submitted to the GPU. On the left-hand side, you can see all of the bound resources, both input resources like textures and output resources or render targets. You can use this first-level screen to make sure the geometry looks reasonable and that the resources that are bound are the ones you expected and are useful. For example, if the diffuse map was incorrectly identified in a Collada file in the art pipeline, you would see it here.

You can click on the textures to enter the Texture Inspector (see Figure 21.5), which allows you to inspect each slice of a 3D texture, face of a cubemap, and mip level to make sure that the data is correct: maybe the texture is supposed to be compressed but is not. Since you can see size and format information as well, these types of bugs are easy to spot. Even the view information can be inspected to determine, for instance, if the proper sampling method is being used. For example, you may wonder "why is anisotropic filtering enabled for screen aligned billboards?" That would be some wasted performance.

Another good use of the Texture Page is to debug generated textures, even ones produced by DirectCompute calls. You can click on the resource, look at it in the inspector, and even click the link in the lower left-hand corner to inspect the resource as a data buffer instead of as a texture. From the data view, you can recast the data as unsigned-integer or floating-point values, looking for values that are incorrect.

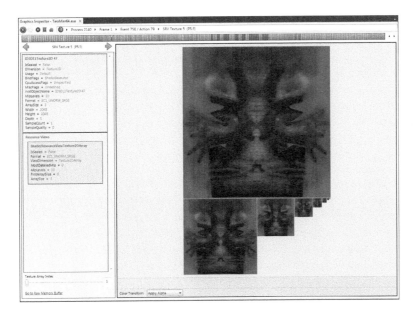

Figure 21.5. The Texture Page. (See Color Plate XXVIII.)

For depth textures and other floating-point data, you can use the histogram feature to remap the float values into the 0.0–1.0 display space. If a certain part of the dynamic range is more populated in the histogram, move the sliders to either side of the range to remap it for easy display, allowing you to see details that might have otherwise remained invisible.

21.2.5 Inspecting API State

The next area of inspection is seen on the left-hand side of the screen. Every point along the GPU pipeline exposed via the Direct3D API has an entry in the graph. You can click, for instance, on the Output Merger stage and look at blend state. Maybe the scrubber (shown at the top of the window) is on a draw call that is part of the opaque geometry (as annotated by the Direct3D performance markers), but blending is enabled. This could cause issues with pixel throughput, hurting performance.

Every bit of the Direct3D state can be easily inspected from these screens. While scrubbing through your depth prepass or your shadow pass, make sure, for instance, that color writes are disabled. Another problematic setting can be the winding order for backface culling. Don't see geometry on the screen? Enter the Graphics Inspector, make sure the pretransform geometry is correct, and look at the winding order.

21.2.6 Using Pixel History

A common question asked when looking at the final output of the renderer is, "Why is this pixel the color that it is?" In the past, you would have to use some difficult debugging techniques to try and see all fragments that contributed to a given pixel, like eliminating draw calls, limiting the geometry for a given draw call, maybe even using printf! Parallel Nsight has a feature to show you exactly why a pixel wound up a certain color: Pixel History (see Figure 21.6).

The way to access this feature is to use the scrubber to the point in the frame, or beyond, where you see the rendering issue. Then, go to the Draw Call Page, as detailed above, and click on the render target that shows the pixel in question. In the lower-right corner is a link called Pick Pixel. This will change the cursor to red and allow you to select the pixel of interest. Once you do, you will see a list of fragments that were blended to create the pixel. Select the one with the output color that seems to be the problem and you can then select Debug Pixel, and the debugger will put a sophisticated conditional breakpoint into the code to isolate the fragment in question. This will allow you to step through the pixel shader and inspect local variables, as well as calculation results, to determine what went wrong.

Because the Pixel History feature utilizes many of the HLSL debugger features, you will need to run this on a remote machine to ensure that the Visual Studio GUI remains accessible.

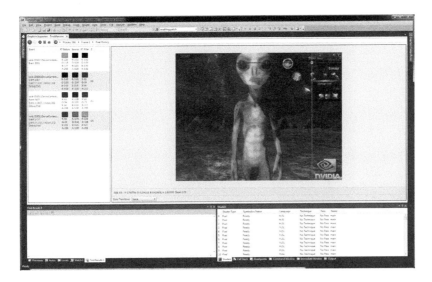

Figure 21.6. The Pixel History Page.

21.3 Debugging an HLSL Shader

The Parallel Nsight Shader Debugger allows the debugging of any type of Direct3D HLSL shader, including pixel, vertex, geometry, tessellation, and compute shaders. In addition, it does so using the same Microsoft Visual Studio user interface and key bindings used for debugging CPU code.

Parallel Nsight actually debugs graphics and computes shaders directly on the GPU hardware, so debugging shaders inside a game is significantly faster and more accurate. Because this requires special hardware features, it is only available on NVIDIA hardware.

The following sections cover how to debug shaders in Parallel Nsight, including how to find the shader you'd like to debug, how to set breakpoints (including hardware conditional breakpoints), and how to inspect shader variables.

21.3.1 Finding a Shader to Debug

One difference between debugging your code on the CPU and debugging shader code on the GPU is that the game must submit shader code to the GPU through an API, such as Direct3D. Shader code also often does not reside on disk, and it can be generated at runtime or embedded in CPU source code directly as a literal and may be pieced together from a number of snippets. Thus, the only way to find the source code for a particular shader is to use the Parallel Nsight Shaders tool window or the Debug this Pixel link from a Pixel History.

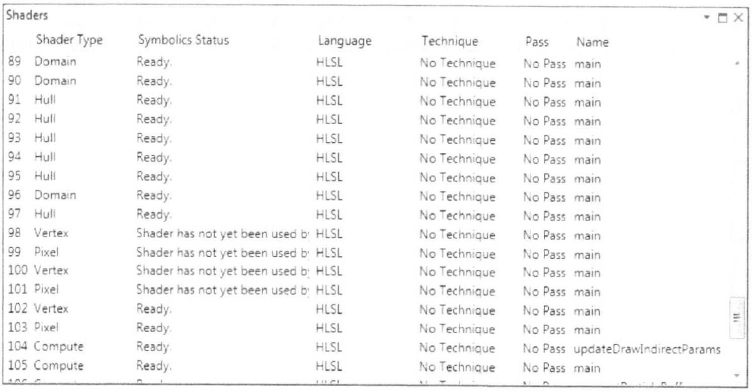

Figure 21.7. The Shaders tool window.

Using the shaders tool window. The Parallel Nsight Shaders tool window offers a straightforward way to see all shaders that have been loaded by your application. Once your game is launched and starts loading shaders, this tool window automatically populates with information about these shaders (see Figure 21.7).

Double-clicking a shader in this window will open the source code for that shader, and at that point the shader can be debugged like other source code in Visual Studio (described in Section 21.3.2).

Using the Debug Pixel in Pixel History. Pixel History (see Section 21.2.6) offers another way to find and debug a shader specific to pixel shaders. This feature shows all operations (draw and clear calls) that affected a given pixel on a render target. Once you have run the Pixel History, described above, you can select Debug Pixel to focus the debugger on the given pixel and shader.

21.3.2   Source Debugging of Shaders

Once the desired shader is identified, debugging a shader is nearly identical to debugging any other type of code inside Microsoft Visual Studio. Halt execution anywhere in the shader using standard breakpoints, view local variables and conditionals, switch to other active primitives in flight using the Graphics Debug Focus, and even set conditional breakpoints that execute on the hardware to detect and halt on any specific user-defined reason. The major advantage is that everything is running on the hardware, so it is very fast, and you are seeing the exact values the hardware is using to calculate any given output instead of a CPU simulation of them.

Breakpoints. A key feature of any source debugger is the ability to set a breakpoint at a particular line of source code, such that the executing code halts at the location of the breakpoint. Once halted, the state of the program and the state of the hardware can be examined in detail.

Parallel Nsight allows source breakpoints to be set in HLSL source code using the standard Visual Studio keybindings and mouse gestures by either left-clicking at the left of the line of source, or by using the Debug > Toggle Breakpoint menu item.

Parallel Nsight also supports parallel and graphics-aware conditional breakpoints, in which a breakpoint only halts at a line of source if a user-supplied conditional expression evaluates to true. Using conditional breakpoints in Parallel Nsight is an incredibly powerful way to debug highly parallel problems on the GPU, as using a parallel-aware expression can allow you to stop the execution of GPU on exactly the graphics primitives or threads desired.

For example, take the following pixel shader:

```
PS_OUTPUT RenderScenePS( VS_OUTPUT In,
                         uniform bool bTexture )
{
    PS_OUTPUT Output;

    // Lookup mesh texture and
    // modulate it with diffuse
    if( bTexture )
        Output.RGBColor = tex2D(MeshTextureSampler,
                                In.TextureUV)
                                * In.Diffuse;
    else
        Output.RGBColor = In.Diffuse;

    return Output;
}
```

If this shader at times appears to generate fragments with the red component incorrectly high, simply add a breakpoint to the last line of the shader, and then add a conditional expression to the breakpoint:

```
Output.RGBColor.r > .9
```

This breakpoint will only break when that shader is executed and when the color values' red component has a value greater than .9. You can specify complex conditionals and still maintain great performance because everything is evaluated in hardware. There is virtually no penalty for conditionals.

Stepping through shader or compute code. Another key feature of a source debugger is the ability to step line by line over subsequent lines of code, once halted at a breakpoint. Stepping in this fashion allows a developer to debug control logic, such as series of if/then/else statements, or to debug mathematical expressions by stepping and watching how the variable values change after each step.

Parallel Nsight supports two stepping commands: Step In and Step Over. On a line of source code that contains no function calls, both of these step commands simply execute the current line of source code pointed to by the program counter and moves the program counter to the next line of source.

However, if the source line does contain a function call, Step In will step to the actual next line of source code to be executed, which is the first line in the function called from the current line of source. Conversely, Step Over will execute all instructions executed by the function call and will increment the program counter to the next line of source code in the current scope.

You can also use the Run To Cursor functionality of Visual Studio, but as of Version 1.5 of Parallel Nsight, the Set Next Statement function does not work when debugging HLSL shader code.

Inspecting variables and evaluating expressions while debugging. Once stopped at the source line of interest, another important capability is the ability to see the values of variables in the source code.

To accomplish this, Parallel Nsight fully supports the built-in Visual Studio Locals and Watches tool windows. These windows are active once the debugger has stopped at a particular line of code and show you the value of variables (Locals) or user-defined expressions (Watches) in the current debug focus.

The Locals Window is populated automatically with all variables local to the scope where the program counter is pointing, while the Watches window allows a developer to enter an arbitrary expression to be evaluated in that same context. Both windows can be used in combination with breakpoints and stepping to view the values at particular places in the computation. As of Version 1.5 of Parallel Nsight, you cannot set the value for any variables.

The Graphics Debug Focus. Thus far, the functionality of the Parallel Nsight shader debugger has focused on debugging a single primitive, for example, a pixel. However, GPUs are inherently parallel processors, and as such, there are often several primitives in flight on the GPU at any one time. When halted at a breakpoint in a shader, the Graphics Debug Focus tool window offers a way to switch focus to any other active primitive on the GPU (see Figure 21.8). Switching focus will also switch the Locals and the Watch tool windows to show information and evaluate expressions in the context of the newly focused primitive's code.

Switching focus to a different primitive type or shader will also switch the current program counter in Visual Studio. The Graphics Debug Focus always opens on a summary page, which shows you all of the different primitives currently in flight. Primitive-specific context and visualization can be found by switching to the primitive-specific tabs, such as the pixel or the vertex tab.

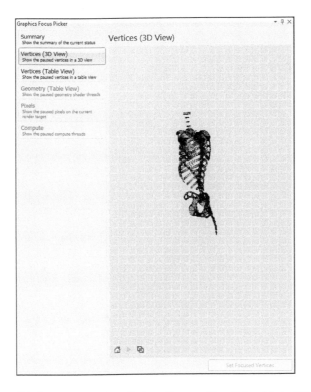

Figure 21.8. The Graphics Debug Focus. (See Color Plate XXIX.)

The pixel tab shows all the render targets currently bound and overlays in red the active pixels currently being processed for each target. Double-clicking on an active pixel will switch the debugger's focus to that pixel.

The vertex tab similarly shows a point cloud of the submitted geometry, with the vertices currently in flight on the GPU highlighted. Double-clicking a vertex will switch focus to that vertex. There is also a tabular view of vertex data available.

21.4 Profiling a Direct3D Frame using GPU Hardware Counters

21.4.1 CPU versus GPU Bound

When tuning your application in a heterogeneous, multiprocessor setup, you first need to determine which processor is your bottleneck. This is best determined in the HUD while looking at the performance graphs that are overlaid on your application (see Figure 21.9).

Figure 21.9. The HUD showing performance graphs. (See Color Plate XXX.)

There are many performance counters that are available for graphing in this application, and they vary from GPU to GPU. In general, they are either counting something (vertices processed, pixels generated, etc.) or giving overall utilization percentages (`gpu_busy`, shader unit busy, etc.). These are set up on the host by selecting the Graphics HUD Control entry from the Nsight menu. This will bring up the HUD Configuration screen, which will allow you to create new graphs, remove graphs, change the signals and names on each graph, etc.

In order to determine if you are CPU or GPU bound, the easiest test is to graph the `gpu_idle` signal. If this falls to approximately 10% or less, you are likely getting GPU bound, and tuning your frame on the GPU would make sense. If you are 10% or more `gpu_idle`, then your bottleneck is likely on the CPU, and tools like Intel VTune or AMD CodeAnalyst will be helpful in tuning your CPU code.

21.4.2   Finding Expensive Draw Calls

Once you have determined that you are GPU bound, you can use Parallel Nsight to profile an exemplary frame and give you real feedback on where the bottlenecks are in the GPU pipeline. Start by finding a scene that shows the poor performance you are trying to analyze. When you have found it, enter the Graphics Inspector by pressing the space bar on the HUD or by selecting the Pause and Capture Frame entry in the Nsight menu in Visual Studio. This will capture the frame as outlined

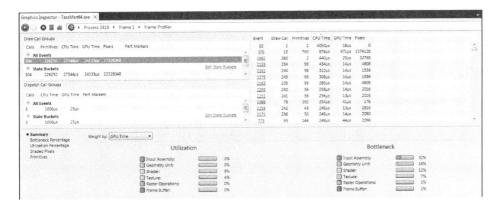

Figure 21.10. The Frame Profiler Results Page.

in Section 21.2.1. You can profile the frame by clicking the Profile Frame link in the lower-left corner of the Frames Page.

Once you have selected the Frame Profiler, Parallel Nsight will run a series of experiments on the captured frame, collecting bottleneck and utilization data-key points in the GPU pipeline. Depending on the GPU architecture, this can take 40–50 passes on the same frame, so be patient, and you will be rewarded. If you are running on non-NVIDIA hardware, you will see a limited amount of information, including primitive counts and draw call duration.

When the profiler is finished, it will show a number of lists on the top of the screen along with some graphs below (see Figure 21.10). If you select the top-most entry on the top-left list, this will show you, in the list box to the right, all of the draw calls in the frame along with some useful data. First, the draw calls will be sorted by GPU time consumed. You can of course select other columns to sort by, but if you are GPU bound, this is helpful to determine which draw call is the most expensive (more on this in Section 21.4.3). The draw call list also shows CPU time spent, primitives drawn, and pixels drawn. If you want to see all of the details about a given draw call, click the link in the first column, and it will bring you to the Draw Call Page discussed in Section 21.2.3. From there, you can check for things like missing mipmaps and blending modes set improperly, etc. More on this in Section 21.4.4. To get back to the Frame Profiler Results Page, simply select the back arrow in the navigation bar.

Another important thing to look for in this list is draw calls that take a long time and potentially render a lot of primitives but only modify a few pixels. This means you are spending a lot of precious resources on something that does not contribute much to the scene. You can fix this by using level of detail (LOD) models, shaders, and/or resources to reduce the workload on the GPU for these less important objects in the scene.

21.4.3   Grouping Draw Calls by State

Another useful feature of the Frame Profiler Results Page is the ability to group draw calls by common state, or what we call a State Bucket. The general idea is that you can make a single improvement that applies to a whole bucket of draw calls, the sum or which is actually greater than the single largest draw call. By clicking on the Create State Buckets link, a dialog will come up allowing you to use any state criteria to group the draw calls. If you are more shader bound, then grouping by shader is a good way to see all of the draw calls that share a shader or group of shaders. One optimization to the shader will possibly result in the performance improving for all of the draw calls.

21.4.4   Using Bottleneck and Utilization to Direct Optimization

Now that you have all of this data, how do you analyze it to determine where to focus your optimization energy? Start by selecting the draw call or state bucket that is most interesting to you. This could be the one with the most elapsed GPU or CPU time, highest number of primitives drawn or pixels generated, etc. When you select this, you will see multiple graphs on the bottom of the screen that show you both state bucket and per-draw call information.

The Summary Graph gives bottleneck and utilization information for all draw calls in the current bucket. These can be weighted by a number of different factors including pixel or primitive count and GPU time. This is useful in finding situations as stated above: draw calls that don't contribute a lot to the scene or don't consume a lot of GPU time causing you to focus your efforts on a GPU pipeline state that doesn't give the largest optimization return. So, if you care more about GPU time, sort by that. If percent contribution to the scene makes more sense, sort by pixel count.

The graphs show utilization and bottleneck information measured at six locations in the GPU pipeline. Utilization is a measurement of activity, and ideally, you want this to be high, as it means that you are giving plenty of work to the GPU to keep it busy. Bottleneck is a measurement of how often the given unit prevents downstream units from getting work done. This will help you determine where to reduce work, or at least how to make it more efficient, in order to improve overall performance and frame rate.

Input Assembly. This is the unit that brings together all of the vertex input streams and constructs the attributes for a given vertex. This can be a bottleneck if you have too many attributes for the given hardware you are running on. Packing attributes as much as possible, or using smaller attribute types like 16-bit indices or bytes instead of floats, is the key for solving this bottleneck. Also, if you click on one of the draw call IDs, make sure that you aren't passing unneeded vertex attributes to the call, such as unused texture coordinates, etc.

Geometry Unit. This unit is responsible for distributing the primitives to various computational units. If this is the bottleneck, the only likely solution is to reduce geometric complexity. Now, if you look at the pixel count, you might see, as stated earlier, that you have a high primitive count with a low pixel count, which means you are wasting all of that geometry and should look at your level of detail (LOD) system to help.

Shader. This is the workhorse of the modern GPU. All of your shaders, vertex through pixel, get processed by this unit. Even though this is true, if the Shader Unit is your bottleneck, you can still potentially see some improvements by rebalancing where you perform work. Ask yourself: Do all of the operations in your pixel shader have to be computed per pixel? Can this work be done per vertex and interpolated across the triangle face? Can the calculation be prebaked into a texture and made into a simple sampling call? Back to LOD: is the contribution of this shader so small or unlikely to be appreciated because of distance to the camera that you can actually run a simpler shader? All of these techniques still apply even though the units are shared because it can reduce the number of times you run the shader since they are all just threads running in the Shader Unit.

Texture. The Texture Unit can feed the Shader Unit no matter what type of shader it is running. Textures aren't just for pixel shaders, but can be displacement maps for vertex or geometry shaders. If the bottleneck information reads high for the Texture Unit, the main things to look at are compression, mipmaps, and sampling setup. There can be quality concerns, but most diffuse textures can be compressed with no loss of image fidelity. Normal maps and other textures that contain mathematical data can be a little more susceptible to artifacts, but experimentation is the only way to determine if it will be a concern. If possible, make sure you are using mipmaps to help with memory access locality. Click on one of the draw calls to inspect the input resources. You can also see if the appropriate sampling mode (point, bilinear, anisotropic, etc.) is being used, and be judicious with your choice of sampling. Bilinear and trilinear can handle many cases just fine. Anisotropic is expensive and will show no improvement for rendering that is always screen aligned. Finally, if you have shader cycles to spare (look at the utilization graph for the Shader Unit), you can consider moving a precalculated texture (like noise or something similar) into the shader, saving some of the texture work

Raster operations. This unit is also called Output Merger in the DirectX specifications. This is where the read/modify/write operation is done when blending is enabled, but can also have work when performing a lot of z-comparisons or converting the output of your shader into a different format. The best optimization strategy for the Raster Operations unit is to limit what it has to do. Can you disable blending? Can you disable it based on level of detail? Of course, making sure that you render your opaque geometry front to back will help as well and will also potentially free up Shader and Texture Unit cycles along the way. Finally, reducing the size of render targets, especially if they are intermediate targets, can be helpful here as well.

Frame buffer. This is the interface into the memory subsystem, and all requests for reads and writes go through the Frame Buffer unit. Because it is shared, many of the suggestions mentioned above apply, but the biggest culprit of bottleneck is typically related to pixel throughput. Since pixels are likely your highest number of items, or threads, processed, reducing them is going to reduce Frame Buffer overhead. Along with that, make sure you are using only the render target and resource formats you have to use. Compressing textures whenever you can and using floating-point formats sparingly are all good ways to reduce Frame Buffer activity and free up this bottleneck.

21.5 Tracing Activity across Your CPU and GPU

Games are among the most demanding applications that a PC can run. They stress all parts of the system, including the CPU, the GPU, and the system bus (PCI-E). Typical profilers, including the Parallel Nsight Frame Profiler (Section 21.4), focus on only a single API or subsystem, but offer no clues as to how well the different APIs and subsystems work together. The Parallel Nsight Analyzer is a post-mortem tool that addresses this need by collecting and visualizing data about how the game utilizes the system across several subsystems and APIs.

Supported subsystems and APIs include the CPU (threads, processes, cores, and custom events), graphics APIs (Direct3D, OpenGL), and GPGPU APIs (CUDA C/C++, OpenCL, DirectCompute). In addition, while many profiling tools significantly change the runtime characteristics of the game they are profiling, the Analyzer's system trace is very low-overhead, and thus delivers an accurate picture of system activity, with only minimal timing changes due to the trace itself. The Analyzer works on any CPU and GPU hardware, but no GPU Performance Counters are available on non-NVIDIA hardware.

21.5.1 Configuring and Capturing a Trace

Configuring a trace is simple and requires only specifying the APIs and options to be traced (see Figure 21.11). For most of the subsystems, no instrumentation, either manual or automatic, is required, and you may run the trace on any program, even programs that are binary-only or lack symbols. The one exception to this rule is NVIDIA Tools Extension events, which are powerful custom events.

Each API/subsystem has several options where you can enable and disable the tracing of specific event types. In particular, consider the expected frequency of an event when choosing to trace it. First, high frequency events contribute to overhead of the trace, as there are approximately two microseconds of overhead

Figure 21.11. System trace configuration.

per API call traced. The overhead for tracing other events is significantly smaller. Second, high frequency events can dominate the Timeline and other reporting views, leading to large number of irrelevant events to sort through. While the Timeline has powerful filtering capabilities, it is often still more efficient to disable the trace of high frequency events in favor of concentrating on the events of interest.

21.5.2 Viewing CPU, GPGPU, and Graphics Workloads on the Timeline

CPU utilization and core allocation. The Timeline View displays data from your CPU across the capture period, including utilization graphs per CPU Core, and CPU Core allocation events (see Figure 21.12).

The Core Allocation rows (one per CPU core) are particularly interesting, as each interval on one of these rows represents a CPU thread that was allocated onto the core. Threads from the game process are highlighted (in green), allowing fast visual searching for other processes that also got allocated to a core during the capture period.

CPU Thread state is also shown on separate thread rows underneath the process node, with red areas indicating that the thread was in a wait state and green areas indicating that the thread was executing normally. Games with a large number of

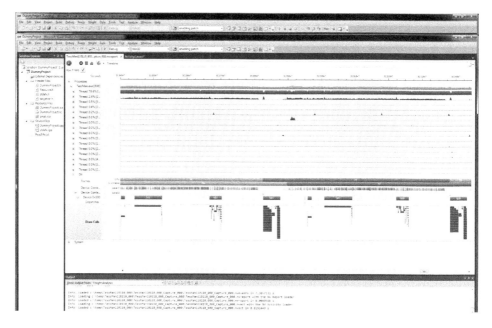

Figure 21.12. CPU utilization from the trace.

threads waiting are either not CPU bound or may not be efficiently utilizing the available cores.

GPU workloads and memory transfers. The Parallel Nsight Analyzer is also capable of displaying workloads as they are executed on the GPU, including draw calls and memory transfer events (see Figure 21.13).

This information is useful for determining when a given draw call is actually executed on the GPU and what calls are potentially stalled waiting for the results of a previous draw call.

Using custom ranges and markers. The Parallel Nsight Analyzer visualizes a large amount of data automatically from a number of data sources. However, ultimately, the goal of the data is to help analyze the data in light of a particular game's logical runtime structure and processes.

Parallel Nsight Analyzer offers a simple C API called NVIDIA Tools Extension (nvtx), which can be used to inject custom events into the capture. These developer-defined events can help annotate the timeline view with game-specific markers and ranges, thereby overlaying title-specific logic and structure onto the Timeline View. You can gain access to these in your code by including nvToolsExt.h in your list of header files and linking with nvToolsExt.lib.

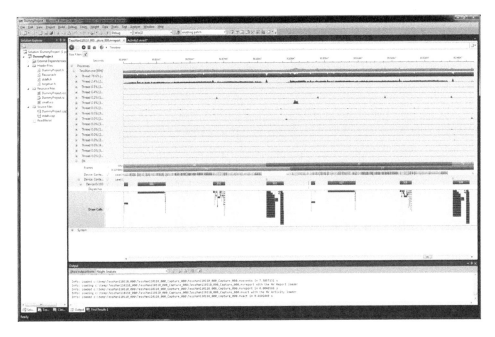

Figure 21.13. Tracing GPU workloads.

Custom markers can be used to annotate one-time instantaneous events, whether they are from gameplay, simulation, or rendering code. For instance, emitting a nvtx marker each time a character dies can give context to other performance data on the Timeline:

```
nvtxMark("Character terminated");
```

Custom ranges can be used to annotate time intervals on the Timeline with an arbitrary string. This can be done either for simple labeling purposes (Cloth Simulation #1) but can additionally be used to compare timing of a range across many frames. Consistent use of custom ranges allow for the fast visual inspection of the major time sinks for a frame or a set of frames: You can even nest ranges to delineate subsections of the running code.

```
nvtxRangePushA("Calculating Physics");

nvtxRangePop();
```

21.6   Conclusion

NVIDIA Parallel Nsight integrates GPU debugging and profiling capabilities into Microsoft's Visual Studio to provide a rich, seamless development environment for writing GPU-centric code. The Graphics Debugger is a fully hardware-accelerated source-code debugger that fully utilizes the Visual Studio GUI to provide the same experience when debugging HLSL code on the GPU as you have when debugging C/C++ on the CPU. The Graphics Inspector exposes the settings inside of the Direct3D runtime for each draw call, as well as showing the scene as it is constructed by scrubbing through draw calls and visualizing the data provided to it by your content pipeline and engine. The Pixel History feature helps answer the question: "Why is this pixel the color that it is?" giving access to the context that colored a given fragment.

On the performance side, the Frame Profiler helps you determine exactly where your bottleneck is, without having to resort to experiments to isolate different GPU subunits. Finally, the Analyzer allows you to perform a complete system trace and watch workflows on the CPU kick off calculations on the GPU to see a holistic view of your application running in a multiprocessor/multicore system.

22

FBX Games Development Tools

Trevor Adams and Mark Davies

22.1 Introduction

FBX technology allows you to translate and exchange 3D assets and media from a variety of sources quickly and easily. In the games community, FBX is used to move artist content from digital content creation (DCC) tools to the game development framework.

Autodesk FBX, as it is properly called, is developed by the Media & Entertainment division of Autodesk, Inc. Accordingly, FBX is supported by most Autodesk DCC products, as well as by a number of tools by other vendors.

Commercial game development frameworks that support FBX include the Epic Unreal Engine and the Unity game development tool. As well, many game development companies (game developers) have proprietary tool sets that use FBX.

This article will describe FBX technology, and will provide guidelines and tips on how to use specific tools to get content from the DCC into your game.

22.2 Exporting and Importing Game Assets

Game assets are usually created by artists who use digital content creation packages such as Autodesk Maya, Autodesk 3ds Max, and Autodesk Softimage software, as well as many more specialized products. Each DCC normally saves assets in its own proprietary file format.

Certain game engines would have a hard time reading the native file formats of all these applications. Instead, the game engines depend on interchange formats such as FBX and COLLADA.

Most 3D applications can export (save) meshes, UVs, and animations to the FBX file format without losing too much or any of the data in the process. Often the export operation requires converting data from formats or data structures used by the DCC to ones better suited for gaming. For example, textures can be converted to TIFF, and patches can be converted to meshes.

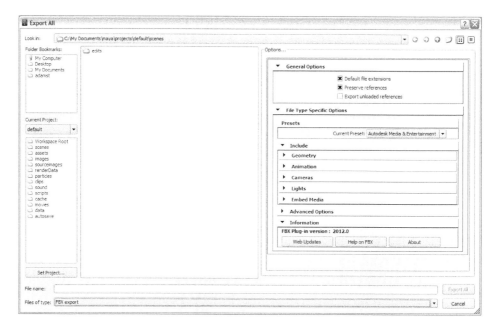

Figure 22.1. FBX Export options in Maya 2011.Choose the Autodesk Media & Entertainment import or export preset to set options suited for most game pipelines. The rollouts found in the File Type Specific Options area of the Maya Export dialog can be expanded to expose the individual preset options for further customization.

The software component that handles the export is called an exporter; exporters are often implemented as a plugin to the 3D application. The FBX exporters for Autodesk products are general purpose, and feature GUIs that give the user considerable control over what gets exported and how conversions are performed (see Figure 22.1).

Similarly, a game development tool uses an importer to read FBX files. A full-functioned importer also lets the user control what gets imported. Since FBX technology supports COLLADA and other non-FBX file formats, an importer built on FBX technology can import COLLADA files as well as FBX files.

22.2.1   Pipeline Architectures

A simple game development pipeline looks something like this:

DCC → FBX exporter → FBX file → FBX importer → Game engine.

If a game asset needs to be processed by more than one DCC, the pipeline looks something like this:

DCC1 → FBX exporter → FBX file → FBX importer

→ DCC2 → FBX exporter → FBX file → FBX importer → Game engine.

While most game developers reply on plugin exporters and importers, FBX technology includes a freestanding converter application that imports files of various formats, processes the data, and exports it to another file format. Game developers can also use FBX SDK (see Section 22.3) to write their own importers.

There are a number of things to always keep in mind when creating your game assets and preparing them for compatibility with the FBX format and your target game engine. In this section of the article, you will learn how to effectively use FBX plugins to get your data exported out of your DCC and be readily usable within a game development pipeline.

22.2.2   FBX Plugin Default Presets

The Autodesk Media and Entertainment FBX plugin presets for both 3ds Max and Maya contain most of the ideal settings for successfully exporting a scene to the FBX file format and importing into another application or game engine.

You can modify this preset to your liking by simply clicking the Edit button in the Exporter or Importer UI. If you make changes to the default preset, you have the option to save a new user preset that you can use for every subsequent export operation. It's always good practice to create a unique preset for your game pipeline and share this XML file with everyone in your project who creates and exports 3D assets.

Commonly, DCC users export as much data as possible to the FBX file so that only one export is required. When importing assets into the game engine, use the options found in the game engine's importer to import only the parts of the FBX scene that you need instead of importing the whole file.

If your game engine's FBX importer doesn't support any of the exported data types in the FBX file, it simply gets dropped during the import process.

22.2.3   Compatibility

FBX Compatibility charts are available online (at http://www.autodesk.com/fbx) to provide you with accurate information regarding the compatibility of 3ds Max, Maya, Softimage, Autodesk MotionBuilder, and Autodesk Mudbox software with the FBX file format.

TRS data.   In general, most DCC objects with translation, rotation, and scale data (TRS) are supported by FBX, either directly or through a conversion process. Pivot points, object names, vertex colors, normals, tangents, binormals, multiple UV sets, bones, animations, image map channels, hardware shaders, and materials can be retained when exporting to FBX for use in certain game engines.

Materials. For great results with materials, you'll want to stick with standard materials and common map channels. The 3ds Max FBX exporter can support the following map channels when applied to a standard material: ambient color, diffuse color, specular level, glossiness, self-illumination (i.e., lightmaps), opacity, bump, reflection, and displacement. The Maya FBX exporter can support the following material attributes in a standard Phong material: color, transparency, ambient color, incandescence, bump mapping, diffuse, cosine power, specular color, reflectivity, and reflected color.

Geometry. Geometry needs to be triangulated to be renderable in a game engine. It's a good idea to avoid letting the renderer do the triangulation itself. In some cases, it's better to leave this triangulation process up to the game engine's importer (rather than triangulating the meshes yourself in the DCC).

Your polygon count in your DCC will usually not be exactly equal to what's being rendered in your game engine; the count will most likely grow on its way to the final render. Sometimes this is simply because some materials require the mesh's triangles to be sent to the renderer twice. The more hard edges found on your geometry, the more triangles will be used to display the mesh in the renderer.

If you want to get a good idea of how many triangles are going to be rendered, you can collapse your modifier stack in 3ds Max to an editable mesh object that is a triangulated mesh object and view the face count. Editable meshes are exported as such using the 3ds Max FBX plugin.

Editable poly objects in 3ds Max are exported as polygonal meshes with hidden and visible edges; in other words, they are not necessarily composed of triangles.

Editable poly edges that are identified as hidden can be turned by the user, but the FBX Exporter plugin for 3ds Max will not retain the direction of these turned edges. This means that if you edit the hidden edge direction of an editable poly and export that geometry to FBX, the topology most likely will not be written to file properly.

The 3ds Max FBX Exporter will identify when there are turned edges and convert the editable poly to an editable mesh during the export process. Edge directions are retained by triangulating the mesh and baking/exposing all hidden and visible edges. To avoid the automatic triangulation of your mesh during the export process when hidden-edge modifications are detected by the plug-in, disable the Preserve Edge Orientation option found in the Include rollout of the FBX exporter.

You need to activate the option to Export Tangents and Binormals in the Maya and 3ds Max FBX Exporters if you want that information saved to FBX and later imported into a game engine. This avoids having the importer generate tangents and binormals on its own, using generic and potentially inaccurate user-specified smoothing angles. This will increase the size of the resulting FBX file, but it's ultimately worth it, if these elements need to be used and respected in your game engine.

In Maya, it is a good practice to delete all construction history of objects in your scene before exporting to FBX. This should provide the highest fidelity possible. You can do so in Maya by simply selecting Delete All by Type in the Edit History menu.

22.2.4 Objects and Transforms

Less Is faster. Game assets should have as few separate elements as possible. When constructing your final mesh, you should make sure to use as few textures and materials as possible to improve efficiency. Also try combining your meshes together; the more separate nodes that exist in your object, the heavier the scene becomes for the game engine and the renderer to process.

Orienting assets in the DCC. The position of each game asset in your DCC should be at $(0, 0, 0)$, i.e., at the world origin, to avoid any potential problems with placing the assets in your game environment.

Most DCCs follow a y-up world, in that the up axis for geometry created in the application's world coordinates is the y-axis.

However, certain applications like 3ds Max use the z-axis as the world coordinate system's up-axis. Since this up-axis cannot be changed in 3ds Max, you have the option to convert the scene's world coordinate system upon exporting to FBX. By default, the FBX exporter will convert the axis system to y-up, unless otherwise specified.

Since most game engines are y-up as well, it's recommended to leave this setting to its default value. When a scene is converted from z-up to a y-up world coordinate system, all scene root objects' pivots are rotated by 90 degrees in the negative x-axis or 270 degrees on the positive x-axis. All animation is affected by this conversion. You will notice (for instance when exporting from 3ds Max to FBX) that scene objects will import into Unity with a 270 degree rotation on the x-axis and all rotation animation is resampled as a result of the up-axis conversion process.

Accordingly, if you have a scene to export that consists of several root objects, we suggest that you parent a null or dummy object to all objects in the scene before exporting to FBX in the y-up world coordinate system. This will add only one rotation to the parent object of the scene and avoid animation re-sampling, while all other child objects and their ancestors retain their original $(0, 0, 0)$ rotation values.

Maya allows the user to convert the up-axis system to a z-up axis world coordinate system as well, but it is recommended to remain in the y-up world in Maya, to avoid any axis conversion issues while exporting to FBX or importing into your game engine.

Scaling and units. You'll want to avoid any unnecessary scaling of your objects when importing FBX files into your game engine. If you import a scene into your game engine with a scale factor already applied, it can quickly get confusing to work within the game engine's units once additional scaling of the object is applied.

This confusion can be avoided by simply working in and exporting to the unit system of your target application or game engine. For instance, since Unity's system unit works in meters (its physics system assumes that 1 unit is equal to 1 meter), you'll want to work in meters in 3ds Max. Do not adjust Display Units in 3ds Max; it's best to keep them generic. 3ds Max uses inches as its default System Units setting. You can change this by simply going to the Customize menu, to the Units Setup dialog and setting your System Unit Setup to 1 unit = 1 meter, in this case. From thereon in, you will be exporting to the FBX file format in meters by default (since the unit system in the default FBX exporter dynamically adjusts to match your host application's unit settings), thereby retaining its 100% scale. Once that scene is imported, the scale remains unmodified at 100% (or $(1, 1, 1)$).

If you cannot change the unit system of your DCC or simply choose not to, that's fine as well. In Maya and MotionBuilder for instance, the default system unit is centimeters and is again your choice whether or not you adjust the unit setting in the host application or apply a scale to the FBX objects being exported. You will simply need to disable the Automatic option in the Unit settings rollout found in the Advanced Options rollout of the FBX exporter and set your units to match those of your target application. Most game engines will adjust this automatically for you during the import process, but it's good practice to export to the proper unit system in case your specific game engine importer doesn't recognize a file's scale factor.

Any objects exported to a different unit system will be scaled; that is to say that the vertex positions of all objects in the scene remain the same while the local scale of the object changes. For instance, a 1 cm cubed box will export out of 3ds Max to FBX in meters as 1 unit cubed with a scale factor of 0.01.

22.2.5 Embedded Media

It's common for game developers to import scenes without embedded media into a game engine and afterwards apply the media, but this isn't necessary. You will most likely want your exported FBX files to be portable and self-contained, in that everything you need in that file is in the file and not located on another path on your hard drive. If all related media is contained within an FBX file, opening that scene anywhere else (i.e., on another computer) removes the hassle of having to research the locations of those missing texture files that are no longer in the same location. A lot of time is saved and confusion avoided when you choose to embed all media of a scene when exporting to the FBX file format.

To embed media during the FBX export process, simply select the Embed Media option found in the Include rollout of the FBX exporter. All image files associated with the materials assigned to objects in your scene will be embedded in the FBX file itself. Of course, this will have an impact on file size. If this file is imported into another DCC, a folder will be created in the same location as the FBX file during the import process, and all textures will be extracted into that folder (so that the DCC can reference the location of those texture files). The same happens when importing an FBX file with embedded media in a game engine. Once texture files are embedded, simply dragging and dropping an FBX file into your game engine will allow the engine to automatically assign textures to their proper material without needing your manual assistance.

If you must export to the FBX ASCII file format, it is important to know that media embedding is impossible when exporting to the FBX 2010 version and earlier versions. ASCII embedding is only supported in the FBX 2011 version and above. Certain game engines currently support the FBX 2010 and other earlier versions, so you will need to understand the limitations of your target game engine before creating any FBX files.

22.2.6 File Format and Versioning

One of the most important things to figure out before working between DCCs and game engines is the version of FBX in both. When a new version of FBX technology is made available, several plugins are offered to support older versions of the host applications. For instance, 3ds Max and Maya FBX plugins support the current and previous two versions of the software, while the Softimage FBX plugin version is included only in the latest release. This is important information because if a file is exported to a newer version of FBX than the target application's importer, errors will most likely occur. You need to determine the FBX importer version of your game engine as a first step. For instance, Unity 2.6 supports FBX 2010 and earlier versions. That is to say, all FBX 2010 plugins (i.e., 2010.0.02, 2010.1, and 2010.2) will export FBX files that can be properly imported by Unity 2.6. However, an FBX 2011 file will not properly import into Unity 2.6 (i.e., animation is lost since animation data is written in a way that FBX 2010 importers don't understand).

If you only have the option to use an FBX plugin that is more recent than the FBX version of your game engine (for instance, you are using Maya 2011 and the FBX 2011 plug-in, with Unity 2.6), you have two options for full compatibility between the two applications. You can simply choose to export to an older version of FBX by choosing the appropriate version in the Version dropdown list found in the FBX File Format rollout in the Advanced Options rollout. Otherwise, you can export to the FBX 2011 format and use the FBX Converter to convert your FBX 2011 file to a previous version that's compatible with Unity 2.6, like FBX 2010. Either way, the resulting file will be compatible with your older FBX importer found in your game engine. Usually, with a new release of a popular game engine, the FBX version is updated to Autodesk's latest release, so this problem shouldn't arise all that often, but it is worth paying attention to. As a case in point, Unity 3.0 supports FBX 2011 files.

You should always have the latest FBX plugin installed, because you can always export to previous versions for compatibility reasons while also having the latest release with the newest features and bug fixes.

22.2.7 Animation

It's more efficient to store all your animations in one FBX file along a single timeline rather than have an FBX file for each animation. If you are using MotionBuilder to create and save your animations to the FBX file format, you have the option to store each animation separately using animation takes. Alternatively, you can use the FBX Converter's Take Manager tool to extract animation takes from FBX files; i.e., an FBX file containing five animation takes can be separated into five unique FBX files. Be sure to verify whether or not your target game engine supports the reading of animation takes in an FBX file before making this decision.

Shape and morpher animation isn't always supported by game engines. In these cases, use bone deformations instead. When using bone deformations use the bake option to retain all animation during the FBX Export process. You will end up with one key per frame; which allows for 100% animation fidelity between host and destination applications. The bake animation process converts all IK solving to FK, removing the dependency on the solvers required to represent the animation data properly. For instance, since only some game engines support HIK, it's safer to just bake (resample) the animation on the way out. If you are using set driven keys in Maya, it's a good idea to set at least one key on your drivers so that baking is done properly.

When using Biped Layers in 3ds Max, you'll want to select the uppermost layer before exporting to FBX. If the uppermost layer is selected, all active layers underneath are considered. The bake animation option must be active in order to evaluate all layers. Alternatively, you can also simply collapse all Biped animation layers in 3ds Max before exporting to FBX.

22.3 Extracting the Information from the .fbx File

The .fbx file is used as a common currency between a variety of content creation tools. To the artist using these tools, the concern is of compatibility, options, and availability in the tool of choice. This section discusses how to extract the information from the .fbx file so that it can be used to add rich content to your game.

There are a number of commercially available game development tools that provide FBX import. The main way for a game developer to get access to the data contained within an FBX file is via the FBX-SDK. The FBX-SDK is available free from www.autodesk.com/fbx. This site contains the SDK as well as other utilities:

the Quicktime Viewer and FBX Converter. Also included is a full reference manual, an introductory programmers guide, and many examples in C++ and Python to aid your development.

22.4   FBX for QuickTime as a Game Development Tool

In a game development pipeline, assets are exported, imported, opened, modified, and resaved frequently. The FBX plugin for the QuickTime application program is a tool that can allow you to monitor your assets as they travel their way through your pipeline (see Figure 22.2). FBX files, whether exported from a digital content creation package like Maya and 3ds Max or saved in an application like Motion-Builder, can be viewed with this tool. It essentially allows you to have viewing access to your game assets without a requirement for a 3D application to be installed and run.

22.4.1   A Tool for Previsualization

The FBX plugin for QuickTime allows you to view, interact with, and share 3D scenes in a standalone player or embedded on a webpage. The experience of viewing the file is similar to that of opening FBX files in MotionBuilder, as it's built from the same technology. You have the freedom to orbit, pan, and dolly the scene using familiar viewport controls. You can switch between camera views and animation takes to evaluate the contents of your scene. The tool is commonly used in game

Figure 22.2. FBX file opened in QuickTime Player.

and film pipelines for previsualization purposes. You can share your models and animation with leads and directors by simply sending the FBX file to them and not having to worry about which versions of software they might have installed or simply whether they know how to use them.

As a game artist, you can use the tool for visualizing edge flows using the Wireframe display mode. Texture work can be analyzed in the Shaders and Textures display mode. An X-Ray viewing mode is also available for users who would like to see their models and the joints/bones driving their animated characters simultaneously. If you're looking for a specific animation take to merge onto a game asset in a 3D application, you can save some time by cycling through the saved animation takes in an FBX file in QuickTime first, instead of having to install and run MotionBuilder and open the file there. Lead animators often use the player as an evaluation tool, cycling through hundreds of files and animation takes, giving feedback to their fellow animators, again without having to open a 3D application. Basically, the FBX plugin for QuickTime opens the door to a lot of previsualization possibilities.

22.4.2 A Tool for Data Asset Management Systems

Game companies choose to store their assets in a format that can be read by multiple applications, including their game engine. By storing FBX files, you avoid a number of versioning and software compatibility issues. If you've decided to store your game assets as FBX files, the QuickTime Player can act as your data asset management system viewer. FBX technology is backwards-compatible, so if you've exported FBX scenes from 3ds Max 9.0 or Maya 2010, the files should open and play back in the player seamlessly; there's no need to worry about versioning so long as the FBX plugin for QuickTime is the latest version.

Since the QuickTime Player can be embedded in a webpage, you can share your FBX files with a broader audience by allowing users to view them on the internet. Each end user needs to install the QuickTime Player FBX plugin to view the files embedded on the webpage. This becomes a simple remote connection to your data asset management system, enabling you to view files from anywhere there's internet access. Many large game companies have set up their pipelines this way to provide teams working in multiple locations direct and visual access to a common set of assets.

Whether you're a game developer, artist, or director, the FBX plugin for QuickTime as a game development tool should help to improve the visibility of your game assets in your pipeline.

Note. Autodesk, FBX, Maya, MotionBuilder, Mudbox, Softimage, and 3ds Max are registered trademarks or trademarks of Autodesk, Inc., and/or its subsidiaries and/or affiliates in the USA and/or other countries.

About the Contributors

Trevor Adams is a Quality Assurance Team Lead of Media & Entertainment products at Autodesk in Montréal, Canada. He has been working in the quality assurance field since 2005, having started his career testing console videogames and ending up leading a team of QA specialists who test interoperability and user workflows between Autodesk Media & Entertainment applications, such as Maya, 3ds Max, Softimage, MotionBuilder, Mudbox, and Smoke. Trevor has also held a number of positions in independent film productions, such as visual effects supervisor and lead animator. In his part time, he's currently working slowly on a video game of his own which may eventually see the light of day :) (awkwardanimations@gmail.com)

Rémi Arnaud is the Chief Software Architect at Screampoint. Rémi's involvement with real-time graphics started in the R&D department of Thomson Training & Simulation (now Thales) designing and then leading the Space Magic real-time visual system for training simulators.He then relocated to California to join Silicon Graphics's IRIS Performer team, working on advanced features such as calligraphic light points for training pilots. Later he cofounded Intrinsic Graphics where he codesigned the Alchemy engine, a middleware targeting cross-platform game development for PS2, Xbox, GameCube, and PC. Alchemy is still in use today as the core technology in games and 3D applications such as Google Earth. He was brought on as Graphics Architect at Sony Computer Entertainment US R&D, working on the PLAYSTATION3 SDK graphics API and joined the Khronos Group to create the COLLADA asset exchange standard, which is currently adopted by most 3D tools and applications such as 3dsMax, Maya, Photoshop, Sketchup, Unity, Flash, and Mac OSX. More recently, Remi was at Intel where he created and lead the Larrabee Game Engine Technology team.(remi@acm.org)

Marwan Y. Ansari is a software engineer for a Chicago-based games company. He has a B.S. in Computer Science and Math from DePaul University and an M.S. from the University of Illinois at Chicago. He has over 15 years of experience ranging from console games development, OpenGL drivers and demos, military simulators, and application and tools development and has worked for Number Nine Visual Technologies, ATI, and Midway Games just to name a few. He specializes in 3D computer graphics and has been published in *ShaderX*^{2} and *Game Programming Gems 4*. (marwan@gamedevelopmenttools.com)

Jeffrey Aydelotte is a programmer at Bigpoint, where he works on streaming techniques and 3D graphics for browser games. Most recently he's been working on developing the content pipeline and asset streaming system for Bigpoint's *Ruined.* He got his start working on browser games as part of the demo team at Unity Technologies. (jeff.aydelotte@gmail.com)

Matthew Baranowski is an independent mobile game developer at www.Studio-MFB.com. Previously he worked at Day 1 Studios in Chicago where he had a chance to implement a CSG editor to augment the production workflow for *F.E.A.R 3.* Before that he worked at Midway Games as a graphics and engine programmer on *John Woo Presents: Stranglehold* and the cult classic *Psi-Ops: The Mindgate Conspiracy.* His big break into the game industry came after releasing several popular modding tools for the Quake 3 engine with Sander van Rossen. (mfbaranow@gmail.com)

Craig Barr is a technical marketing specialist in the Media and Entertainment Division of Autodesk. In this role, he focuses on the creation of demo content to showcase the latest features for Mudbox and Maya. Prior to joining Alias/Autodesk in 2005, Craig worked in production for feature films, games and commercials. He also runs the Mudbox blog on *The Area* (http://the-area.com/blogs/craig) (craig.barr@autodesk.com)

Samuel Boivin is a research scientist at INRIA currently on a leave of absence. He is the head of Research and Development at SolidAnim, a company specializing in visual effects for movies and video games. He obtained a Ph.D. in computer graphics in 2001 from Ecole Polytechnique in Palaiseau (France). He has published several papers about computer graphics in many conferences including SIGGRAPH. His research interests include photorealistic real-time rendering, real-time augmented reality, fluid dynamics, and inverse techniques for acquiring material properties (photometric, mechanical) from videos. (sam@solidanim.com)

Gustavo Carazoni is a software engineer and game developer with over ten years of experience. He has worked as tools lead programmer and lead programmer at Pyro Studios, where he shipped the titles *Commandos Strike Force* and *Planet 51—The Game.* He is currently working on a new game at Virtual Toys in Madrid. (guscarrazoni@gmail.com)

Mark Davies is a technical product manager with Autodesk in Toronto, Canada. Mark has been in software development for around 20 years. Initially working in computer aided design (CAD) in the United Kingdom, Mark joined Autodesk and has worked on Power Animator, Alias, and Maya as a developer. Mark is usually found looking at or developing API's. Previous to all of this Mark was part of the first bedroom programmer community making games for the Sinclair ZX81 and Spectrum. (mdavies860@gmail.com)

Dave Eberly is the Chief Technology Officer of Geometric Tools, LLC. His introduction to the game industry was as the Director of Engineering for Numerical Design Ltd., developing NetImmerse/Gamebryo. Most recently, he was part of the production of *Baja: Edge of Control* (2XL Games, THQ). He has M.S. and Ph.D. degrees in mathematics from the University of Colorado at Boulder and M.S. and Ph.D. degrees in computer science from the University of North Carolina at Chapel Hill. Dave is the author of *3D Game Engine Design*, *3D Game Engine Architecture*, *Game Physics*, and (with Philip Schneider) *Geometric Tools for Computer Graphics*. (deberly@geometrictools.com)

Amir Ebrahimi is a senior software engineering consultant working primarily on Unity-based projects. He has been working professionally in game development since 2003 after receiving his B.S. in computer science from Georgia Tech. Amir has worked on multiple AAA titles and for a variety of companies including Unity, Flagship Studios, Activision, and Naughty Dog. (gdt@aebrahimi.com)

Simon Franco started programming on the Commodore Amiga by writing a *Pong* clone in AMOS and has been coding ever since. He joined the games industry in 2000, after completing a degree in computer science. He started at The Creative Assembly in 2004, where he has been to this day. When he's not keeping his baby daughter entertained, he'll be playing the latest game or writing assembly code for the ZX spectrum. (simon_franco@hotmail.com)

Matt Greene is a technical artist at Volition, Inc. and has worked on several recent titles including *Red Faction: Guerrilla* and *Red Faction: Armageddon*. He has most recently been involved in building complete asset development pipelines, exporters, and numerous custom art tools. He is a graduate from the computer animation program at Full Sail in Florida. (MGreeneTD@gmail.com)

Frank E. Hernandez is a member of the special interest group on game development (SIG-Games) at Florida International University (FIU) wherehe gives workshops on different aspects of game development. He received an M.S. in computer science at FIU in 2008. Frank is currently a Ph.D. student in computer science at FIU where he is specializing in the developmentof domain-specific languages for multitier application. (Hernandez.f@rouninlabs.com)

Jaewon Jung has been a game developer since 1999. After he spent almost a decade dealing with several gamedev projects in South Korea, he's now at Crytek in Germany to meet new people, new challenges, and enrich his experience. He's happy to be a journeyman constantly improving his skills, learning new things and speaking new languages. (jaewon@crytek.com)

Jeff Kiel is the manager of graphics tools at NVIDIA. His responsibilities include development and oversight of the graphics side for performance and debugging tools used by developers, including Parallel Nsight, PerfHUD, etc. Before coming to NVIDIA, Jeff worked on PC and console games at Interactive Magic and Sinister Games/Ubisoft. Jeff has given presentations at many GDC and SIGGRAPH conferences and contributed articles to graphics-related publications. His passion for the art started in the G-Lab at the University of North Carolina at Chapel Hill where he received his B.Ss in mathematical sciences. (JKiel@nvidia.com)

Alan Kimball is a principal software engineer at Vicarious Visions in Albany, New York and has been programming games professionally since 2002. He has been a graphics, network, and gameplay programmer on a variety of different platforms. In 2005 he started the tools group at Vicarious Visions and has been lead tools programmer on several titles, including *Spider-Man 3* (DS/GameCube/Wii) and *Marvel Ultimate Alliance: 2.* (akimball@vvisions.com)

Kumar Iyer is a Product Manager of Developer Tools at NVIDIA, where he works on the most advanced GPU development tools in the world. Prior to his work at NVIDIA, Kumar worked on PC and console games at Electronic Arts, and in virtual reality research at the USC Institute for Creative Technologies. Kumar holds a BS in Computer Science from UCLA, and a MBA from the UCLA Anderson School of Management.

Ichiro Lambe is founder and president of Dejobaan Games, LLC, an independent Boston-area game development studio. He has worked in the industry since 1993, co-founding Worlds Apart Productions (now Sony Online Entertainment, Denver) in 1995 and Dejobaan Games in 1999. Since Dejobaan's founding, he's led development on the studio's 14 titles, working on titles for mobile and desktop PCs. He doesn't take himself too seriously, but takes game development very seriously. (ilambe@dejobaan.com)

Yannis Minadakis is a software engineer at Intel and has focused on performance optimization for graphics and computer vision since 1999. He developed the Windows Experience Index for graphics and gaming in Windows Vista while at Microsoft. Working as a third-party engineer since 2006, he has contributed to many games including *Assassins Creed* and *Civilization V.* (2yannis@gmail.com)

Fernando Navarro works as lead technical artist for Lionhead Studios (Microsoft Games Studios) where he has just released *Fable III.* Prior to joining the lions, he directed different R&D departments at several production houses. His work on vfx, feature films, commercials, and games has received many awards including several Goya of the Spanish Academy of Cinematography and the Bafta for the best action and adventure game. He has an M.Sc. from the University of Zaragoza and is currently earning a Ph.D. in Computer Science, focused on advanced rendering algorithms. (fernandn@microsoft.com)

Sebastien Noury is a Ph.D. student in computer science at Paris-Sud University in Orsay, France, where he received his M.Sc. in software engineering in 2009. He also studied game development in Montreal and interned at independent game studios in Paris and Singapore before joining the VENISE team of the CNRS/LIMSI lab to work on real-time fluid dynamics for virtual reality. His research interests include GPU acceleration of dynamic simulations, real-time rendering, and human-computer interaction. (sebastien.noury@limsi.fr)

Mike O'Connor is a software engineer at Iron Galaxy Studios, where he is currently working on an upcoming XBLA/PSN title for Capcom. He graduated from the University of Illinois at Urbana-Champaign with a degree in computer engineering in 2004 and was previously employed at Midway Games (RIP). He has enjoyed writing an article for *Game Development Tools* and hopes that you will find it helpful. (mike.oconnor@gmail.com)

Francisco Ortega started programming in Basic on an Atari 65XE at the age of 11. He has been professionally developing applications since the age of 18. He has earned a B.S. and M.S. in computer science from Florida International University. He is currently a computer science Ph.Dd student at Florida International University interested in human-computer interaction with special emphasis in multitouch 3D navigation, computer graphics, microprocessors, and domain-specific languages that deal with gaming, 3D navigation, and effective computing. (ortega.f@rouninlabs.com)

Steven Ramirez is a game engineer at Schell Games located in Pittsburgh, Pennsylvania, whose focus is tools and system-level code. He fulfilled his dream of getting into games after receiving his diploma from Full Sail University in 2007. Since then he has contributed to a wide variety of games such as *The Lord Of The Rings: Conquest* and *Toy Story Mania TV Games Deluxe.* (sramirez@schellgames.com)

Sander van Rossen is an independent game developer. He taught himself programming as a child and has loved programming ever since. He released several popular modding tools for the Quake 3 engine together with Matthew Baranowski. When he isn't working on games, he blogs about CSG, virtual texturing, and other computer graphics experiments at sandervanrossen.blogspot.com. (s.v.rossen@synthesis.nl)

Atlas Roufas is founder of Spiral Graphics Inc, where he leads development of the seamless texture editor Genetica. In this role, he is responsible for the creation of new image-processing algorithms and tools that have been used by countless artists working on game titles for desktop, console, web, and mobile platforms. (atlas@spiralgraphics.biz)

William Smith is a technical artist at Volition, Inc. and is responsible for tools and workflow programming, building complete art-asset pipelines, and integrating design and art using new and existing technologies. He is a graduate of the University of Illinois at Urbana-Champaign and has been making games for as long as he can remember. His most recent projects at Volition include *Saints Row 2* and *Red Faction: Armageddon.* (william.smith.linkedin@gmail.com)

Index